CD INSIDE BACK COVER

Managing Global Development Risk

Other Auerbach Publications in Software Development, Software Engineering, and Project Management

Accelerating Process Improvement Using Agile Techniques
Deb Jacobs
ISBN: 0-8493-3796-8

Advanced Server Virtualization: VMware and Microsoft Platforms in the Virtual Data Center
David Marshall, Wade A. Reynolds and Dave McCrory
ISBN: 0-8493-3931-6

Antipatterns: Identification, Refactoring, and Management
Phillip A. Laplante and Colin J. Neill
ISBN: 0-8493-2994-9

Applied Software Risk Management: A Guide for Software Project Managers
C. Ravindranath Pandian
ISBN: 0849305241

The Art of Software Modeling
Benjamin A. Lieberman
ISBN: 1-4200-4462-1

Building Software: A Practitioner's Guide
Nikhilesh Krishnamurthy and Amitabh Saran
ISBN: 0-8493-7303-4

Business Process Management Systems
James F. Chang
ISBN: 0-8493-2310-X

The Debugger's Handbook
J.F. DiMarzio
ISBN: 0-8493-8034-0

Effective Software Maintenance and Evolution: A Reuse-Based Approach
Stanislaw Jarzabek
ISBN: 0-8493-3592-2

Embedded Linux System Design and Development
P. Raghavan, Amol Lad and Sriram Neelakandan
ISBN: 0-8493-4058-6

Flexible Software Design: Systems Development for Changing Requirements
Bruce Johnson, Walter W. Woolfolk, Robert Miller and Cindy Johnson
ISBN: 0-8493-2650-8

Global Software Development Handbook
Raghvinder Sangwan, Matthew Bass, Neel Mullick, Daniel J. Paulish and Juergen Kazmeier
ISBN: 0-8493-9384-1

The Handbook of Mobile Middleware
Paolo Bellavista and Antonio Corradi
ISBN: 0-8493-3833-6

Implementing Electronic Document and Record Management Systems
Azad Adam
ISBN: 0-8493-8059-6

Process-Based Software Project Management
F. Alan Goodman
ISBN: 0-8493-7304-2

Service Oriented Enterprises
Setrag Khoshafian
ISBN: 0-8493-5360-2

Software Engineering Foundations: A Software Science Perspective
Yingxu Wang
ISBN: 0-8493-1931-5

Software Engineering Quality Practices
Ronald Kirk Kandt
ISBN: 0-8493-4633-9

Software Sizing, Estimation, and Risk Management
Daniel D. Galorath and Michael W. Evans
ISBN: 0-8493-3593-0

Software Specification and Design: An Engineering Approach
John C. Munson
ISBN: 0-8493-1992-7

Testing Code Security
Maura A. van der Linden
ISBN: 0-8493-9251-9

Six Sigma Software Development, Second Edition
Christine B. Tayntor
ISBN: 1-4200-4426-5

Successful Packaged Software Implementation
Christine B. Tayntor
ISBN: 0-8493-3410-1

UML for Developing Knowledge Management Systems
Anthony J. Rhem
ISBN: 0-8493-2723-7

X Internet: The Executable and Extendable Internet
Jessica Keyes
ISBN: 0-8493-0418-0

AUERBACH PUBLICATIONS

www.auerbach-publications.com
To Order Call:1-800-272-7737 • Fax: 1-800-374-3401
E-mail: orders@crcpress.com

Managing Global Development Risk

James M. Hussey
Steven E. Hall

Auerbach Publications
Taylor & Francis Group
Boca Raton   New York

Auerbach Publications is an imprint of the
Taylor & Francis Group, an **informa** business

Auerbach Publications
Taylor & Francis Group
6000 Broken Sound Parkway NW, Suite 300
Boca Raton, FL 33487-2742

© 2008 by Taylor & Francis Group, LLC
Auerbach is an imprint of Taylor & Francis Group, an Informa business

No claim to original U.S. Government works
Printed in the United States of America on acid-free paper
10 9 8 7 6 5 4 3 2 1

International Standard Book Number-13: 978-1-4200-5520-7 (Hardcover)

Library of Congress Cataloging-in-Publication Data

Hussey, James M.
    Managing global development risk / James M. Hussey and Steven E. Hall.
       p. cm.
    Includes bibliographical references and index.
    ISBN 978-1-4200-5520-7 (alk. paper)
       1. Computer software industry--Subcontracting--Management. 2. Computer software--Development--Management. 3. Offshore outsourcing--Management. 4. Project management. I. Hall, Steven E. II. Title.

HD9696.63.A2H87 2008
004.068'4--dc22   2007025612

Visit the Taylor & Francis Web site at
http://www.taylorandfrancis.com

and the Auerbach Web site at
http://www.auerbach-publications.com

Acknowledgments

The principles presented in Managing Global Development Risk began to take shape in 2001 as we found ourselves managing offshore projects under less than positive settings. It was the dotcom bubble burst and suddenly US-based software development project managers were dealing with the emotional impact of the decision to offshore outsource. While there was widespread resistance, there were a few managers who embraced the new model and managed to succeed.

Managing Global Development Risk is the culmination of our experiences as members of these incredible teams as they transitioned their development organizations. While there are simply too many individuals to name for their contribution, we would like to thank the customers who accepted our support, the individuals who truly embraced our recommended approaches and TPI who, as an organization, understands sourcing is truly a joining of expertise across multiple organizations and cultures.

Above all, we would like to thank our families for their ongoing support and commitment. Being a part of the offshore outsourcing community does require extensive travel and execution focus, all of which is only possible with their support. We look forward to receiving your thoughts on Managing Global Development Risk and hope you take the opportunity to join the MGDRisk.com users group as a way to extend your participation with fellow Global Development Managers.

Steven Hall
TPI

Contents

Introduction

Offshore outsourcing, a trend that dominated the news headlines a few short months ago, has quietly evolved into global outsourcing: utilization of software development resources across the globe with the goal of reducing cost while improving efficiency and quality. Although global outsourcing has expanded dramatically in terms of activities, there remain consistent challenges facing organizations that have made such an outsourcing decision: maximizing the opportunity, fully realizing the potential gains, and managing the inherent risks of global development.

Managing Global Development Risk has been produced to address the growing gap between software project management skills and the realities of managing global development projects. Although companies today continue to start or expand their use of global resources, little is being done to help their retained organization of project managers, business analysts, architects, and others succeed in this new environment. Built on real world experience, *Managing Global Development Risk* provides actionable tools, templates, and practical advice specifically designed to help this new breed of project managers succeed in the global development market.

In our years of experience supporting customers in their efforts to achieve global outsourcing success, we have consistently observed similar challenges and issues. This book represents the summation of our experience. We can share with confidence that the recommendations and advice provided will greatly enhance your ability to execute global projects, evolving from your current role to truly becoming a global development manager.

Managing Global Development Risk has been organized to serve as an ongoing resource. Each section is clearly aligned in logical project management activities so you can easily refer to this book over time and quickly locate information that can be put to immediate use.

Good luck in your journey to becoming a global development manager.

About the Authors

Jim Hussey is a senior advisor with TPI, the global leader in outsourcing advisory. Jim has extensive knowledge and expertise related to global outsourcing, marketing, communications, strategy, and negotiations. He has extensive experience establishing global outsourcing operations including operational models, such as build-operate-transfer (BOT) agreements, and dedicated offshore development centers. In addition to his role as senior advisor, Jim supports TPI's global outsourcing research efforts. In 2005, Jim led the execution of TPI's Global Service Delivery Report, which isolated the characteristics and key attributes of an organization's offshore outsourcing maturity. He has long focused on the behavioral and interpersonal impact global outsourcing has within an information technology organization. He has developed multiple workshops and targeted assessments on this issue. He continues to explore behavioral challenges that surface after a global outsourcing environment has been created and activities that will unite and empower the integrated global development team.

Before joining TPI, Jim was Offshore Advocate for Covansys Corporation, a global service delivery provider, where he supported delivery and major account efforts. He was responsible for strategy and negotiations for development of large applications and maintenance agreements with ISV organizations. Prior to joining Covansys, Jim was chief operating officer of Offshore Development Group where he directed market research and publishing operations focused on offshore outsourcing. As founder of Offshoredev.com, he conceived, designed, launched, and managed the largest single online content repository dedicated to offshore outsourcing, called www.offshoredev.com. In 2001, he produced the Offshore Benchmark Report, the largest and most extensive quantitative analysis of offshore buying trends among U.S. organizations. The survey isolated these trends by industry, company size, and individual role in the offshore outsourcing decision process.

Jim lives in Denver, Colorado, and has three teenagers (Kristin, Dana, and Patrick), who have been very supportive of the travel demands of this market. He looks forward to his upcoming marriage to Kim and to continuing his studies on the impact of global outsourcing and how companies can successfully harness these talents.

Steven Hall is a project director with TPI, the global leader in outsourcing advisory. Steve has extensive knowledge and expertise related to global outsourcing, application development maintenance, software development, and project management. He has successfully implemented large-scale software projects using a global team and established global outsourcing models, such as BOT agreements and dedicated development centers. He regularly helps clients assess their outsourcing capabilities and advises them on best practices.

Steve's experience includes all aspects of the software development process, application maintenance development, offshore delivery, project management, and implementation of multiple software development methodologies. His knowledge derives from practical implementation experience and advising large multinational corporations in their outsourcing strategies. Steve's unique outsourcing experiences were gained from both a client and offshore outsourcing perspective. Steve's extensive software development and project management expertise was gained at Citigroup Diners Club and MCI. At Diners Club, he directed delivery and maintenance of multiple large-scale software projects. Steve's offshore experience was gained at Covansys, an international outsourcing company, where he led multiple offshoring projects and was engaged in sales, offshore strategy, and delivery. He supported development of business cases for multiple clients and overall strategy for offshore projects and e-commerce initiatives. Earlier in his career, Steve worked at MCI Corporation as Software Development Manager, Unisys Corporation as Quality Assurance Manager and Senior Systems Analyst, and at FlightSafety Corporation as Subject Matter Expert and Software Developer. Steve lives in Denver with his wife Michelle and two teenagers (Chelsea and Justin). When not traveling for business, he enjoys relaxing with the family, skiing, golf, and international travel.

Steve holds a bachelor of science degree in computer science from Regis University, Denver.

Chapter 1

The Emergence of Global Development Managers

A. Introduction

There has been a great deal of press coverage over the past several years concerning the growth of offshore outsourcing. There is no doubt the trend toward global outsourcing and development is real. The challenge we face today is not how we will stop or prevent this inevitability, but how will we embrace this reality and expand our skills to meet these global challenges.

The purpose behind *Managing Global Development Risk* is to provide project managers (PMs) and subject matter experts (SMEs) — individuals who typically are responsible for interfacing with offshore resources — with the tools, techniques, and knowledge necessary to achieve project success. Today, ill-prepared PMs and SMEs are thrown into the role of interacting with offshore suppliers. *Managing Global Development Risk* is designed to educate PMs and SMEs in these critical management and leadership positions on the road to becoming global development managers (GDMs). As such, their skills will expand and diversify beyond project management and software development processes to encompass true, multi-dimensional capabilities sensitive to the realities of managing globally dispersed and diverse teams.

B. Managing Global Development Risk — What You Will Learn

Over the course of the following pages, attachments, and tables, you will learn the core skills necessary to successfully manage globally dispersed software development projects. You will be exposed to the critical management techniques and approaches that have helped organizations achieve success regardless of their global sourcing operational model. *Managing Global Development Risk* has been built on a compilation of best and current practices along with suggestions on how individuals can combine learned activities and "good ole" common sense to succeed.

By reading and utilizing the templates within *Managing Global Development Risk*, you will acquire the following skills along with the ability to apply the principles immediately to your unique work requirements. These skills include:

- Thorough knowledge of project management principles and their unique application for global projects
- Thorough knowledge of software development processes and their unique application for global development projects
- Insight into the diverse personalities that will comprise your global development team and the appropriate management and communications style to achieve success
- An awareness of cultural issues and mannerisms to enhance your ability to guide all team members to achieve and exceed required productivity levels

Why is this important? To truly extract the benefit of global development, a proper mix of local and offshore resources is essential to achieve the desired cost and "follow-the-sun" efficiencies. Simply adopting staff augmentation and establishing an onsite team of offshore resources will not get your organization to the desired end game. Your skills and experience in managing global development team members will enable you to succeed, regardless of the operational model chosen by your organization. *Managing Global Development Risk* is an important tool to help you gain this necessary competency and expand your skills in this critical area, positioning your global development management skills at a point where such skills are in great demand!

In addition to this critical knowledge, when you finish reading this book you will find a series of templates and tools designed to guide you through all aspects of the global development process. These tools include:

- Risk-issue-decision (RID) log
- Project selection and applicability tool
- Offshore ramp-up sheet
- Offshore staffing plan
- Metric development template

- Change control log
- Software quality assurance (SQA) template (tollgate deliverables)
- Service level agreement template

C. Why Is This Important To You?

During the 2004 presidential election, there was a great deal of discussion around the loss of jobs in the United States as information technology (IT) and business process positions were moving to low-cost locations around the globe. What received little attention or analysis was the fact that this trend is creating a very important high-value role, a U.S.-based role for individuals who can effectively design, implement, manage, and deliver software development projects successfully in a global model: GDMs.

Today, GDMs are in great demand. Due to the manner in which offshore outsourcing has grown, there is a very limited universe of American software development managers who have had to truly manage complex global development projects. Many times, the use of offshore resources has been in an onsite, staff augmentation role; or the offshore provider has "carved out" an activity, and the offshore onsite "coordinator" simply keeps the development manager posted — a parallel activity to those you are actively managing.

As these words are being typed, a chief information officer for a major Fortune 100 firm has shared with us that she is desperately seeking PMs and SMEs who have true hands-on experience and knowledge of managing global development projects. When we shared with her the focus of *Managing Global Development Risk* and our goal of preparing GDMs to execute global projects effectively, she urged us to get it done quickly as her peers "are clamoring for individuals with these skills."

Managing Global Development Risk is the tool that will start you down this important path, the path to becoming a GDM.

Chapter 2

Offshore Trends

A. Introduction

Offshore outsourcing has grown significantly in the past 10 years. This growth has significantly expanded the number of options available to organizations of all sizes and across all industries. No longer strictly the domain of large organizations, offshore development has permeated all the way to venture-backed operations looking to accelerate development cycles to the largest multinational operations.

At this time, we are witnessing a saturation of the offshore market. This multi-level dynamic is forcing the growth of many new and diverse models, approaches, and applications of global development models. At the same time, it is creating a significant vacuum of project managers and software development managers capable of handling the ever-increasing complexity of software development or applications development and maintenance. The reason this is important to understand is that your organization may start or approach offshore outsourcing from a number of different entry points, ranging from staff augmentation all the way to possibly

> **Section Key Concepts: Offshore Trends**
>
> ➤ Offshore Destination Evaluation Criteria
> ➤ Offshore Supplier Categories
> ➤ Offshore Operational Models
> ➤ Global Pricing Dynamics

Figure 2.1   Section II Key Concepts

establishing a captive center. As the global development manager (GDM), you need to understand the implications.

This section of *Managing Global Development Risk* is intended to provide a high-level backdrop of the shifting global sourcing market. Insight and sensitivity to these trends will be essential to manage global projects effectively because the formula you have today could quickly evolve to encompass resources in different parts of the globe.

Let's take a quick look at what has become a very interesting, multidimensional sourcing solution; the genesis of which was simple staff augmentation.

B. Offshore Market Dynamics

Most (if not all) service providers today boast some level of offshore development capacity. Gone are the days where they would discredit the approach. Clearly it has been customer demand that has forced these developments. It is the consumer of global development resources that is driving the response of service providers in every phase of the market. Those service providers who are aware and sensitive to consumer buying patterns have enjoyed great success over the past 10 to 15 years. The question we ask is which service providers are best positioned for the coming 10 years. It is a fascinating debate.

1. Offshore Development — The Perfect Storm

In some respects it is amazing to look at where the large Indian service providers have come from. Although there is no shortage of success case studies, awards, and accolades to go around, Indian offshore service providers simply served demand — they did not create the demand. I know that counts for something, and they have made some very good decisions, but the concern we have is other countries continue to "study" India as the model to adopt and to launch their outsourcing efforts. The complicating factor is that customers' needs, issues, and challenges are rapidly evolving, and we feel too few are studying the customers.

a. Staff Augmentation

Although large multinational firms, such as General Electric and Texas Instruments, were establishing significant operations in India during the 1970s, the seeds were being planted that would begin to create a wealth of young Indian development talent. In and of itself, this did not dictate success. The combination of a large and growing Indian community in the United States, severe skill shortage of information technology (IT) while the market was red hot, and liberal visa policies made more liberal through legislation all contributed to a flood of Indian developers entering the United States and European workplace in the early to mid-1990s.

What is also important to recognize is that cost was not an issue. Indian firms were placing their resources at U.S. comparable rates. These organizations quickly began to scale with little attention to methodologies of the capability maturity model (CMM) or project management professionals (PMPs). Their focus was on managing the visa process, acquiring proper resource training, and applying a tremendous work ethic.

b. Onsite Projects

Based on the success gained through staff augmentation, customers began to ask providers of offshore resources if they could take on projects. As offshore firms began to take on these projects, they were pushed to acquire and put into practice project management skills. Not typically a role well suited for Indian development executives working at a U.S. customer site, they turned to industry-accepted and proven processes, a decision that set a spectacular stage of growth.

c. "Over-the-Wall" Project Development

With proven technical capabilities and a growing level of process discipline, customers began to ask if their offshore suppliers could do more: could they take a project, execute, and bring it back fully tested and ready to deploy? The shift to global sourcing had begun.

Although there are more than enough examples of failure and customers pulling projects back in-house, there were enough successes, cost savings, and added value to establish sufficient momentum to start the boulder down the hill.

d. Offshore Development

The ball was now rolling. Indian firms applied a fanatical approach to process discipline and adherence to evolving standards, such as Carnegie Mellon's CMM and International Standards Organization (ISO) standards. As you will read later, Software Engineering Institute (SEI) CMM methodologies were established within the U.S. Department of Defense as a means to establish the software development rigor necessary for complex, mission-critical applications. Although the methodologies were applied within the Department of Defense and the systems integrators that support their unique environments, SEI CMM had little impact in the commercial marketplace, that is, until now.

Indian offshore firms quickly combined the basics of project management with the discipline of CMM software development methodologies. Suddenly there was a real offering; although U.S. developers may not desire to practice it, they understood the risk reduction associated with the methodology.

We could say the rest has been "all history" from that point; however we are still very much midstream in the global sourcing market. True winners are yet to be crowned. The market continues to splinter and morph, putting firms that were seen to be clear winners suddenly being hunted as takeover candidates.

C.   Offshore Adoption Model

Offshore outsourcing, in the initial stages, appeared to be aligning nicely with this traditional adoption pattern. However, in the past few years the global sourcing market has developed multiple dimensions or layers of global sourcing customers entering the global sourcing market at various entry points. As an example, a firm new to global sourcing has never done so before, but believing it important, hires an advisory firm to help establish a sourcing strategy. The decision is made to develop a captive center, an operational model where the company establishes its own dedicated facility. They have bypassed the "traditional" adoption of offshore outsourcing and taken the strategic step to win control and accept the associated risk.

We cite this example to demonstrate that as the global sourcing segment has matured and become less intimidating to customers, organizations are evaluating various sourcing operational models versus immediately calling an Infosys or Wipro to come give a price quote. This is a major reason why the true winners in the global sourcing segment have yet to be crowned, and so many other global destinations continue to enter the fray.

D   Offshore Destinations

There are a few key ingredients necessary for countries to be taken seriously on the global sourcing stage:

- ◾ Attractive tax and business incentives
- ◾ Qualified resource pool in terms of skills, experience, and size
- ◾ Long-term commitment to educational systems necessary to produce required talent
- ◾ Mature processes or the work ethic to apply these processes
- ◾ Quality technology infrastructure

The Internet has significantly altered the barrier of entry for many countries. Internet access and the availability of high-speed data lines mean every country with the proper focus and incentives can claim a viable global sourcing alternative;

however if scale, quality of resource pool, and maturity are the driving factors, there are only a handful of true, low-cost, leading global sourcing destinations.

1. Global Sourcing Macro-Region Issues

Before we begin to look at the individual countries that comprise the global sourcing community today, it is important to identify those key evaluation criteria that will determine those locations that best suit your individual needs. Independent research continues to document the core drivers that organizations use to establish their global sourcing locations. These criteria are: language capabilities, the size and skill of the perceived available workforce, quality and pervasiveness of the educational system, attrition levels, and the potential corporate leverage an organization can extract from an investment in a specific geography.

Although this is not an exhaustive list and there may be some very important items for your unique situation, we have found that some combination of these factors typically occupies the top spots. One item that is not on the list and could have a very significant impact on your global sourcing operation is a change in a country's tax structure or incentives.

Perhaps one reason we have not seen this as a key factor in determining a location is the relative parity among many of the world's global sourcing locations; however, it is critical to understand the length of time that tax incentives and structures will be in place or the time horizon for potential change. For example, India is the dominant location for information technology outsourcing (ITO) and business processing outsourcing (BPO) today. Many organizations have tapped this country based on the above core criteria as well as on an attractive tax and business environment. Today, however, as India has become so dominant, significant tax debates are occurring in their centers of government that could significantly impact the cost of using India as a global sourcing destination. The old adage "consumer beware" is very, very true as well as an "educated consumer is the best customer."

a. Language Capabilities

There are many overstated claims about a country or region's English capabilities and multilingual capabilities. These items are challenging to really evaluate on a single due diligence visit or two, as many of the individuals you will meet are not the people who will be running your offshore development center. In fact, it may not really sink in until you are well into your first project: speaking English and understanding or comprehending English are two very different things.

Our experience has been that the Philippines may have the best overall comprehension capabilities, followed by India and South America. China is trying very hard to improve in this area; however, it will take time for this to take root.

Although it is incredibly challenging today, we are confident they will continue to make strides.

We have found that one way to uncover the depth of language capabilities at a potential supplier or location is to insist that all conversation during the workday be in English or the language required by your operation. Regardless of position or role on the team, suppliers must speak the assigned language. As you mingle and interact with those at developer levels all the way through senior management of the offshore operation, you will easily sense the true language capability and facilitate continued improvement. We will touch on additional mechanisms that can be used to help in this important area once you have established an offshore operation.

b. Resource Capabilities

Every offshore destination claims incredible skills, a large and eager workforce waiting to help you with your challenge, and an educational system that promises to keep your resource pipeline full of world-class talent. The single best example of bringing this challenge into perspective is the tremendous skill shortage being experienced in China today.

Our opinion is that an analysis of a country's resource capability needs to incorporate an understanding of the skills you require in combination with the overall general skill universe. Although India and China are the most populated nations on the globe, both are not a certainty to attract and retain the talent you require. In fact, they are experiencing challenges not unlike Silicon Valley in the 1980s and 1990s.

When considering a global sourcing destination, we suggest you understand a few dimensions about the countries you are considering. These include:

■ Number of years involved with global sourcing
■ Number of cities or major centers within the country that have focused on outsourcing the types of services you are seeking
■ The relative perception of these types of positions within the local economy and culture. For example, Indian developers aggressively and joyously seek application maintenance roles, which are viewed as a means to get ahead, whereas in Russia, a computer scientist may begrudgingly accept this type of position; waiting for the first opportunity to secure a more challenging role more fitting of his or her skills.

Clearly there are dynamics that only become visible after spending a significant amount of time in a country and conducting interviews with many differing constituencies, but it is possible to understand the relative strength of a country or region. Here are some suggestions for you if you are in a situation to evaluate global sourcing locations.

Skill of Labor Pool

We believe the following criteria are essential to uncover the skills available within a country or a supplier's capabilities:

- Number of development teams in excess of 100 FTEs
- Length of time supporting FTE teams that are larger than 100
- Number of project managers who have managed projects greater than 50,000 hours
- Number of years the country has been actively (and successfully) involved in the global sourcing market
- Career advancement track for both project managers and technical resources

Size of Labor Pool

Size isn't everything, but when you suddenly have a critical position to replace and there are no resources of the experience and skills you require, size matters. Again, we're not talking about simple raw numbers, but the ability to build, retain, and grow the core competencies required.

There are strategies to work around these issues, but each will require a sizeable universe to pull required foundation skills that can be built on. Our suggestions are to build an appropriate buffer pool and training curriculum with the necessary resource levels to cover possible market dynamics.

Educational System

Not all university programs are the same. Although many countries are making great strides in this area, their focus on IT education has been driven by the success they have witnessed in India. Clearly countries such as Israel, Ireland, and Canada have many positives as does India, and have all offered superior IT education for two decades or more. Others simply cannot point to this record of focus and investment. We believe China will continue to grow in this area and perhaps in the next five years, begin to see the depth of resources in experience and skills required to truly compete with India.

Secondary educational markets also play an important and growing role in preparing a steady stream of "freshies" to an IT or BPO organization. Firms such as NIIT in India have helped shape the global sourcing landscape as they apply their strong educational curriculum in new regions and countries around the globe. (We all wanted to make it to the finest universities, but some of us just didn't make the grade.) I have found this secondary market can produce individuals who are incredibly driven; don't discount this important pool. We have spent many hours talking with senior executives at some of the IT community's most prestigious organizations and to a man, they all want the best and brightest. Competition for the top graduates from leading universities is fierce, and we have yet to see an equally high correlation of loyalty.

c. Attrition

We find it ironic that the business trend that gave birth to the offshore outsourcing market now poses a significant challenge to global service providers in their own backyards. Do not be fooled or lulled into thinking this is a temporary situation or a short-lived business cycle. As global sourcing grows in various countries around the world, each sub-market will experience a maturing process that at a logical and predictable point will encounter attrition.

Our advice is not to try and run away from the issue, but be aware of it, understand the drivers, and plan appropriate measures with your service provider or leaders of your captive operation. Later in the book we will touch on different techniques to build into your global software development project plan to help elevate the impact a high level of attrition can have on productivity, but the reason to add this ingredient to your macro-market evaluation is that attrition has a predictable and direct impact on cost and the long-term sustainability of your operation. In addition, we have found global sourcing providers, leading Indian providers, as well as multi-national corporations (MNCs) such as IBM and EDS, as well as multinational corporations (MNCs), all seem to want to wish the challenge away; worse yet, they want their customers to assume the risk. They do this by negotiating aggressive currency fluctuation and cost-of-living adjustment clauses into their contracts based more on emotion and superficial data than true detail.

In our experience, as of this writing, offshore outsourcing rates have stabilized slightly, and in certain cases at appropriate volume and term commitments, they are still coming down. We will discuss this shortly.

We discuss attrition on a country level later on in this book as well as ways to address the impact of attrition on global software development projects, negotiation strategies for dealing with your global service provider on a project or company-wide level, and recruitment tactics to ensure you maintain continuity. Clearly we feel this is an important reality to get your hands around early and often.

d. Corporate Leverage

Most of the time those of us running a software development project really don't care very much about what in-country leverage our firm may have gained by selecting one offshore location versus another. In fact, it may never be articulated outside the sourcing team, executive level, or boardroom.

However, there is always a criterion for the selection of a short list of countries to consider. Look at China: foreign direct investment (FDI) is pouring into the country. Leading firms from all industries are hiring consultants and leading business strategists to help them "get into" China. If we simply looked at the criteria we have already listed — language capabilities, resource capabilities, and attrition — China may not be a top-three choice. However, they offer so much potential to an organization as a consumer of their products and services that they cannot be ignored. In fact, the criteria may be so strong that they will override all dimensions of the evaluation.

Recent independent research has shown that organizations that have more than three years of experience leveraging offshore resources begin to expand into other countries as a means of diversification on multiple levels: resource skills, tax liability, improved customer service, and enhancing their opportunity for revenue growth.

In summary, the global sourcing market is experiencing rapid and dynamic change on multiple levels. Although the surface waters may appear calm, there is a great deal of education and time required to gain a credible level of knowledge of the market.

Now that you have made that all-important investment in time and focus to learning the macro trends of the global outsourcing community, it is time to take a deeper look at a few of the leading countries that have probably scored high on your analysis.

2. Global Sourcing Country Issues

An understanding of the macro-economic forces and critical regional selection criteria prepares us to now look at the global regions that are competing to win your offshore outsourcing investment. By all measures India is the dominant country selection today and into the foreseeable future. It is our opinion that although the gap between India and the other countries will narrow, India's unique combination of language, skills, and size of workforce will fortify their grip on No. 1. The apparent resistance of Indian Pure Plays to truly "globalize" their organizations will allow other regions of the world to secure sizeable portions of the market.

The following analysis of global sourcing countries is not intended to be an exhaustive list. Our goal is to help you understand the relative strengths of the players today, provide some insight to the dynamics that could impact your near- and long-term operations, and help you anticipate potential changes.

a. India

1. The clear leader of the global sourcing landscape today, India leveraged its many strengths to be the destination of choice. Regardless of the selected global sourcing operational model or required skills, India has had the proper mix of government incentives, skilled workforce, and sensitivity to business dealings.

2. Where we believe India is vulnerable is on several important fronts:
    a. The physical infrastructure remains poor and, despite best efforts, seems to be losing ground to regions such as China and other Asian destinations.
    b. Indian pure play firms have struggled with middle management and seasoned resource attrition, trying to pass the financial impact of these trends to the customer.
    c. The Indian government, in particular the Treasury Ministry, continues to suffer from rumors of tax incentive repeals and other activities that could make it difficult to project the cost of doing business in India.
3. Regardless, we believe India will remain the leading choice on the global sourcing landscape, but will see its dominant position reduced.

b. China

1. For the past several years, analyst firms have been predicting that this country is only a matter of three to five years away from being a true contender on the global sourcing stage. We can tell you from firsthand, on-the-ground experience that although we also believe China as a country will be a significant player in the global sourcing community, the manner in which this growth is realized will be very different from that of India.
2. China has a tremendous internal physical infrastructure. Clearly the level of FDI that has been pouring into the country has enabled them to place that investment in very obvious areas such as highways, airports, buildings, etc.
3. In addition, China continues to provide excellent business incentives on a provincial basis that, when combined with the lure of cracking this large consumer market, organizations are finding it difficult to pass up.
4. The central government has also eased the restrictions around foreign-owned business with the introduction of the wholly owned foreign enterprise (WOFE).
5. Where China does suffer is in several very basic and critical areas:
    a. **Language.** Several years ago, the government and universities announced an initiative to improve their English language capabilities, in essence, an effort to overcome the most basic of obstacles. We do not for a moment doubt that in time this initiative will pay significant dividends; however, today English language capabilities are weak.
    b. **Seasoned skills.** We all have this mental image of an endless stream of qualified resources at the ready; however this long line of qualified resources becomes short very quickly when experienced developers and managers are sought. This has already forced a level of attrition and pay pressure for qualified resources to those levels found today in Bangalore, India.
    c. **Middle management.** Basically there is none. The market has grown so dramatically and the entrepreneurial spirit is so strong, it is hard to find

a quality mid-level management layer in most of the Chinese indigenous global sourcing organizations.

d. **Process.** In general, China has not fully embraced the Project Management Institute (PMI) style for project management techniques. In fact, after interviews of over 30 different indigenous Chinese sourcing providers, they seem most intent on having complete projects carved out with sufficient documentation that they can execute fully from the Chinese location, and on completion, send the finished product back to the customer.

    i. During the interview process and extensive site visits, it also became apparent that another reason for the perceived avoidance of establishing a true onsite-offshore model is the visa process within China.

    ii. One of the most frequently cited means to work around this issue by the Chinese providers is to attract expatriates back to China who have U.S. or European experience at managing software development projects.

e. **Intellectual property.** Yes, intellectual property (IP) is an issue. Culturally, it appears the Chinese approach is to develop a thorough understanding of how something works and make it better or adopt it to their unique culture, regardless of ownership. The firms we met with that have taken appropriate measures within their development environment to reduce IP infringement appear to suffer a higher level of attrition than those that have not. Although we are confident this will continue to improve over time, it needs to be a top item of concern.

f. **Work ethic.** After many interviews with Chinese executives running substantial development operations in China, there was a consistent undertone when we spoke of the typical Chinese software developer. These themes included:

    i. Strong technical skills; more innovative than those of India

    ii. Government-managed 40-hour work week with overtime pay escalations

    iii. The "single child" generation; hardship in managing and driving productivity

    iv. Limited mobility due to government HUKOW (similar to our social security system) that reduces individuals' benefits when they move from their designated province to another

6. Despite these issues, China will firmly establish its position as the second leading global sourcing destination for ITO and continue to expand its role as the BPO destination for organizations to service their Asian customers.

7. We believe in China. The major beneficiaries of the growth of global sourcing will be the Chinese provinces, as they attract a tremendous number of captive centers to their technology parks, and the MNCs such as Accenture, EDS, IBM Global Services, and Bearing Point.

8. Indigenous Chinese global sourcing providers seem most capable of serving the variable staffing needs of these firms versus being able to build a sizeable U.S. footprint and pipeline of U.S. projects for U.S. deployment.

c. Russia

1. We must say that this has to us, been the biggest disappointment of the global sourcing community. Filled with promise, the Russian software development community has achieved little broad success in North America. Combined with the current state of affairs in Russia today such as the Yukos debacle, the VimpleCom tax situation, and President Putin's continued reassertion of government control, Russia has lost momentum and faces ever-growing competition.
2. FDI has slowed significantly; making it more challenging for continued investment in necessary infrastructure.
3. Russia is also encountering a challenge with the emergence of Eastern Europe as a desirable global sourcing destination, in BPO activities in particular. There are several significant reasons for this that we will touch on in a moment.

d. Philippines

1. The Philippines continues to play a significant role in the global sourcing portfolio. Perhaps the most successful way to tap the quality resources in this country is through an MNC service provider. There are some local organizations, but few have achieved critical mass.
2. The Philippines, with a U.S.-aligned tax and accounting structure along with excellent English skills, should continue to be a top-five consideration for organizations looking to establish or expand their global sourcing portfolio.

e. Eastern Europe

1. Eastern Europe as a global sourcing destination has become a 'must consider' when developing a global sourcing portfolio. Although as a category, the countries that comprise Eastern Europe are somewhat young and lack scale such as India and China, we have found excellent skills for both IT outsourcing and business process outsourcing.
2. We define Eastern Europe today as:
     i. Lithuania
    ii. Latvia
   iii. Estonia
    iv. Slovakia
     v. Slovenia

    vi. Poland

   vii. Czech Republic

  viii. Hungary

3. Some of the significant strengths these countries embody today are:
   i. A strong educational system inherited from their Soviet heritage to support world-class scientists from a broad range of disciplines
   ii. Strong multilingual capabilities
   iii. Excellent geographic location to establish distributed 24/7 operations
   iv. Exciting economic incentives from each country
4. The interest and use of Eastern Europe will only grow with the planned European Union (EU) expansion that will include Romania in 2007.

f. South America

We continue to see growing interest in this part of the world. There are several industries that have taken root in South America in regions such as Brazil and Argentina. Financial services and automotive industries are strong today and have helped spawn a community of local IT service providers as well as attract the leading MNCs. Other parts of South America and Central America such as Costa Rica also continue to attract attention. We are confident that as the offshore market matures, South America will continue to play an increasing role.

g. Near-Shore Alternatives

1. Canada, Mexico and the emerging global sourcing markets of South America, particularly Brazil and Argentina, are credible locations for North American firms to consider. Although the weakening U.S. dollar has robbed Canada of some of its price advantage, management oversight and many of the expenses necessary to manage an offshore facility are significantly reduced. In addition, the quality of the development staff and experience of the project management team will be well aligned.
2. We also have observed that the major offshore service providers continue to expand their presence in these regions, which will help continue the vitality of the near-shore offering. A possible driver behind this development is the continued visa challenges offshore firms encounter due to the current limitations and strict guidelines; these do not exist in Canada, South America, and Mexico.
3. Our recommendation is that if your service provider is aggressively promoting a near-shore component, make certain you truly know what it is you are receiving. We have heard stories of a customer doing a site visit in Halifax and feeling like he had walked into a development center in Bangalore. Although he was satisfied with the work, he felt as if he was overpaying as he had not

gone through the exercise of pricing the critical "offshore working onsite" category in his agreement.

4. Mexico continues to expand in terms of its IT capabilities, but is still viewed as a region that lacks the ability to scale quality IT staff.

5. South America as a global sourcing destination is growing in popularity and its ability to deliver. Argentina and Brazil have very strong capabilities, evident through large MNCs, such as EDS and IBM.

6. All of these near-shore regions, in addition to countries of the Caribbean and Central America, are enjoying strong growth in the BPO and call-center markets.

h. Other Players

You may find it surprising that we have not covered Ireland, Israel, Singapore, and some of the other vanguards of the global sourcing market. Our focus has been on locations that are perceived to offer a solid cost advantage over North America. Although these regions have excellent quality, they don't necessarily provide significant cost savings; however, they should not be ruled out too quickly as they continue to innovate their offerings and expand their advanced capabilities.

3. Supplier Categories

A look at the countries and regions competing on the global sourcing stage is only a partial analysis of the market. To gain a true understanding of the global sourcing segment, we need to take a look at the activities of global sourcing providers to better understand the dynamics of the game. As we mentioned earlier, the global sourcing game is far from over, and we believe the winners are yet to be crowned. In fact, it is our opinion that the competitive landscape is going to become very exciting to observe over the next 24 to 36 months.

For the purposes of our discussion, we have identified three distinct market categories: MNCs, pure plays (defined below), and you as a Captive Center.

a. Multinational Corporations

These organizations appear to have done one of two things as offshore outsourcing began to grow:

1. Adopted a global sourcing delivery model to their internal development operations to lower cost while publicly advising against the trend

2. Publicly advised clients and prospects against the use of offshore resources and shoved their heads in the sand

Table 2.1   2006 Managing Global Development Risk Top Service Providers

TCS	Wipro	Infosys	HCL	Cognizant
Syntel	Satyam	iGate	Covansys	MindTree
Patni	L&T	Polaris	Hexaware	NIIT

In some respects, the lack of aggressive movement on the part of the MNCs allowed the offshore pure plays to become established, but as the overall size of the offshore outsourcing market is still below 15 percent of the total sourcing market, it may seem that the MNCs have suffered little.

Once we got past the initial wave, leaders such as IBM Global Services, EDS, ACS to name a few, continued to build their global capabilities and slowly evolved their sourcing message to encompass global delivery. Some firms have done a better job of it than others, but by and large, if you are talking today to an MNC, the odds are very good that they have strong offshore capabilities that are CMM certified and that they manage a diversity of work. Combined with their proven project management capabilities, the MNCs are increasingly offering compelling solutions.

b.   Pure Plays

We define pure play global service providers as organizations whose true operational execution resides in a global sourcing location. We draw this distinction because many of the leading offshore firms may present themselves as having U.S. or U.K. headquarters with a wholly owned subsidiary in India. Although this may be an accurate description of their legal entity, the powerbase of the offshore service provider will typically be at the offshore location.

For the sake of this conversation we will limit our focus to the Indian pure plays as today they represent the most significant players. By several independent estimates, better than 70 percent of all offshore outsourcing dollars are spent in India on both ITO and BPO activities. This has helped spawn an entire category of global service provider that in its infancy was little more than staff augmentation firms and today is pushing into comprehensive solution providers.

We need to keep in mind that the three largest of these pure plays (TCS, Infosys, and Wipro) will eclipse the $2-billion mark in total revenue shortly. Although they are enjoying strong sequential growth, they are still very small when compared to a leading MNC. They also tend to focus on applications support and have quietly been expanding into infrastructure support as a means to expand their services.

What these firms typically do not do is what could be termed total outsourcing: they resist "re-badge" employees, take over existing data center operations, or assume risk. What they will do is take on your applications and remote managed services work and apply their structured processes to deliver quality at a fair price. It is our opinion, and a driving vision of this book, that to drive global sourcing to the next level, U.S.-based project managers and technical leaders will need to become expert in managing remote resources to harness their capability.

The focus of our time together is on *Managing Global Development Risk*; however, the global sourcing market has pushed well into the BPO market and, as previously mentioned, is expanding quickly into IT infrastructure and remote managed services. Combined, these facets of the global sourcing market promise to fuel continued growth for the providers and refine the processes and methodologies to manage these projects.

c. Captive Centers

Why would we include captive centers in the supplier category? The reason is that as the offshore market has matured and people have become more comfortable with leveraging offshore resources, they have questioned the need of using a global service provider. Establishing your own foreign wholly owned subsidiary essentially places captive centers in the global sourcing market, although typically the sole customer is internal.

By virtue of establishing an offshore operation, captive centers are now competing with the MNCs and pure plays for resources, office locations, and all other operational needs they may have in establishing a functioning and productive development organization. The upfront investment is significantly more than establishing a partnership with a global sourcing provider; the long-term financial impact is very positive.

It is important to point out that this is not a new or emerging trend. In fact, many of the leaders such as Texas Instruments, General Electric, and Motorola have long-standing global development centers. What has emerged is the surprising level of interest and activity by small and mid-sized organizations to open their own captive centers.

4. Offshore Operating Models

The global sourcing market continues to evolve very quickly. As noted earlier, it is our belief that the customer is ultimately driving supplier behavior and service offering. This has led to the creation of four distinct operational models in the global sourcing space. Although there may be variations of these four, most operations can be broadly grouped into one of the following.

a. Offshore Development Center

Offshore pure plays love to talk about the establishment of a customer's dedicated offshore development center (ODC). Although the marketing aspect of this is very appealing, for a company to achieve a true ODC there are a number of unique issues that need to be tackled such as security, development, environment, and connectivity to ensure the work activity is truly isolated and protected. After many due diligence visits to offshore facilities, it is clear that ODCs are the primary manner in which offshore resources are engaged. It is also clear that it is project-based work or staff augmentation capacity versus true, ongoing application development and maintenance or remote monitoring activity. Typically at this point, the service provider will seek additional investment to create a true stand-alone area for your growing operation, which in our opinion, is of great value.

Making certain that your ODC is a unique and defined space helps you begin to build a personality and dynamic within the work environment. Compared with being placed in a large room where there are numerous customers being supported, a true ODC begins to take on the personality of the customer. We have found that productivity is enhanced, morale improves, and shortly thereafter, the type of work being done also expands.

The characteristics of the ODC are the following:

- The resources are employees of the service provider.
- These resources can expand or contract based on work load.
- Typically the cost of the space and all technical needs other than communications cost are baked into the hourly bill rate.
- Your area is one of many ODCs in a defined area.
- The typical billing relationship is on a time and material basis or a fixed headcount level with a defined utilization band to adjust level.

b. Build Operate Transfer

This operational model was all the rage in 2003 and 2004. Every service provider we spoke with from the very largest of offshore pure plays to the absolute smallest, *all* claimed deep experience with helping clients establish true build–operate–transfer (BOT) facilities; what we found to be fact was quite different.

Let's take a look at the concept of the BOT: the service provider helps your organization build up an offshore capability and then after some event or trigger for which the supplier is compensated, they hand you the key and say goodbye to continued billing. Is it understandable then that the offshore pure play service provider, although they may have worked with you to create a BOT option in the contract, really does not want you to execute the transfer? If you do, then you can understand why this much-promoted operational model has in fact had little real impact. The service providers do not want this to occur. They will do what they can to convince you that it is not in your best interest, and ultimately you will fail without their expert methodologies and processes.

We believe it is this dynamic that we have just described that has helped accelerate the growth of captive centers. Until offshore firms can clearly document productivity and the benefit of CMM Level 5 processes in terms of quality and overall cost, organizations will naturally begin to look at alternative models.

When evaluating a BOT as an operational model, many of the strategic considerations are the same as those for a captive center. Tax issues, incorporation processes, human resources, and a host of business elements need to be addressed prior to entering into a BOT agreement, even if it is just a clause in a standard ODC type of agreement.

c. Joint Venture

The joint venture (JV) model remains a viable alternative for organizations that view global sourcing or offshoring as strategic to overall corporate direction, but that may be hesitant to make a large investment. We are also seeing an increase in the use of the JV operational model as organizations expand their global sourcing portfolio to include new countries and locations. In many respects, a JV can be viewed as a means to enter a market with a partner who has insider status and is well connected, or the potential of establishing a revenue-generating arm in addition to securing the required internal support; whatever the driver, JVs present a viable alternative.

Perhaps the challenge with a JV is that when it fails, it tends to get a high level of attention. Similar to the spectacular coverage failed JVs will receive here at home, those formed to serve a global development need tend to collapse due to a mismatch of personality or expectations. Despite this potential, we believe JVs will continue to prove a viable alternative, especially with the continued expansion by firms into multiple country locations.

d. Captive Center

As the global sourcing market matures, we have seen a significant increase in captive centers. Interestingly, it was the captive centers of leaders such as General Electric, Motorola, IBM, and Texas Instruments that gave rise to the offshore outsourcing segment. Today, firms large and small are evaluating and selecting captive centers as part of an overall global sourcing strategy.

There are several primary drivers that contribute to the determination of a captive center as a viable option for your firm. These include the following:

- Global sourcing is a long-term strategic corporate direction.
- Your organization is looking to move beyond simple application development and maintenance (ADM) or project support to truly integrate and expand capabilities.

- There already exist or there is a true commitment to establish a stand-alone entity in the selected country.
- Cost analysis and current financial baselines support the investment with a return on investment (ROI) in a reasonable and defined period of time.
- Labor arbitrage is viewed as the initial financial benefit; allowing a longer path to productivity.

To us, the interesting development around captive centers is the multiple dimensions impacting the offshore outsourcing market today. Organizations that have been leveraging offshore for a period of time and have grown comfortable with the model are increasingly establishing captive center operations, many in parallel with their ODCs maintained by a supplier. Over time, the majority of work — if not all — transfers into the captive center. Additionally, we are observing smaller organizations as well as those who are first evaluating offshore outsourcing, looking at and selecting the captive center operational model. Perhaps it is because they feel the suppliers simply are not aggressive in meeting their needs or there is an immediate desire for control and building an asset. Whatever the reason, captive centers have developed into a significant competitive threat for both the large MNCs as well as the Indian pure plays.

What you will hear from the service provider community is that the captive center choice is far more expensive than what your financial models will indicate. The premise is that by going it alone, you will struggle with productivity, attrition, and operational efficiencies that will balloon all of your estimates. However, what we have observed (and a central driver behind *Managing Global Development Risk*) is the use of an offshore partner does not guarantee productivity, reduced attrition, or accurate budgets. In fact, once you have worked through the initial stages of establishing a captive center, this may in fact be the only way to ensure ongoing productivity and control.

It is our opinion that the continued growth of captive centers, combined with the BOT and JV models, will continue to change the overall global sourcing landscape.

5. Global Sourcing Pricing Dynamics

We spend so much time talking about hourly bill rates for individual full-time equivalents (FTEs) that we lose sight of the real cost of global outsourcing. This is evident in the number of firms that continue to struggle with developing accurate budgets, many of which have extensive experience with offshore outsourcing. The introduction of offshore or global outsourcing impacts internal team cost every bit as much as the cost associated with the global resources regardless of an operational model. However, in an attempt to provide some perspective, we have provided below our thoughts and insight on the following cost drivers of global outsourcing.

a. Rates

The offshore or global outsourcing market is one controlled by "rate envy." I'm certain you are familiar with this concept. Everyone likes to brag about the absolutely incredible offshore rates he or she successfully negotiated. What we need to be cognizant of are the many drivers that can quickly take what appears to be a reasonable rate and make the overall exercise incredibly expensive. Here are a few of the items we recommend you pay particular attention to:

1. "Freshies." Offshore firms are continually recruiting recent graduates to their organizations. Use of these talented but raw resources is a significant way in which offshore firms build margin.
2. Offshore resources working onsite. Another very interesting pricing dynamic is what appears to be a complete focus on negotiating the offshore rate, with little attention paid to the rates paid for offshore resources working at the customer location onsite. As we will touch on in a moment, not only can the onsite-offshore ratio quickly change your budget, but the impact is compounded when you are paying an onsite rate commensurate with a U.S. consultant for an offshore resource.
3. Category definitions. Based on Point 2 above, we strongly recommend three core categories of resources for your global sourcing agreement:
   a. Offshore resources
   b. Offshore-onsite resources
   c. Onsite resources, typically U.S. citizens, green card holders, or H1-B visa holders
4. Travel. Many times we have observed that the negotiated rates do not include or account for travel. There are logical times when travel costs are high such as during knowledge acquisition or knowledge transfer, but travel occurs throughout the full duration of the project or running of the ODC. Who is responsible for this cost? Is it a staffing plan that you feel is justified, or is it a means by which the service provider is rotating staff at your expense?
5. Communications cost. Does your rate include the communication links to your U.S. or European centers? Are they sufficient to handle the type of work activity?
6. Standard desktop. What is included in the service providers standard desktop for their resources? Will it support your current and potential work?
7. Training. Beyond the training of resources new to the project, is there ongoing training? What is the minimum training for each resource coming onto your project or ODC?
8. Buffer. Does your service provider provide buffer resources to help offset the impact of attrition or support overall staffing ramp plans?

These are some of the key areas you need to define before you can determine the real cost of an offshore resource.

b. Onsite-Offshore Ratio

We have already touched on the impact of onsite resources from a cost perspective. We believe the true culprit with an onsite-offshore ratio is that customers quickly become very comfortable with a large onsite staff during the knowledge acquisition and knowledge transfer stage of the relationship. As the resources transition, you increasingly feel exposed, and your internal project managers struggle. As the offshore resources working onsite move back to the offshore facility, many times the project managers are now just becoming aware of what they are committed to. Again, this has been a key driver behind the creation of *Managing Global Development Risk* as a means to prepare you to successfully adapt to this transition.

c. Visa Considerations

The majority of the time, you have little to no awareness of the issues that impact a supplier and their visa management strategy. Although we are not recommending necessarily a detailed analysis of each onsite resource visa status, we are recommending that you are aware of the overall visa mix of your onsite staff as it will have significant implications that could impact continuity and overall cost.

There are several broad categories of visas:

- L-1. Typically this is a long-term visa that allows a resource to stay in the U.S. for up to 1 year. Many times, this resource has a standard rate plus a per diem of some sort and typically requires a return to India to renew the visa.
- B-1. Typically this is a short-term visa that allows managers to be in the U.S. for up to 90 days, and typically requires a return to India to renew the visa.
- H1-B. Typically this can be renewed on an annual basis and does not require the resource to be in India. This is the visa that the U.S. government has significantly reduced over the past several years, but in reality, it is the most expensive resource for the global service provider to place at your worksite.

The use of the other visa categories has increased significantly as it enables suppliers to maximize margins, and if not carefully negotiated around travel as staff move into and out of the customer site, the supplier has potentially eliminated any liability.

d. Staffing Models

All of the above elements contribute to the overall staffing plan or model that ultimately will drive the final cost. As you can see, rates are a single input to the formula with a number of key variables. The staffing model, which is the culmination of the onsite-offshore ratio; movement of staff during the knowledge acquisition, knowledge, and steady-state phases; and the length of these phases all need to be closely studied and understood so you can agree with the overall rhythm of the global sourcing operation.

6. Pricing Options

The offshore category has seen a number of operational models as well as pricing options take shape over the past few years; however, it is important to understand that this is a community that started and grew up through staff augmentation: billable hours. This has made the evolution of pricing options somewhat limited or, should we say, an empty promise because at the end of the day, the suppliers want time and material agreements.

Our belief is that as offshore service providers mature, we will see an increase in the number of pricing models actively accepted. Let us take a moment to talk about the pricing options that are in common practice today in an ADM environment.

a. Fixed Price

We have not come across a supplier who will openly say they do not do fixed price projects; however, once they actually structure the cost, you will see they attempt to push all of the risk to the customer. Their hesitation centers around the fact that a fixed price bid will require clear and understood requirements and specifications. It also will require the provider to develop a project plan that is accurate and complete. Typically the fixed price bid is going to be based on a rate card and some risk factor to account for a customer's inability to estimate or provide the required input for a project plan as well as the supplier's "fudge factor."

Fixed price projects can and should cover the full spectrum of ADM work. In particular, we have found that application construct, test, deployment, and sustainment of activities work very well. When working with your supplier on a fixed price project, you need to be aware of and focused on the structure of the change process and the expenses associated with the project:

1. Change process. The agreed to change process is a trigger designed to help suppliers more comfortably bid fixed price projects in the event the customer completely missed some items that have material impact to effort and scope; it is not meant to be the vehicle by which the supplier manipulates the system. With a fixed price project, a customer will typically receive a long list of supplier "assumptions." Before you agree to the project cost, make certain to work through these assumptions with your supplier as they *will* come back as an issue. Make certain there is an agreed to escalation process that will allow you to quickly determine the validity of a change request. If a supplier simply missed the issue, it is not the customer's fault. If this was a competitive situation, why allow a supplier who provided a lower bid to simply

and methodically raise your price because he did not include certain project elements? With several of our clients we have had to do a great deal of education on these issues because the project manager will tend to be at the level where these items arise and are executed. If you are not careful, your fixed price can quickly run out of control.

2. Expenses. Perhaps a holdover from the fact that many of the suppliers have grown through staff augmentation, we find a surprising number of fixed price projects that do not include the necessary expenses associated with executing the project. Believe us when we say that the suppliers have done a very thorough analysis of the cost associated with executing project, and they have factored expenses into the equation. This is again another effort to push project risk to the customer and in our opinion dramatically reduces the supplier's obligation to efficiently manage the project. If expenses are to be paid by the customer, what is the concern for the supplier to fly in a resource from another city versus one that is local? Can they be a little more efficient using their time with the customer? Our belief is that a fixed price project should absolutely include the cost associated with executing the project. If the customer then requests travel separate from or in addition to the established project plan, at that point a change request should be issued.

b. Time and Material

By far the supplier's preferred pricing option, a time and material (T&M) project, enables the supplier to more comfortably provide services. The vast portion of *Managing Global Development Risk* is dedicated to helping project managers execute their tasks. T&M agreements, in our opinion, require a substantial amount of oversight to ensure you succeed. These individual areas are well documented throughout this book. In this particular area, we want to speak to the business issues behind these elements and the value they bring if you are dealing with a T&M billing relationship.

1. Service levels. The value of service levels in a T&M project is that it provides very real evidence of how the project is proceeding. Service levels can be metric-based measurements, as described in *Managing Global Development Risk,* or they can be simple deliverable-based items such as artifacts from key stages of the project. If your supplier is missing the dates and if costs are running high, you need to escalate.
2. Management oversight. We believe that T&M agreements require a significant amount of management overhead as detailed within *Managing Global Development Risk.*

3. Staffing plan. Typically with T&M projects, expenses are billed to the customer. If this is the case, the benefit of seeing a project staffing plan is that you are able to question staff dynamics such as time on site, travel, etc.

4. Utilization rate. This issue tends to be more critical if you are in an application-sustained type of project that requires a set number of ongoing staff. We have seen suppliers combine the T&M billing approach to a set number of resources to create the appearance of a fixed price or fixed fee billing relationship. If this is a situation you are considering or currently find yourself in, the inclusion of a resource or team utilization rate is essential. Make certain to define the activities that are to be included in the utilization calculation so there is no confusion. Now that you have an established utilization rate, you have a mechanism to establish a utilization "band" that controls the addition or removal of billable resources. This pushes some responsibility to the supplier to make certain the resources are being productive and contributing versus waiting for the next piece of work.

5. Project plan. Much like the staffing plan, once the project plan is established and agreed to, you manage the supplier to perform per the project plan. When combined with service levels, staffing, and utilization, there is a significant ability to proactively manage the project.

c. Cost Plus

This is a very interesting and challenging approach to offshore outsourcing typically reserved for very large, multiyear engagements, but we wanted to touch on it as we believe this can be an emerging pricing model for offshore outsourcing; despite the cries of the supplier community.

The theory behind a cost plus billing structure is that the supplier divulges all of his fixed cost and the customer and supplier negotiate a fair and equitable margin that the supplier can charge above the agreed to cost. Clearly this requires complete insight into the supplier's business operation and a total understanding of how he determines cost. Obviously, today there are only a select group of customers who can exert the appropriate leverage to nudge the suppliers to utilize this billing structure. Many times we find that the suppliers have made a flat statement that the cost of a resource by various categories is x and then there is a flat percentage above that rate. This is done with no real visibility into the elements that comprise the "cost" rate.

One reason we believe this pricing model will grow is the continued push of organizations to open their own offshore captive centers.

d. Other

As in most industries, there will be many variations of pricing options. Some will be combinations of the above core approaches whereas many will be rather creative.

7. Negotiation Posture

Negotiations tend to happen on multiple levels throughout the global sourcing life cycle. Of course the major negotiations will tend to be at the point your organization has established a request for proposal (RFP) and goes through the process of selecting an offshore partner or operational model that now provides you offshore resources. But do not be fooled; negotiations with the supplier are just starting. What we have observed is that the competition is fierce up until a supplier is selected, at which point the goal of the chosen supplier is to manage the relationship in as profitable a manner as possible. Sound project management skills and principles described throughout this book will help you more effectively manage and anticipate the dynamics of your global sourcing provider. This section is intended to help you understand the potential negotiation position during the major selection process as well as project-specific negotiation patterns you will most likely encounter.

a. Multinational Corporations

Here we want to take a few moments to discuss how the leading MNCs tend to handle themselves in an ITO scenario at two levels: the partnership negotiation and the execution negotiation levels.

Partnership Negotiation Level

1. It is at this level of negotiations that the MNCs are able to demonstrate their sophistication and capabilities. Years of honing their business development processes combined with strong marketing materials make MNCs a formidable contestant for your business.
2. Be certain to see through this and focus on service levels, metrics, their CMM capabilities, and how they will be assimilated by your organization. Understand their experience with your unique need based on a thorough evaluation of provided references.
3. Focus on establishing the core components of a master service agreement including areas such as:
   a. Comprehensive rate card
      i. Rates by skill level or category

      ii. The three recommended resource categories of onsite, offshore working onsite, and offshore

      iii. Length of resource commitment

      iv. Visa category

  b. Service levels

      i. Clear and concise service levels based on the principle of continuous improvement

      ii. Based on agreed to metric collection and measurement processes

      iii. Based on existing benchmark data

  c. Payment provisions

  d. Governance model and process

      i. Project management organization (PMO) structure

      ii. Escalation process

Execution Negotiation Level

1. This is the unglamorous level of negotiations typically at the project manager level with some IT management or director oversight. Execution negotiations, in our opinion, tend to be where the work will actually get accomplished.

2. What is interesting about these negotiations is that the supplier will typically push and say that all the parameters that drive their price have been negotiated. Although this is true of the major issues such as price, it typically does not lock resource mix, staffing plan, or model. This means there is a fair amount of negotiation to be done by the project management team on an ongoing basis.

3. MNCs are excellent at expanding their account footprint, understanding the manner in which your organization will contract for additional services, and making certain to somehow gain leverage as they work an ever-expanding array of projects.

4. Our recommendation is to keep them focused on executing projects in a linear fashion. We have seen a number of projects fail due to scope-creep and the supplier's complete focus on bagging the next great project.

b. Pure Plays

Here we want to take a few moments to discuss how the leading Indian pure plays tend to handle themselves in an IT outsourcing scenario at two levels: the partnership negotiation and the execution negotiation level. As a general statement, there appear to be very different strategies and approaches for the Indian firms for each of these negotiation events. It appears that they have learned that once they have gained access to a customer through some very tough negotiations, they are able to substantially improve their financial position on the individual projects that always pile on after they have successfully executed the first piece of work.

Partnership Negotiation Level

1. At this strategic level of negotiations, Indian firms will focus on their rate, the benefits of their CMM development processes, and the power of their experience project managing similar ADM projects.
2. They will work very hard to avoid or delay service level discussions.
   a. They will focus on negotiating a period of time to get comfortable with the application and environment in which to establish baselines.
   b. Many will engage the concept of continuous improvement and sharing the rewards, but we have not seen this placed into practice consistently.
3. In short, there will be a great deal of yeses with few direct nos to your RFP.
4. They will also want to build in rate escalation for multiyear periods.
   a. Make certain the focus is on cost of living adjustments versus currency fluctuation or the impact of attrition on the service provider's operating margins.
   b. It is not your responsibility to help them pay their employees more to retain them. We believe this to be their management challenge and one they need to come to grips with versus passing the risk along to you.

Execution Negotiation Level

This is where the Indian firms shine in terms of negotiation skills relative to the U.S. project manager. Hidden behind a veil of "communication or cultural" misunderstandings, Indian offshore pure plays do a tremendous job of building margin into the individual projects. Remember, they have won the deal because their rates were attractive so you don't have the option to push on price, but what you need to pay attention to are:

- Onsite-offshore ratios
- Team composition
- Staffing model
- Adherence to service levels
- Productivity levels
- Travel expenses and who is responsible
- Project level assumptions
- Trigger to change request

8. Summary — Negotiation Posture

You may be wondering why we have spent so much time on this subject. As a GDM responsible for the successful execution of projects, it is essential you understand these nuances because you will be managing your global service provider to execute your unique statement of work (SOW). Your SOW lives within the context of the overall master services agreement and is impacted by the selection your company has made on all the above topics. Our focus is to make certain you understand overall context.

For the purpose of this book, we are going to assume that you have just been handed a project that will require the use of global resources, and you have been handed an initial SOW and a brief outline of the terms and conditions that bind the relationship with the global service provider through the MSA. Good luck!

9. Global Sourcing Contract Structure

There are many components to a service contract or MSA between a customer and global service provider. For you to dig in and gain knowledge of the entire agreement would be a daunting task; however to effectively manage your project, there are a few key areas you should focus on and get clarification from your PMO or whichever authority is responsible for the overall relationship with the global service provider.

Here is a brief list of the items you must understand:

a. **Service levels** — Service levels tend to be a hotly contested subject during contract negotiations. There are multiple key measurements, timing, penalties, and definitions painstakingly agreed to, many of which will never be thought of postcontract execution. As GPM, your job is to dig into these agreed to service levels and identify which are most pertinent to your project and truly understand the impact, management, and communications of these important tools. It is also essential to understand what room you may have to negotiate a project-specific service level agreement (SLA) because the supplier will certainly not initiate this type of conversation. We suggest you look at service levels along the following multiple dimensions:

1. Critical deliverables — As we are primarily focused on applications development and maintenance projects, there tend to be several critical path items for your project. Does the supplier equally provide incentives to hit their project plan and the embedded milestones as you do? If they miss key deliverables, will they be penalized? Do you feel it sufficient for the nature of your project which is typically defined by application classification? What are these deliverables, joint review sessions, tollgates?

2. Metrics measurement and reporting. As we move away from application plan and define and build activities toward deployment and ongoing

maintenance, critical deliverables will be typically married with ongoing project metrics. Typically the MSA will feature SLAs for the overall relationship of which your project will be a part. Again, having confirmed your ability to add unique project-level SLAs and appropriate metrics is critical to fully leveraging this important contract dimension. How are these metrics being gathered? Are they relevant to your needs? How are they being communicated? Does this provide time for corrective action? How are these metrics communicated throughout the global supplier organization? Do you actively manage and communicate these metrics across the entire global team?

3. Project-specific tracking

a. Once you have a complete understanding of what SLAs have already been negotiated and agreed to between your firm and the global service provider, it is important to identify other project-specific metrics that you believe are essential to monitor. Although there may be no financial incentive or penalty for your partner, keeping these elements highly visible and monitored can help overall project execution.

b. In particular if you are managing a long-term maintenance type of agreement, we would urge you to preserve a clause that allows you to elevate project-specific metrics to the status of critical deliverable in the event you deem it appropriate.

b. **Staffing models** — This may seem odd to you, but there are a number of characteristics associated with a global supplier's staffing plan that can quickly impact your project's overall cost as well as the overall financial impact of the MSA. It is important to understand each of the following elements from a project level as well as from the overall MSA. Don't make the assumption that this has been addressed completely in the MSA, and the supplier may look at those requirements as minimums or guidelines versus requirements. The areas to evaluate and make certain you are comfortable with are the following:

■ Onsite-offshore ratio
■ Length of knowledge acquisition stage
■ Length of knowledge transfer stage
■ Offshore resource training effectiveness
■ Project management versus contributor resources

c. **Resource skill category and definitions** — Make certain you understand completely the description for each resource skill category that will be assigned to your project. You may believe a senior developer has +5 years of relevant experience, but the contract may say a generic +5 years. Because each resource category will have a corresponding rate, suppliers are more than happy to grab senior resources (as defined in the MSA) and bill accordingly. Make certain you know what is required and what is a "nice to have"; you may need to compromise a bit or at the minimum, be honest about the skills and experience needed to succeed.

d. **Resource rate card** — As we just discussed, resource skill categories will carry an associated cost that have been negotiated as part of your firm's overall agreement. Although there may be some volume discounts that could kick in during the span of your project, we suggest you use the contract base rates to form your project's financial baseline. The reasons you need to truly understand the rate card in combination with the resource skill categories and definitions are because:

1. It will help you understand how the supplier is proposing to staff your project and the possible "pockets" of cost that you may be able to adjust.

2. It will help you identify where you may be able to increase experience and skills for your project with little cost impact and what areas you can perhaps reduce or change for significant financial benefit with little increase in project risk.

3. It will help you provide solid financial and resource management throughout the project.

e. **Travel policy** — We have seen too many contracts that ineffectively deal with the subject of travel. Although this is covered in several other sections of the book, it is important to look at travel and the impact to cost and productivity at the project level of your project. First, dig into the staffing plan and understand the movement of the proposed resources. Does it seem reasonable to you? Are there specific periods or events in your project plan that may necessitate additional or incremental movement between offshore resources coming on site or vice versa? Who is paying for this travel? In the case of a T&M project, it will most likely be you. Can the travel be dictated by a resource's current visa status more so than actual project need? We suggest you dig in and really understand. Question! You also need to look at the travel that will be required by your team to the offshore development facility. Many times we see this is a pure afterthought, and although it can have a very positive impact on overall project productivity and success, it can quickly impact cost.

f. **Reporting process** — Typically a master service agreement will contain the minimum level of reporting required for ADM projects. They can run from very basic to somewhat involved. The question to deliberate on is what is the appropriate level of reporting for your project? Are there additional needs you may have that are not covered sufficiently in the MSA? If so, you need to discuss them while developing the final statement of work with your supplier because your additional reporting needs may require additional effort, hence additional cost.

A quick point we need to address is that your partner is probably running a CMM Level 5 development process that captures a significant amount of data. There should be little additional work required on the part of the supplier to capture this data and make it available to you. If they continue to complain or make this an issue, we would recommend a deeper look at their overall development processes.

g. **Escalation process** — Understanding the escalation process and knowing when to initiate the actual process and who is responsible to do so are critical. We have seen several projects face major challenges because the supplier project manager did not want to alert his or her superiors in India that there were project-level challenges. Remember, the project management position at an offshore pure play is a hotly contested position, and once achieved, there is a great deal of competition to hold the position. Enacting the escalation process is a major red mark for the supplier project manager — even more so than here at home — and they will do everything possible to correct the situation without intervention.

Your challenge is to understand the chain of command and maintain interaction and visibility with all. At the end of the day, it will benefit your ability to escalate and gain timely intervention while the project timeline is not compromised.

h. **Warranty period** — What is the standard warranty language in the master service agreement? If you are managing a build-and-deploy project, is this warranty sufficient? If you are managing a maintenance or sustain type of project, how does the warranty relate to minor modifications, fixes, or other types of development work? Be aware that any changes to the warranty will quickly (read closely, immediately) impact your project price. Do you understand the staffing plan and how it coordinates with the warranty period? Are you paying for resources of those who are performing warranty work? Question. Question. Question.

i. **Payment provisions** — How is the supplier being compensated for your project? Is it possible they have 90 percent of their payment before the project is successfully deployed? Are you comfortable that you both have equal skin in the successful completion of the project, or does the payment fall unfairly to one side? Is it deliverable-based or simply based on hours billed? A thorough understanding will help you align supplier activity.

In summary, time spent becoming familiar with the overall master service agreement and how it interacts with your specific SOW will prove of great value as you execute your project. One suggestion we would like to offer is once you have a strong understanding of the above outlined contract dimensions, sit down with your global service provider counterpart and review language and your interpretation of what the language dictates. This may in fact be the first time this individual may see the contract details as they are more than likely taking direction from corporate heads. We have seen on more than one occasion a global sourcing supplier absolutely dig his heels in and deny or charge additional fees for support that is clearly defined in the contract. This exercise will also help identify any potential challenges, force each of you to get clarification prior to project initiation, and at the minimum, give you a good appreciation of what to expect when the project is underway.

10. Offshore Governance

This is a critically important topic and one that has such broad implications that there are volumes dedicated to the subject. There is a great deal of theory applied to this critical link, but for our purpose and the focus of this book, we will limit our discussion to the necessary elements to successfully execute a project that has a defined beginning and end, more so than "governance" of the overall supplier relationship, which we assure you is a significant task and not to be underestimated.

For GDMs, the goal is to have the necessary communications and oversight to achieve success; defined as delivering the project on time and within budget while limiting surprises during the project.

Our recommendation is to discuss governance activities with your global service provider's project management team so they fully understand why you are managing the project in such a manner. Clearly this will be a different conversation if you are looking at an ongoing maintenance project rather than a build project, but helping the global service provider understand will reduce the time necessary to make adjustments downstream.

Chapter 3

The Foundation of Global Development Management

A.   Introduction

The growth of offshore outsourcing is a steady trend that is estimated to result in over 3.1 million information technology (IT) jobs being sent offshore from the United States over the next three years. As this trend continues, development organizations will face new challenges because they are held accountable for delivering business value with a global diverse workforce. Managing global development risks will be the critical skill that project managers (PMs) must master to be successful, essentially having their current skills evolve to become true global development managers (GDMs). Global development will require mastery of core project management principles such as budgeting and estimating, resource optimization, and measuring and tracking productivity combined with cultural awareness.

> **Section Key Concepts:**
> - GDM Essential Skills
> - Global Project Management Requirements
> - Global Development Models

Figure 3.1   Section III Key Concepts

To be successful, GDMs must learn to apply new tools along with the techniques to engage all development team members. The GDM must be a skilled practitioner who can monitor metrics and key performance indicators (KPIs) to keep projects on track. They must understand and track service level agreements (SLAs) in new ways to drive performance. GDMs must enhance their communication skills and be cognizant of cultural differences that will often cloud effective communications. They must understand the political and cultural environment of the service providers so that issues are escalated appropriately.

If this sounds a bit daunting, we assure you *Managing Global Development Risk* will prepare you to succeed. Throughout this journey, we will help you anticipate the challenges, putting you in the position to succeed. We provide a roadmap and tools to help you successfully manage your global development project.

B. Role of the Global Development Manager

Why the focus on the GDM? If the world is quickly moving to an outsourced model and the offshore firms are praising CMMi Level 5, PCCM, ITIL, Six Sigma, ISO 9000 certifications, and a host of other certifications to help sell their services, then why would the GDM make a difference? Wouldn't the GDM be just one more outsourced position? The answer surprisingly is no and can be substantiated in multiple surveys.

Consistently, the majority of IT executives have selected staff augmentation and project-based consulting as their primary vehicles for integrating offshore into their organizations. With both of these models, offshore vendors perform various tasks, but the implementation responsibility and the risk remain with the customer. Your organization's primary interface with the global service provider is going to be you and your peers: GDMs executing numerous parallel development activities.

The GDM is responsible for setting the course, managing the scope, tracking the project, and ultimately for the project's overall success. In a globally sourced development environment, the role of the GDM is even more critical because as we have already seen, many companies initially select the global outsourcing route to save development cost through lower labor arbitrage. However, what these organizations do not do is make internal adjustments to prepare existing staff and processes for the new global model. What quickly becomes evident are the significant challenges, unanticipated management costs, and the simple frustrations associated with the global delivery model.

When problems occur, which they will, senior management looks to the GDM to solve the issue and still deliver the project. If you are unlucky enough to be with a company that is moving offshore with the goal of dramatically reducing their expenses to show profitability, then you will have the added challenge of management "helping" you move the project along at a quicker pace. The management team may begin to focus on integrating the teams faster and accelerating the learning curve, which often shifts the focus from capacity to cost savings.

Table 3.1   Essential Global Development Management Skills

Role	Essential Global Development Management Skills
Leadership	■ Establishing direction — developing the vision and strategies ■ Aligning people — communicating the vision ■ Motivating and inspiring — helping people energize themselves to overcome barriers
Communication	■ Ensuring the message is clear, unambiguous, and precise ■ Ensuring information is received in its entirety ■ Having strong written and oral communication skills ■ Having listening skills ■ Choosing correct media (written, verbal, formal, informal)
Negotiation	■ Managing the scope, schedule, and budget of project ■ Adjusting to changes in scope, schedule, or budget ■ Negotiating contract terms and conditions ■ Negotiating assignments ■ Negotiating resources
Problem solving	■ Defining the problem— distinguishing between cause and effect ■ Analyzing problem to determine viable solutions ■ Selecting the "right" choice ■ Implementing decisions
Influencing the organization	■ Getting things done ■ Understanding formal and informal organizational structure ■ Understanding the mechanics of power and politics

GDMs must demonstrate their capabilities in each of the following areas: leadership, communication, negotiation, problem solving, and organizational understanding. Each of these skills outlined in Table 3.1 is an important management function, but becomes even more vital when layered with the added dimensions of culture, individual personality, communications content and style, combined with distance and time. In addition, in an outsourced environment, the GDM must be able to establish these capabilities with fellow employees as well as supplier personnel.

Core technical skills have the least influence on a PM's success. It is the soft skills that ultimately determine success. How would this apply for a globally dispersed team featuring a combination of employees and contractors? Do you see the challenge? Project management core skills are not in the areas in which developers are typically comfortable. We have found that the area developers will gravitate to when uncomfortable is talking technology, the common language.

What we mean by this is that over the years we have observed U.S.-based PMs visit their development facilities in India and truly miss the opportunity to engage the global team. During these visits, the PM will focus on technical issues such as processes, implementation of new technology, quality assurance, break-fix, and the like. Little is actually focused in the other five areas identified in project management: a managerial approach other than what the global service provider has scheduled to welcome their valued customer.

Ignoring these areas or not taking the time to become sensitive to the issues has a direct impact on productivity. As you will learn, there are simple activities and techniques that can be applied to fully leverage your time at the global development center. Understanding the importance of soft skills and combining these with standard technical management capabilities will determine your success. Successful GDMs are skilled at combining all these important core skills.

An interesting study was conducted by Andrew Dainty, Mei-I Cheng, and David Moore. Their research was based on behavioral event interviews that examined the attributes that differentiated superior and average performing PMs. Their study identified 6 major groupings and 13 core competencies, which we have highlighted in Table 3.2

For global development perspective, the above findings provide a foundation on which additional dimensions or competencies will need to be mastered as you evolve into a GDM (see Table 3.3). These competencies are covered in detail throughout *Managing Global Development Risk* providing the tools, templates, and suggestions.

C. Global Development Manager Leadership Requirements

Global outsourcing will introduce complexities that even the best PMs will struggle with. Numerous leadership books have identified three overarching characteristics that strong leaders possess:

- **Vision** — the ability to see solutions in chaotic situations
- **Influence** — the capability to effectively engage your offshore team and business partners in a way that doesn't depend on the power of your position
- **Execution** — the bottom-line ability to deliver time and again

Vision, influence, and execution are just as critical for the GDM as they are for the chief executive officer (CEO) or the chief information officer (CIO). Your ability to articulate the global delivery vision, see solutions where others don't, negotiate and manage interactions with the global service provider, and deliver projects in a global model will set the stage for success in future endeavors.

D. Global Software Project Management Methodologies

Historically, the decision to outsource is an internal tug of war between two distinct groups: those who see savings as the major driver for outsourcing versus those

Table 3.2   Core Competencies of Successful Project Managers

Core Grouping	PM Competencies
Achievement and action-oriented competencies — focused on actions toward task accomplishment	1. **Achievement** — concern for working well toward a standard of excellence (completeness of action, achievement impact, degree of innovation) 2. **Initiative** — taking action and seizing opportunities; higher degree of self-motivation, sustained periods of performance, ability to involve others in accomplishment of key tasks (effective delegation) 3. **Information seeking** — underlying curiosity to know about things, propensity to seek first-hand information on issues, innate ability to scan for wider information that could be of future use
Human service-oriented competencies — related to meeting others' needs	4. **Customer service** — Strong desire to meet customer's needs, propensity for seeking information about the real, underlying needs of a client; responsible attitude toward dealing with problems rapidly and efficiently
Impact and influence-based competencies — effect on others and organizational behavior	5. **Impact and influence** — ability to gain support for a course of action, leading or directing a group, breadth of understanding, and influence within organization 6. **Organizational awareness** — ability to understand the power relationships within an organization (getting buy-in and political astuteness); ability to understand client's needs and articulate those to other team members; ability to rapidly assimilate organizational information; ability to expedite decisions
Managerial competencies	7. **Teamwork and cooperation** — genuine desire to work cooperatively as part of a team (fosters teamwork and engages others in team activities) 8. **Team leadership** — intention to take on the role of a leader and desire to lead others; strong desires to lead others, improve teamwork, and foster cooperation 9. **Directiveness or assertiveness** — appropriate use of positional power; not as prevalent with client PMs and employed less often by high-performing PMs; implies that project management requires a more diplomatic or conciliatory management approach

continued

Table 3.2 (continued) Core Competencies of Successful Project Managers

Core Grouping	PM Competencies
Cognitive competencies — intellectual version of initiative that helps the PM understand the situation or task; ability to apply intelligence to resolve a problem	10. **Analytic thinking** — ability to understand a situation by decomposing it or tracing the implications of a situation in a causal way; ability to analyze complex problems 11. **Conceptual thinking** — ability to see the bigger picture through the identification of patterns or interconnections between situations that are not obviously related * Provides strong support for importance of emotional intelligence among PMs, which is the ability to recognize feelings of one's self and those of others, for managing one's emotions, and for self-motivation
Personal effectiveness — reflect intellectual and behavioral maturity in relation to others and to work	12. **Self-control** — ability to remain composed, restrain negative actions, and cope well, even when confronted with stressful situations; ability to remain calm and not be easily provoked, a cross-cutting theme that underpins all effective management behaviors, high levels of competency in this behavior being particularly predictive of superior performance; proves to be a fundamental requirement for PMs (to remain reasoned and composed, even in high-pressure situations) 13. **Flexibility** — ability to adapt approach or behavior in a variety of situations (breadth of change and speed of change)

who fear the loss of quality and control. This debate is only intensified when the element of offshore outsourcing is introduced. Depending on your organization's personality and management team, the dynamics can quickly encompass reaction by your local community, security of your corporate intellectual property, and loss of key strategic positions to a third party on the other side of the world.

The savings camp has had a major influence in the growth of the offshore market. To address quality and resource retention concerns, global service providers began introducing standardized processes into their development methodologies.

Offshore firms embraced the Project Management Institute® (PMI) Project Management Professional (PMP) certifications, Software Engineering Institute (SEI) Capability Maturity Model (CMM), International Standards Organization (ISO) 9000, Six Sigma, and other quality initiatives to measure, track, and report quality improvements.

Table 3.3   Essential Global Delivery Competencies

Core Grouping	Global Competencies
Achievement and action	**GDM 1** — Proactiveness. Proactively identifying, tracking, measuring, and improving KPIs that drive global projects. **GDM 2** — Collaboration. Collaborate with service provider to resolve issues versus escalating issues
Human service	**GDM 3** — Team building. Nurture and build team interaction at all levels; create multiple integrated teams **GDM 4** — Recognition of individual. Observe, guide, and advise on individual interactions; know the individual
Impact and influence	**GDM 5** — Decisiveness. Understand the individual, team, and corporate dynamic; quickly determine supplier key decision makers to effectively resolve issues; do not dwell on decisions; collect data, know decision makers, and move forward
Managerial	**GDM 6** — Service levels. Establish processes and procedures to manage service levels.
Cognitive	**GDM 7** — Analytical thinking. Continuously learn new skills and collaborate with supplier to improve offshore effectiveness
Personal effectiveness	**GDM 8** — Flexibility. Embrace cultural differences and challenges and work with internal teams and the supplier to develop new processes and new ways to address issues

This disciplined approach to software development led to significant improvements in the overall quality of deliverables. It also set expectations that offshore project managers would be PMP certified and global service providers would be assessed or certified in the latest methodologies. A CMM Level 3 or above (often Level 5) assessment and an ISO-9001 certification are almost mandatory for offshore vendors to be competitive. As part of the evaluation process, most companies require proof of these certifications during the proposal process.

Although CMM, ISO 9000, Six Sigma, and other processes mentioned above are only becoming more widely accepted in the general U.S. market, as GDM responsible for the successful execution of the project, it is essential that you and your internal U.S.-based team understand and embrace these principles. Many PMs managing software development projects today are not trained in these disciplines and resist their use. Today, with your team distributed in multiple cities and time zones, the nomenclature from the processes will form the basic communication that holds activity together. Lack of PM discipline and adherence to process methodologies has led to conservative onsite-offshore ratios, and has limited productivity gains and cost savings that can be realized from a robust global delivery model. As GDM managing global development projects, you will have a critical role in understanding these processes and utilizing them to positively impact the project's scope, schedule, and budget.

1. Project Management Institute

The Project Management Institute (PMI) a non-profit organization, is the world's foremost advocate for the project management profession. PMI sets industry standards, conducts research, and provides education, certification, and professional exchange opportunities designed to strengthen and further establish the project management profession. PMP certification involves a rigorous, examination-based process that represents the highest caliber in professional standards. Therefore, PMI professional certification is universally accepted and recognized.

Whereas we strongly endorse PMI and understand the methodologies in depth, we believe global software development requires additional dimensions today that have not as yet been folded into overall PMI training. Although PMI truly understands the challenges encountered when teams are distributed, it does not take into account the communications and cultural and philosophical aspects along with the interpersonal development necessary for a great U.S.-based PM to be equally successful when managing teams in Chennai, Manila, or Krakow.

As a foundation for GDMs, PMI's project management body of knowledge (PMBOK) sets the standard. Although the PMBOK contains a great deal of tools and guidance, we have extracted the tasks that GDMs will be accountable for when leading global software development projects. Though Table 3.4 is not an exhaustive list, it provides a sense for the depth of skills the GDM must have to be successful in managing a global development effort. We will touch on each of these tasks throughout the balance of *Managing Global Development Risk*.

2. The Capability Maturity Model

The capability maturity model (CMM) for software is a framework that describes the key elements of an effective software process. The CMM describes an evolutionary improvement path from an ad hoc, immature process to a mature, disciplined process. It is not a cure-all for software development. It does not guarantee success. It may in fact cost you time and money. This is why GDMs need to understand the unique characteristics of each CMM certification and level to determine exactly what the appropriate level for their unique need is.

As discussed earlier, global service providers grabbed onto the concept of CMM as a means to demonstrate their software development quality and ability

Table 3.4   Core Project Phases and Global Delivery Tasks

PM Phase and Purpose	Global Delivery Tasks
Initiating — Define objective of project, evaluate costs and benefits, and define approach	■ Define project. Evaluate return on investment and Total Cost of Outsourcing (TCO). Get sponsorship. ■ Determine feasibility of global delivery. ■ Commit offshore resources. ■ Define mix of onsite-offshore resources
Planning — Determine how the project will be delivered, and plan all aspects of project, including detailed WBS.	■ Evaluate and modify knowledge acquisition and knowledge transfer templates. ■ Plan and conduct knowledge transfer and knowledge acquisition. ■ Select and hire the best people. ■ Staff offshore teams; the role of the offshore PM and team leaders. ■ Scope management and define the project deliverables. ■ Schedule tasks; detail component level (inch pebbles). ■ Control and report budget. ■ Make quality plan. ■ Facilitate project communications. ■ Determine risk management. ■ Oversee procurement. ■ Oversee logistics (hardware/software for offshore facility)
Executing — "Plan the work and work the plan." Assure the quality of all deliverables	■ Communication, formal and informal communication paths, escalation process, status reporting, and weekly meetings ■ Issue identification and resolution ■ Establish Service Level Agreements ■ Team development; establish teamwork between onsite and offshore teams; travel between sites ■ Quality assurance, ensuring quality of every deliverable ■ Scope verification
Controlling — Continuously measure project performance to determine variance against plan	■ Change control ■ Metrics capture and reporting ■ Managing attrition and staff turnover ■ Earned value analysis (EVA) ■ Estimate to complete, and variance reporting ■ Balanced scorecard ■ Digital dashboard ■ Tollgates and signoff on all deliverables

continued

Table 3.4 (continued)   Core Project Phases and Global Delivery Tasks

PM Phase and Purpose	Global Delivery Tasks
Closing — Final opportunity to gather metrics, reports, and stakeholder conclusions (EBIT validation), and archive project deliverables	■ Sign off on project ■ Gather metrics ■ Validate SLAs ■ Customer acceptance ■ SQA review ■ Lessons learned ■ Check all deliverables ■ Project repository

to successfully execute projects. More than a marketing ploy, CMM dictates the level of documentation and process discipline associated with the process, reducing overall risk. Although CMM is much abused with organizations falsely presenting their capabilities, it did serve as a means of bringing credibility to the overall offshore market.

The CMM covers practices for planning, engineering, and managing software development and maintenance. When followed, these key practices improve the ability of organizations to meet goals for cost, schedule, functionality, and product quality. It has essentially become the way global service providers function. To communicate with representatives from your partner firm, it will be very important that you can converse using the CMM nomenclature.

The CMM is composed of five maturity levels. With the exception of Level 1, each maturity level is composed of several key process areas (KPAs). As organizations establish and improve the software processes by which they develop and maintain their software work products, they progress through levels of maturity. It is this reason that global sourcing relies heavily on the concept of continuous improvement and enhanced productivity over time. Global service providers rely on this as a means to capture some additional revenue because the level of effort to achieve results declines over time. Today, customers are more aware of this concept and are doing a better job developing their contract terms so that customers and global service providers share in these productivity gains.

With CMM, each maturity level provides a layer in the foundation for continuous process improvement. Each KPA comprises a set of goals that, when satisfied, stabilize an important component of the software process. Achieving each level of the maturity model institutionalizes a different component in the software process, resulting in an overall increase in the process capability of the organization.

As GDM, it will be critical for you to honestly and completely assess your team's current process capabilities. As we will discuss later, aligning your current organization today with the process orientation of a global service provider can be very frustrating for team members, causing unnecessary and easily anticipated challenges.

As GDM, your introduction to CMM Level 5 will most likely be through the partnership with an Indian-based global service provider. Most corporate IT departments do not operate at this level, nor do they independently strive to achieve such a lofty level. In some respects, other than global service providers leveraging low-cost development resources, there are few businesses that can sustain such an environment.

The impact of CMM on the success of projects has been widely proven. On average, companies that are less mature in project management KPAs, miss schedule targets by 40%. The cost of projects is 11 to 20 percent higher in corporations that are less mature. In a global development setting, it is very important to combine the global KPAs to ensure your project fully leverages the distributed team in a consistent, repeatable manner.

a. Process Alignment — The Hidden Challenge

It is important to take a few moments to recognize that you will encounter challenges as you align internal processes with those of your service provider. These issues, real and imagined, will have a true impact on project productivity

Take some time to discuss this with your global service provider because they will have a process they follow for this situation. You need to understand their approach and personalize it to your unique needs and the personality of your team. It is also critical to recognize that your global service provider is more comfortable in a "carve out" scenario where they inform your team of their efforts versus truly integrating your processes and theirs.

As GDM, it will be essential to create a path for your internal team as they experience the alignment process. See Table 3.5 for a global process alignment playbook.

3. The Global Service Provider "Badge of Courage"

The CMM has had mixed acceptance in the United States. Many internal IT shops and software houses have "experimented" with various forms of the CMM, but have often found it too burdensome to fully implement. During the middle to late 1990s, many organizations underwent the CMM assessments as a means to garner some control over escalating budgets. Many of these organizations were assessed at the CMM Level 2 (repeatable) and elected not to expend additional resources to achieve higher levels.

It took the threat of outsourcing and the rapid adaptation of CMM by major vendors to "wake up" IT departments and move them to implement much-needed process improvements. Admittedly, some organizations took CMM too far and implemented process for process's sake. But on the whole, the adoption of engineering disciplines within the software development community has led to higher productivity levels and better cost containment, and has increased the probability of success.

Table 3.5 Global Process Alignment Playbook

Global Process Alignment Activity	Benefit/Impact
Schedule deliverables and activities that align methodologies	Alignment of SDLC methodologies will facilitate communication by providing a common language and framework for deliverables. For example, a functional design document will have the same meaning to both parties
Define specific checkpoints or tollgates to validate progress	Even with process alignment, miscommunication often occurs with offshore providers, tollgate reviews, or defined checkpoints in the process align the suppliers work with your internal expectations. It is better to know in Week 5 that more work is required to understand the SDLC than to wait for the end of a project and fail an internal audit because the supplier didn't create the right deliverables. Ongoing tollgate reviews also help ensure the project is proceeding per the plan
Refine processes through continuous learning	CMM Level 5 firms excel at applying lessons learned to project work. Use this to your advantage by applying lessons learned to your development methodology. Many offshore firms have the advantage of working for multiple clients where they have had an opportunity to witness the benefits of a wide variety of development methodologies and tools. Be open-minded about these experiences, and develop new processes that better support global development activities

As previously discussed, CMM has been widely adapted in the offshore market and has become the de facto standard. With the exception of the United States, India and China led all countries in the number of SEI assessments over the past 5 years. Figure 3.2 illustrates CMM maturity in U.S. and non-U.S. organizations. Increasingly, global service providers are touting their CMM Level 5 assessments as a way to differentiate themselves in the offshore market. A high CMM level is not a guarantee of quality or performance — only process. It means that the company has created processes for monitoring and managing software development that companies lower on the CMM scale do not have. But it does not necessarily mean those companies are using the processes well. There is also a difference between an organization's CMM assessment and a project's CMM level assessment. Although your vendor might be a CMM Level 5 assessed organization, this does not necessarily translate to your individual project. As GDM, you need to understand how your global service provider will support your project with its CMM processes; ask if any of their projects have been assessed using the CMM process.

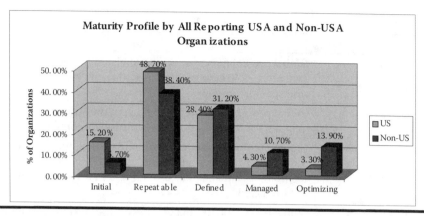

Figure 3.2   CMM Maturity Profiles (US and non-US Organizations)

Areas to push with the global service provider when discussing CMM process include:

- Attrition management
- Offshore PM experience, specifically the individual
- Project Management Office (PMO) and software quality assurance (SQA) oversight: how will they be engaged?
- Training: for both CMM and on your unique environment and its technologies

Also be aware that although a high CMM assessment might have given your organization greater comfort that you are dealing with a credible and quality-oriented offshore development partner, you need to also be aware that this can come at the expense of flexibility and agility. CMM Level 5 might be fine for a mission-critical system, but you might want to think about whether something so important is the right candidate for a global development project. The most important thing to be focused on is how your global development partner adjusts to deviations from its CMM processes. How these differences are managed can influence how well your own organizational processes can work with them.

As the GDM, we suggest this discussion occur prior to the estimation stage.

Please beware of suppliers who use language such as "CMM Level 5 compliant process" or "Self-assessed at a CMM Level 5." The SEI has defined specific criteria and standards for their assessors. The independent organizations are required to assess an organization's maturity level for it to be recognized by the SEI. You should demand this same rigor by requesting a copy of their independent assessment. SEI also publishes guidelines for reassessment every three years. Again, during the proposal process, you should review these documents. If the supplier is not independently assessed, the level of risk you assume, if you select this supplier without diving deeper into the processes, may increase unnecessarily.

Table 3.6 P-CMM KPA Level Global Validation

P-CMM KPA Level	GKPA Validation
Level 2 KPAs	**Global project guide:** specific details outlining the activities, deliverables, and execution of Level 2 KPAs for the specific project
Level 3 KPAs	**Global project baseline:** how each of the sub-KPAs will be aligned for the project and monitored ongoing
Level 4 KPAs	**Global mentoring guide:** quantitative documentation on how each of the global resources will be measured combined with activities to engage and involve customer internal staff
Level 5 KPAs	**Global team growth:** analysis of continuous improvement across the global team

4. The People Capability Maturity Model for Software Management

The current wave of CMM marketing battles is centered around the people capability maturity model (P-CMM). In an effort to address attrition issues and maintain currency in the CMM certifications, global service providers, in particular the leading Indian firms, have latched onto this certification as a means to address marketing concerns and offset some of the pressure they currently feel due to their ongoing attrition challenges.

P-CMM adapts the maturity framework of the CMM for software to managing and developing an organization's workforce. The motivation for the P-CMM is to improve the ability of software organizations to attract, develop, motivate, organize, and retain the talent needed to continuously improve software development capability. The P-CMM is designed to allow software organizations to integrate workforce improvement with software process improvement programs guided by the CMM. The P-CMM can also be used by any kind of organization as a guide for improving their people-related and workforce practices.

When dealing with the P-CMM, it is important to understand how these principles are being applied to the specific project and how the GDM can leverage the concepts with the internal development team. To accomplish this, *Managing Global Development Risk* suggests in Table 3.6 global KPA validation elements are infused with standard project reporting with potential penalties for lack of documentation.

5. Capability Maturity Model Integration

Capability maturity model integration (CMMI) is designed to blend the management and engineering disciplines of software development and systems engineering. Over the past decade, multiple versions of the CMM have been incorporated by various disciplines. CMMI is intended to reduce these duplications and support process and product improvement.

The CMMI includes a common set of process areas, which form the core of an integrated capability model that integrates process improvement guidance for systems engineering, software engineering, and integrated product and process development (IPPD). The CMMI product suite provides an integrated approach to reducing the redundancy and complexity resulting from the use of separate, multiple capability maturity models. The CMMI products should improve the efficiency of and the return on investment for process improvement. The resulting integrated capability models can be tailored to an organization's mission and business objectives.

According to the SEI, the core benefits of CMMI are the following:

- Efficient, effective assessment and improvement across multiple process disciplines in an organization
- Reduced training and assessment costs
- A common, integrated vision of improvement for all elements of an organization
- A means of representing new discipline-specific information in a standard, proven process improvement context

6. International Organization for Standardization 9000

The ISO 9000 is an international standard that gives requirements for an organization's quality management system (QMS). For this reason, you may sometimes hear your suppliers refer to being "ISO 9000 certified," or having an "ISO 9000-compliant QMS." This will normally mean that they are claiming to have a QMS meeting the requirements of ISO 9001:2000, the only standard in the ISO 9000 family that can be used for the purpose of conformity assessment. It is important to understand, however, that ISO is the body that develops and publishes the standard; ISO does not "certify" organizations.

- The objective of ISO 9001:2000 is to provide a set of requirements that, if effectively implemented, will provide you with confidence that your supplier can consistently provide goods and services that meet your needs and expectations and comply with applicable regulations.

The requirements cover a wide range of topics, including your supplier's top management commitment to quality, its customer focus, adequacy of its resources, employee competence, process management (for production, service delivery, and relevant administrative and support processes), quality planning, product design, review of incoming orders, purchasing, monitoring and measurement of its processes and products, calibration of measuring equipment, processes to resolve customer complaints, corrective and preventive actions, and a requirement to drive continual improvement of the QMS. Last but not least, there is a requirement for your supplier to monitor customer perceptions about the quality of the goods and services it provides.

D. Six Sigma

Six Sigma simply means a measure of quality that strives for near perfection. Six Sigma is a disciplined, data-driven approach and methodology for eliminating defects (driving towards six standard deviations between the mean and the nearest specification limit) in any process — from manufacturing to transactional and from product to service.

The statistical representation of Six Sigma describes quantitatively how a process is performing. To achieve Six Sigma, a process must not produce more than 3.4 defects per million opportunities. A Six Sigma defect is defined as anything outside of customer specifications. A Six Sigma opportunity is then the total quantity of chances for a defect.

The core goal of Six Sigma, though, is not to achieve six sigma levels of quality, but to improve profitability. Prior to Six Sigma, improvements brought about by quality programs, such as Total Quality Management (TQM) and ISO 9000 usually had no visible impact on a company's net income. In general, the consequences of immeasurable improvement and invisible impact caused these quality programs gradually to become the fad of the moment.

The fundamental objective of the Six Sigma methodology is the implementation of a measurement-based strategy that focuses on process improvement and variation reduction through the application of Six Sigma improvement projects. This is accomplished through the use of DMAIC (pronounced De-May-Ick). The Six Sigma DMAIC (Define, Measure, Analyze, Improve, Control) process is an improvement system for existing processes falling below specification and looking for incremental improvement.

The Six Sigma processes work extremely well in a global environment. Many offshore firms have fully embraced the continuous process improvement aspects of Six Sigma and as such have trained Six Sigma practitioners (Green Belt and Black Belt). Offshore firms are also very interested in sharing this knowledge and helping their clients achieve higher performance through Six Sigma practices.

E. Summary

GDMs absolutely need to be conversant in all of the above detailed methodologies to effectively manage their global service provider and offer the required guidance to internal team members. CMM and its various flavors are the most prevalent processes used by global service providers' vendors today.

Many less mature organizations (Level 1 and Level 2) often do not understand the cost of CMM, or as it is coined in the outsourcing world, "the cost of quality." A prime example of this is peer reviews, which is a required Level 3 KPA. In most global service providers, peer reviews are conducted for every deliverable, including every software component that is developed. Although this may sound like a great idea and should in fact improve the overall quality, it comes at a cost. This cost typically crystallizes when you review project estimates.

Software quality assurance (SQA) or software quality management (SQM) is another SEI Level 4 KPA that comes at a cost. Most global service provider organizations have formal SQA organizations that develop and track metrics for a quantitative understanding of the quality of the project's software products. They strive to achieve higher levels of quality within an organization by understanding the root cause of errors. GDMs need to fully understand how these organizations operate, how they benefit your project, and how you can most successfully engage them. Again, on the surface, this is a great process and should be embraced. But it often comes at an unexpected cost. The offshore SQA organization will most likely bill back their effort to the project. These unexpected costs may result in cost overruns.

During the project planning phase, it is advisable to set process expectations. If you want CMM Level 5 processes, great. But you will pay for these, and they may not add immediate value. Peer reviews and SQA audits could be negotiated in the statement of work (SOW). For example, you may state that peer reviews are required for all deliverables defined in the SOW and all new software components and components that meet a defined level of criticality or change (e.g., 25% or more of the code was modified). Any additional reviews conducted by the vendor would be at his cost and would not impact the project schedules.

Now that we have taken the time to truly dig into the PM philosophies and development methodologies to manage our global development project, it's time to dig into the project itself.

Chapter 4

Initiating the Global Development Project

A.   Introduction

Up to this point, *Managing Global Development Risk* has reviewed overall trends and developments of the global sourcing market in addition to defining the core skills required of global development managers (GDMs). We have also reviewed the methodologies and process used for software development including Software Engineering Institute Capability Maturity Model (SEI CMM), International Standards Organization (ISO), and Six Sigma, while calling out those unique dimensions that need to be addressed to successfully manage global development projects.

It is now time to dive into global development. Starting with project initiation, *Managing Global Development Risk* will provide the tools, templates, examples, and guidance to execute your role of GDM.

In this section, *Managing Global Development Risk* will cover the following core components of global software development project initiation:

> **Section Key Concepts: INITIATING**
> - ➤ Productivity of offshore teams
> - ➤ Accuracy of Budget
> - ➤ Conservative Use of onsite/offshore resources

Figure 4.1   Section IV Key Concepts

- Global measures of success
- Global project and approach definition
- Global development feasibility and checklist
- Onsite-Offshore global development staff profile
- Global development procedure manual
- Global development roles and responsibilities
- Global success factors:
    - Service level agreements
    - Global metric definition
- Global risk identification
- Issue management and global issue management process
- Global development initiation phase deliverables

As a GDM, the initiation of a project often involves negotiations around the unique scope of work and completion of a statement of work (SOW) or a work order. This phase defines the high-level work that will be accomplished offshore and the preliminary plans for completing the project. The initiation phase enables the GDM and the global development teams to determine the best approach to the project. Unlike the initiation phase in a standard project, the offshore initiation phase does not focus on the project charter or determine the go, no-go of a project: it focuses on execution.

Global development projects are often initiated by the Chief Information Officer (CIO), Chief Financial Officer (CFO), or through a central procurement office. The selection of a global service provider is typically the result of an extended request for proposal (RFP) process and negotiation. Many organizations will conduct site visits and select two or three vendors to meet their offshore needs. In most cases, lengthy negotiations have occurred outlining the nature of the relationship, and a master service agreement (MSA) and contract have been signed.

Earlier in *Managing Global Development Risk* we spoke of the need for GDMs to review the MSA to understand the overall relationship between your firm and the selected global service provider. Now, as you prepare to initiate your project, we assume you have done this careful review and are prepared to interact with your assigned global project team. It is important to remember that the team assigned by the global service provider to support your development efforts more than likely has little to no real knowledge of the agreement. Despite what they may say to your direct questions, they have probably never seen the documents or have been "briefed" by their executives or sales representatives. Ultimately, you need to make certain your project gets the full complement of services and support your organization has negotiated. As the GDM, you may want to schedule a review session with the internal sourcing organization and your offshore teams to ensure all parties understand the contractual framework, the specific expectations of both parties, and the performance expectations (i.e., service levels). This also provides an opportunity to review or agree to specific reports that will measure and track the ongoing performance.

The MSA forms the basis for the overall relationship. The SOW for your project will define the manner in which your global service provider will support and execute your requirements. Make certain your SOW encompasses the following:

1. Description of Services
   a. Requirements
   b. Deliverables, including acceptance criteria for deliverables
   c. Roles and responsibilities
   d. Project plan inclusive of all key milestones and required gate reviews
   e. Staffing model and definition
2. Warranties
3. Service Level Agreements (SLAs) and process to measure them
4. Expenses
   a. Costs and rates — onshore and offshore per labor category and years of experience. Labor categories to include:
      i. Onsite
      ii. Offshore-onsite
      iii. Offshore
   b. Travel-related expenses
   c. Other related expenses such as network usage, one-time setup charge, software license fees, etc.
5. Terms and conditions — length of contract, terms for extending or terminating
6. Payment terms — established fixed price or time and material (T&M) basis
7. Confidentiality and intellectual property right protection, typically defined in the overall MSA; need to validate that the terms are sufficient for your unique project requirements.

Most offshore suppliers will insist on clear acceptance criteria for deliverables and a process to ensure deliverables are accepted within a specified time period. This acceptance process is typically defined in the SOW or other contractual documents. As the GDM, you will be responsible for managing the acceptance process so you should familiarize yourself with it. If it doesn't exist, then you may want to jointly develop one to manage expectations. As a minimum, the acceptance process should address the following:

1. Format for all deliverables (e.g., Microsoft Word, Excel, and Visio, etc.). Where practicable, you should also agree on specific templates for requirements, design documents, test planes, etc. For code-based deliverables, specify the language and process to deliver the source code and object code.
2. Process to specify the acceptable content for each deliverable. For example, you should collaborate with the supplier to specify the contents of the design document and the level of detail that is required.

3. Process that defines both parties' responsibilities if the deliverable is rejected. The process should include:
   a. Identification of areas of document that are to be corrected for the supplier to accomplish corrections.
   b. Timeline for correcting issues. Nonconforming deliverables must be corrected within five business days (or within the number of days specified by the supplier for that deliverable) and returned for review.
   c. Final review and acceptance process.
4. Process that defines type of problems and resolution (i.e., Sev 1, Sev 2, and Sev 3 issues).
   a. Severity 1 issues are essential to the scope and criteria for the deliverable. A Severity 1 issue should be resolved before the baseline version of the document is released. Oftentimes Severity 1 issues are related to warranty items and may be resolved at no additional cost.
   b. Severity 2 issues are problems typically found in a deliverable that are out of scope but were identified during the deliverable review. Severity 2 issues should be discussed, and the supplier should provide an estimate to incorporate the changes.
   c. Severity 3 issues are cosmetic in nature and do not substantially affect the content or meaning of the deliverables.
5. Process to approve deliverables within a certain number of days. A word of caution here: many suppliers will try to negotiate an automatic approval clause that essentially states the deliverable is accepted if not approved by the client within the specified timeframe. Be on the lookout for this clause, and strike it if possible. As the GDM, you'll want and need to manage the deliverable acceptance process. But automatic approval puts you at a legal disadvantage that may cost you time and money to get nonconforming issues resolved.

Initiating a global development project requires scrutiny and analysis by the executive members and the offshore governance board. As GDM we recommend consistent communications with your internal governance and oversight teams to minimize possible confusion or misunderstandings. Questionnaires and initial analysis models will aid GDMs in determining the feasibility and ease of performing work offshore. In case it is the first interaction between the internal onsite team and global resource staff who will be working on the project, these initial steps will help you identify gaps and possible interpersonal conflicts. Insist on meeting and spending time with the onsite coordinator, and begin integrating processes from both teams. Initial discussions may be conducted at the supplier's site depending on the size or scope of the project, but make certain you overcommunicate and interact with your global service provider counterparts.

As you read through *Managing Global Development Risk*, we will continue to reinforce this theme as well as provide suggestions on how to engage the global resources assigned to support your effort. Because this is initiation of the project, it is the time you quickly establish the personality of your overall team, the manner in which you all will interact, and the level of participation all will have in making your project a success. Do you want an engaged global development staff or a team to "throw it over the wall"? Now is the time you establish this important dynamic that will be the underpinning to productivity and success. Of all the stages, this is the most critical in establishing the team mentality and interaction. Do not let this phase slip by without assembling the plan to address communications and team building.

B. Global Measure of Success

All projects must have a measure of success (MOS) to determine if and when project goals are achieved. The MOS should be relevant to the business sponsor and capture the key goals they want to achieve. The MOS should also state priorities when conflicts occur. For example, if the delivery date is critical due to a legal or regulatory issue, then the scope can be negotiated when issues arise. If the scope is the most critical component, then the date or budget should be negotiable. A MOS typically addresses the following:

- **Scope.** For example, the project must provide users with the ability to display, review, and update mortgage loans.
- **Schedule.** The project must be completed by Nov 1 or within 4 months of project initiation.
- **Budget.** The project must be completed within 10% of estimates or achieve a return on investment (ROI) of X.

Global development projects should also have an MOS that describes both the goals of the project and the goals to be achieved with the global development effort.

The global measure of success (GMOS) will often be different from a standard project MOS. An organization needs to clearly articulate its goals and strategies as it begins integrating global resources. Unlike many other methodologies, management processes, or "flavors of the month," global sourcing will drive rumors and negatively impact morale if the goals are not clearly articulated.

A key component of the GMOS is the *why*. Why are you offshoring? Is it to drive down costs? If so, are the costs savings associated with a consolidation of higher priced onsite contractors or is it to drive overall IT cost reductions by outsourcing major functions that will impact employees? Is it to increase capacity? Is it to help your company establish a global footprint for its products or services? These questions will need to be addressed as the organization begins integrating global delivery.

In general the GMOS should address the following areas:

■ **Timing.** Identify specific dates for knowledge acquisitions and knowledge transfer. This is a great time to have early conversations with the selected global service provider to plan these phases. The timing and project plan need to clearly identify activities across all locations and teams.

■ **ROI.** If the chief executive officer (CEO), CIO, or CFO has established target costs savings or other ROI factors for the offshore project, document these and ensure your plan can meet these goals. Be sure to calculate in the many hidden costs of outsourcing, including knowledge acquisition and knowledge transfer, onsite resources, additional travel, productivity rates, infrastructure costs, and communication costs. You may also want to understand the expected timeframes for achieving the cost reductions. If this is the first offshore project, it is important to remember there are many overhead items that will quickly erode perceived savings.

■ **Increased capacity.** If the core objective is to increase the overall capacity of the organization, then the GMOS may be different. The organization may be gearing up for a large conversion or other project similar to Y2K. In this case, your goals are to meet the ramp strategy with the core skills required to meet future needs.

■ **Schedule.** How quickly do you want to be there? Senior management expectations are important GMOS factors. If they have communicated a global sourcing strategy to the board or shareholders that provides timeframes for achieving productivity levels or achieving cost savings, then as GDM you have the responsibility to deliver a plan that achieves these results or communicate why the results cannot be achieved within the timeframe. Again, this GMOS may change your focus or your level of risk and define how quickly you move headcount to the offshore facility.

For your project's GMOS to be established as overall project guidelines, it is critical that your entire team, including the global resources, clearly understand the GMOS and the full impact it holds for your company. This can be a bit of a challenge at times as your global sourcing partner equates MOS with metrics. Although we will get to the area of accurate project metrics and service levels the goal of establishing the GMOS is to help everyone understand the overall context of the project and impact to your organization. How can you expect all members of your team to be working in the same direction if they don't understand the context in which it will be delivered and how overall business success will be determined? Can you manage to achieve all the metrics associated with a project, yet have development output that misses the mark?

Educate all team members and make them aware of the GMOS targets and how they were developed and why they are important. Seek input. Turn the creation and articulation of the GMOS elements into a team-building exercise.

C.   Global Project and Approach Definition

In global development there are two critical dimensions that will greatly influence your success: selecting the right project for global development and selecting the right process with the right global resource mix throughout the project life cycle. If this is your first global development project, the initiation phase will be critical in establishing future success. The wrong project or the wrong process can have lasting effects on the relationship with the global service provider and the success of future projects. The right project and processes will help establish a long-term collaborative effort. In this section we will discuss the elements of a successful project and process. We will examine why some projects are better candidates for global development than others.

Some projects and services are a poor fit for offshore outsourcing because they require high levels of internal knowledge, process integration, and collaboration, or because their failure would be too costly because they are mission critical. The best candidates are those with clear, well-documented specifications, leveraging a standardized skill set, and with a well-defined owner.

As GDM, you often will not have a choice of the global service provider. Most likely, the supplier has already been selected, and you are now required to deliver the project with them as part of the development solution. However, if you are involved in the selection process or have your choice of suppliers, select a partner with proven expertise in your business and technical domain. As you will soon learn, there are many hurdles GDMs cross at project start-up, try not to allow communication caused by the supplier's lack of domain experience further hinder progress.

So what projects are suitable for offshore? This is the number one question asked by information technology (IT) leaders. In a nutshell, this boils down to projects that are well defined with little anticipated change. We categorize these as follows:

- Staff augmentation
- Discretionary
- Enhancements to stable applications, minimal change
- Maintenance of legacy applications
- Software testing
- Package implementations

1.   Staff Augmentation

Organizations with a large base of contractors (measured as a percentage of overall staff) can typically see immediate cost savings through integrating global resources. Once sourced, these organizations will typically have a higher onsite-offshore ratio (50:50 or greater). Staff augmentation continues to be one of the primary means for companies to engage offshore teams. Unfortunately, it is also one of the least productive, frustrating, and costly.

Many times, we encounter high use of staff augmentation as the global development solution because the project manager (PM) truly has no desire to learn the global paradigm. He or she is forced to have a certain percentage of the team offshore and simply load up by adding offshore resources to the onsite team. Although the PM is able to check the required box, this ultimately will not help the company achieve their global sourcing goals. As the new model of PMs — the GDM — you will need to communicate the offshore advantages to your team, appropriately balance the inherent risks with a blended team, and collaborate with the supplier to achieve the targeted offshore-onsite ratios.

In the staff augmentation model, the entire organization often "feels the pain" of the offshore engagement. Long-term contractors from local or national firms are replaced with contractors from the offshore firm, strictly to lower the labor rate. The problem though is that most organizations do not have well-defined processes or procedures for integrating contract labor, relying on the ability of the PM to assimilate the new resources. They tend to be "part of the team," and breaking up the team can have an immediate, negative effect on productivity. Extensive training must also be completed to ensure that both the onsite and offshore teams are capable of completing their tasks, which also impacts productivity and morale, especially when working on time-based projects. The staff augmentation model tends to be more expensive than other global sourcing operational models because it requires a higher percentage of onsite resources. Essentially, an offsite coordinator is required for each offshore group used, and because processes and procedures haven't been established to manage the offshore work, a higher percentage of workers (developers, testers, etc.) are required on site.

There are some advantages to this model, however, if your primary goal is to augment your existing team with lower-priced contractors and you don't engage the offshore team, or you use them for only limited activities that are closely controlled by the onsite team. The staff augmentation business is a mature industry with eroding margins, tactical value to your corporation, and limited strategic value to the supplier. This tends to mean a "stress-free" environment for both parties. Essentially, you are happy as long as the supplier provides skilled workers that meet your project needs and that save the company some money.

2. Discretionary Projects

Migrations to a new platform, operating system, compiler upgrades, or small enhancements to a well-established application make good candidates for initial global development projects. These projects are typically important to the business (i.e., they may open new markets) but are somewhat more discretionary and not always time critical. They provide a good opportunity for GDMs to understand

and overcome the unique challenges associated with global development, without jeopardizing the project or the company.

Discretionary projects are the recommended for global development engagements. There is a compelling business case that makes the venture important, but there is also a realization that the movement to global sourcing is strategic. This often eliminates some of the time pressures and unrealistic expectations that doom offshore projects.

3. Enhancements to Stable Applications, Minimal Change

Small to mid-size projects to modify existing applications, provided those enhancements do not require a high degree of user interaction, are strong opportunities for global development. This approach has been proven time and time again as many of the leading software vendors use global development to maintain and enhance older versions of their software packages, while internal resources address major new releases.

There is typically extensive training and a longer knowledge acquisition period required for these types of global development projects. As we will review later in *Managing Global Development Risk*, software vendors have become quite astute in applying many of the team-building and integration activities to positively impact productivity. Our experience is that vendors also dig into the entire knowledge acquisition and knowledge transfer process deliverables to ensure truly solid baselines and training regimen. This model should be used when outsourcing is strategic and a long-term component of your delivery model. GDMs will need to take a longer perspective and understand how each individual project contributes to the overall goal. It will be essential that GDMs apply many of the ongoing team-building and integration techniques to achieve consistent success.

4. Maintenance of Legacy Applications

Many legacy applications use a support model of X number of resources to support ongoing maintenance items. The primary goals of these teams are to ensure the Service Level Agreements (SLAs) are consistently satisfied. The SLAs should be clearly defined, including the application up-time, response time, number of change requests supported in a specified period, and the number of resources required to support ongoing maintenance.

This is another application of global development that has had great success when properly documented. This model provides an early ROI, minimizes risks to applications, and typically frees up internal resources to tackle more daunting issues. System documentation and well-defined escalation procedures are usually the early stumbling blocks when outsourcing legacy applications.

The global service provider will help with the system documentation during the knowledge acquisition phase, but as earlier noted, GDMs need to be intimately involved in this process because it will form the baseline for all development activity at the global locations in addition to training staff. GDMs also need to work closely with the global service provider to define the core project management organization (PMO), issue resolution, and escalation path. Approaches include a common trouble-reporting ticket system, well-defined priorities and escalation procedures (i.e., Sev 1, Sev 2, Sev 3), established SLAs, prioritization process, and monthly analysis of trouble tickets. It is also best to maintain some onsite support for Severity 1 (critical) issues until the global development team is completely proficient.

5. Software Testing

Software testing is another great way to start integrating global resources into a development organization. Internal testing teams often lack process and procedures to automate testing. Global development groups can develop automated test tools and scripts for regression testing or implement "follow-the-sun" processes to conduct full-blown system testing offshore.

Although testing is such a natural activity for global development and typically can be aggressively leveraged with a high onsite-offshore ratio of 20:80 or better, it is important for GDMs to appreciate the need to introduce additional development activities over time. This will help keep a more productive and dynamic development environment versus allowing boredom to set in.

6. Package Implementations

Many large-scale package implementations (i.e., Oracle, SAP, etc.) require customized components be developed to integrate the package into the end-users' environments. Although the implementation of the package should be done at the end-user's facility, the development of custom components is well suited for global development. This is extremely effective once a repository of common components is created and needs to be "tweaked" for the specific implementation.

Projects that require a high degree of customer interaction, such as designing a new customer order entry process, or those that are likely to have a high degree of change during development are typically not suitable for initial projects to complete offshore. In the early stages of a global development project, you will get exactly what you ask for including all mistakes and errors, whether obvious or not. It is critical to document everything clearly and not to make assumptions about what is obvious or implied. All members of the global team must practice this discipline, and GDMs must continually look for ways to enhance individual and group communications skills. Projects that are not well understood, thus undergoing a high degree of change, tend to compound this problem.

Although there may be high cost savings associated with higher-risk approaches, the organization needs to determine if those savings are worth the risk and determine if they have skilled GDMs to manage these risks. In an organization with a mature global sourcing model, the reward is often worth the risk and, in fact, can propel an organization to the next level of global sourcing maturity. However, in organizations that have not established a strong global presence or not managed the risks associated with global delivery, the estimated savings are often lost, and the project is put in peril.

D. Global Development Feasibility

First off, it is important to understand that not all software development projects will benefit from the addition of global development; there are many factors that need to be considered when evaluating global development projects. As previously discussed, your organization has made the strategic decision to leverage global sourcing, and your IT development organization is now challenged to leverage the capabilities of the selected partner. We have already discussed project-related factors along with core project management skills and software development processes. In addition, *Managing Global Development Risk* identified the additional skills and capability maturity model (CMM) nuances you will need to master to truly become an effective GDM.

At this time, it is necessary to touch on the cultural and process-related factors you will encounter during global project initiation. The GDM needs to access the capabilities of the internal development team that will be needed to integrate with global resources. These global development factors include the following areas outlined below.

1. *Maturity of Internal Organization*

- Does your development organization require lots of face-to-face meetings, or can meaningful work be accomplished via e-mail, documented processes, etc.?
- What are the activities and process you can put in place to prepare the internal development team to effectively interact with the global resources?
- Are there activities you can assign the internal team that will help them better document requirements more consistently?
- Does your business sponsor tend to change direction frequently or can they be more accurate or communicate change effectively?

2 *Internal Team Composition*

- Is the development organization used to working with contractors or consultants? Have they demonstrated the ability to successfully engage and leverage these resources to achieve success or has there been a fair amount of finger pointing?

■ Is your internal team already culturally diverse or will the introduction of a different culture completely change the team dynamics?

3. Communication and Escalation Plan

■ Does your internal team exhibit the rigor associated with your current internal escalation plan? This will be discussed in more detail during the planning phase, but during the initiation phase Global Development Managers should begin asking the global service provider how issues are resolved. GDMs will need to align this with current internal dynamics to ensure all team members have a common understanding.

■ Many global service providers are highly centralized and decisions are made at a senior level. As the GDM, it is important to understand these relationships, so issues can be appropriately escalated and resolved when they occur. Having a well-designed escalation plan and actually executing against the model are two very different realities. This is equally important for all global development team members.

4. Cultural Misunderstanding

A general understanding of the internal team culture and the culture of your global sourcing partner are critical to managing the risk of global development. Many cultural issues, such as how we listen or acknowledge understanding are magnified in the offshore relationships. For example, the nodding of one's head in U.S. culture generally means we understand and agree with the stated position. In the Indian culture, this simply means that they have heard the discussion. There is neither implied agreement nor understanding of the issue, which is often frustrating if you are not aware of it. There is also a tendency in the Indian culture to not provide feedback on issues. In the centralized process, most decisions on status, issues, etc. are deferred to the PM, and a "rosy" picture may be painted.

E. Onsite and Offshore Global Development Staff Profile

The initiation phase is the time GDMs need to begin thinking about the onsite-offshore mix throughout the entire project plan. This ratio defines the percentage of resources that will be located at the offshore facility and the percentage that will be co-located at your facility. Risk management is the key factor to consider when determining the appropriate offshore-onsite mix. The following factors should be considered within the context of the global development project:

- Cost
- Approach (staff augmentation, project based, etc.)
- Application development maintenance (ADM)
- Increased capacity

In addition to evaluating the appropriate onsite-offshore resource mix for the overall project, it is important during the initiation stage that you develop the overall project staffing model with your global service provider contact. This will help you see the resource mix by project stage and activity. It will also help you see the proposed flow of resources by your global service provider and help you identify logical project milestones when you may consider having key members of your development team travel to be with the offshore development resources.

Remember, rarely is the onsite-offshore mix consistent through all phases of the project. GDMs need to be comfortable with this important concept and manage the accepted project and staffing plan.

1. Cost

The bottom line is offshore resources are significantly less expensive than onsite resources. The common thought is that the higher the number of resources offshore (as a percentage of your total project team), the less expensive the project. As you will see in Section V of this book, this is not always true because of variations in the productivity levels and the additional cost associated with oversight. In general, though, if you are using global development to lower costs, then you will want a higher offshore percentage. Most offshore vendors will recommend an 80:20 mix (80% offshore, 20% onsite) when a project is first initiated. This is a fairly conservative number that provides some comfort to the vendor and the company.

We have already touched on the types of projects a GDM will be able to maximize or be more aggressive with the onsite-offshore mix. Although these are meant to be guidelines, each individual project will have some slight nuances. As GDM, be careful to look at the onsite-offshore mix from a project perspective versus the need to have the extra security that comes with a higher onsite component or a desire for a higher offshore portion if your internal staff is hostile to the concept. Although these issues should not be ignored and *Managing Global Development Risk* offers many tools and techniques for these situations, productivity and ROI will ultimately be dictated by your global resource mix.

2. Staff Augmentation

In a staff augmentation role, it is difficult to drive tasking to the global development team and leverage your skills as a GDM because the offshore resources are typically located throughout the organization and operationally report to various development managers. Many firms use a 50:50 or 60:40 mix in staff augmentation relationships. The onsite resources will typically be developers, testers, or project managers who can perform day-to-day tasks. The offshore coordination role has a limited benefit, functioning as the point of contact for you in the event some activity is sent to an offshore team.

The challenge we have observed is that many believe this application of global resources is truly global development. Staff augmentation does little more than help a project get executed in the same style and process used by your current development organization. Be careful not to fall into this trap because the global service providers are more than happy to load up staff augmentation resources, charge you the hourly billable rate, and have no accountability because it is you and your team who provide direction.

3. Application Development Maintenance

ADM is one of the most common and successful areas of outsourcing software projects. On ADM projects, an entire application is outsourced to the global service provider. Small contingencies of resources are left onsite to manage the relationship and work with the customer to ensure requirements, deliverables, SLAs, etc., are understood, but the vast majority of the development is completed at the global development facility. ADM outsourcing is ideal for companies that are making a long-term investment in global sourcing or need to outsource legacy applications to reallocate internal resources to higher priority projects. Because this is often a cost-saving measure, GDMs should drive to the highest ratio possible (80:20 or 90:10) as quickly as possible.

4. Increased Capacity

Many companies engage in global outsourcing to allow them to quickly ramp up to address a large-scale project, such as a conversion effort. In these situations the ability to ramp up quickly is the key driver. This means that resources can be placed at both facilities as long as the project risks can be appropriately managed. A 40:60 or 50:50 mix is often appropriate in these situations.

As we have already seen, cost is a primary driver in global outsourcing decisions. There are many variables to the cost formula that need to be carefully analyzed. For example, onsite rates are higher than offshore rates. If a typical offshore rate is $25 per hour, the onsite rate will typically be $50 to $75 per hour.

Some global service providers may even offer a blended rate, say $30 per hour regardless of onsite or offshore location. This is a great onsite rate, but the vendor will push to have more resources offshore to increase their margins. Alhough this may be intriguing, you will end up paying more for offshore resources and may not have the right mix to ensure project success.

One of the common trends we have noted over the past several years is that companies appear to take a conservative approach to their onsite-offshore mix. Some of this conservatism is directly related to the issues we have addressed with managing global teams. Some are project related, although the vast majority of issues tend to be interpersonal and team integration issues. However, the conservative approach has eroded the cost savings associated with global delivery and reduced its overall effectiveness. More and more companies are using a staff augmentation model to implement their global teams. This is seen as less threatening to onsite resources, but in practice complicates the transition to a global delivery model and erodes potential cost savings. There are also numerous visa and organizational issues to consider with onsite resources.

As GDMs, it is your responsibility to focus on effective project execution. You may be surprised to learn that during typical negotiations with a global service provider, little attention is paid to onsite-offshore mix by project type or stage of development. The focus tends to be exclusively on resource bill rates. They may not have even addressed the offshore-onsite resource category, which leaves a significant door open for the global service providers to push the team structure that best suits their financial goals. It will ultimately be the GDM's knowledge of global sourcing and project requirements that will allow you to maximize the appropriate staffing ratio to efficiently achieve success.

F. Global Development Procedure Manual

The initiation phase of a global development project is a great time to put the global sourcing governance model and procedures in place to manage the global sourcing relationship. Global development engagements introduce many new processes, such as visa management, on-boarding, and network and computer logistics, that most PMs have not had to address. One of the most important deliverables to create during the initiation process is the Global Development Procedural Manual. This manual defines the global delivery processes and documents the overall relationship guidelines. The purpose of the Global Development Procedural Manual is to do the following:

■ Serve as a guide for both parties so that the delivery can be executed effectively, thereby meeting the objectives of the contract or agreement as well as the project

- Define the execution process of projects and services
- Formulate the necessary guidelines and standards
- Facilitate the global team to consistently follow the defined processes
- Ensure that the quality of deliverables meets the expected standards and improves continuously
- Capture the processes and procedures required, ensuring that the contract objectives are fully met
- Unify all team members in utilizing a unified procedure across the entire project development organization

Managing Global Development Risk recommends the outline in Table 4.1 to serve as the table of contents for your specific Global Development Procedural Manual.

Time tracking is an important dimension for GDMs. SLAs, productivity rates, and base costs are all driven by the number of hours "decked" to a project. Many companies also capitalize a large portion of their software development and use time tracking to determine which phases of a project can be capitalized. If the contract is on a T&M basis, timesheets should be reviewed and approved by the global development management team and the onsite team before being submitted to the GDM for final approval. Even on a fixed price contract, GDMs should ensure time is accurately tracked and reported so that baseline estimates of productivity SLAs and work effort can be established.

It is highly recommended that GDMs execute weekly time reporting. Accurate submission and approval of timesheets should be integrated with the invoicing and accounts payable systems. It is effective to hold up invoicing for inaccurate time reporting — this will certainly get the attention of the global service provider and force corrective action. This also ensures that the full management team is involved in the time reporting process and that invoices are accurately generated. On deliverable-based invoices, GDMs should track the actual hours to complete the deliverable against the estimated hours. This will be discussed further when we address earned value analysis later in *Managing Global Development Risk*.

The typical sets of activities performed during the initiation phase of a global development project are the following:

- Understand and clearly document customer requirements.
- Develop the methodology, processes, and document templates to be used for the global development project.
- Understand the defect information needs for clear and quality defect documentation.
- Prepare knowledge transfer schedule: items to be covered, responsibilities, infrastructure needs (if any), and the schedule.
- Prepare structure and execution of ongoing training of global resources.

Table 4.1   Sample Table of Contents for Global Development Procedural Manual

Table of Contents
Introduction
Objectives
Organizational Structure of Global Service Provider and Corporation, including Detailed Organizational Charts for Both Teams
Global Service Provider Organizational Chart
Global Service Provider Roles and Responsibilities
Corporate Organizational Chart
Corporate Roles and Responsibilities
Global Management Process
On-Boarding Process: Internal and Global Resources
Resource Connectivity — Onsite as well as Offshore
Passwords
Building Access
Billing Process
Visa Regulatory Compliance Process
Performance Monitoring
Governance Model
Procedures for Developing the Statement of Work
Delivery Process
Quality Assurance, Metrics Collection and Analysis
Project Communications, Reporting and Escalation Process
Communication Plan
Status Report Format
Project Issue Tracking and Resolution
Knowledge Acquisition Process and Key Knowledge Assets
KA Deliverable Review and Compliance Process
Knowledge Transfer and Training Guidelines and Expectations
Management Plans and Processes
Time Tracking and Time Reporting Processes

G.   Global Development Roles and Responsibilities

In our experience, we have found GDMs do not spend the necessary amount of time understanding the roles and responsibilities of their global development team or the managers and executives watching the project from the periphery. When GDMs do dig into the issues of roles and responsibilities, they will tend to focus on the global service provider. Although this is understandable, GDMs need to execute an equally diligent and honest assessment of the internal development team and surrounding project stakeholders.

Managing Global Development Risk provides guidance on both organizations as only truly understanding the roles and responsibilities, dynamics, and ultimately the authority of each individual will provide GDMs the insight to execute the project successfully.

1. Global Service Provider Roles and Responsibilities

As a GDM working diligently through the project initiation phase, you will probably be amazed by the number of individuals representing the global service provider whose role is to keep you happy. Knowing the roles and responsibilities of this somewhat convoluted maze will be essential to overall global development success, particularly when rapid escalation is required.

Managing Global Development Risk attempts in Table 4.2 to capture the essence of each possible role the global service provider will dedicate to your project. Dependent on the size and complexity of the global development project, GDMs may see all or only a portion of these roles. What is important to note is that responsibilities, regardless of size, tend to exist within each global project.

As GDM, it is essential that you understand the formal roles and responsibilities for each member proposed by the global service provider. As you read through the list above, you will notice the number of critical responsibilities that are being executed by the global service provider from the offshore development facility or their corporate headquarters versus at your location. Although your partner organization may hesitate providing you this level of detail and may in fact do a nice job of masking individual authority, it points to some interesting management challenges:

- If the key decisions about your project are being made by global service provider management in India, China, or elsewhere, what does the onsite team do?
- How do you ensure these managers are completely engaged and aware of all project developments?
- How do you directly influence the internal communications process of your global service provider to effectively deliver the project without causing problems to a very hierarchical process?

We encourage GDMs to continually develop ways to reach managers and executives at their global service provider as a means to support the formal escalation process. You will find your effort in this area can be extremely valuable at the most critical times.

Table 4.2   Typical Roles and Responsibilities of the Global Service Provider or Supplier

Role	Responsibility
Account executive and global resource manager (GRM) (Offshore and Onsite)	■ Accountable for entire engagement ■ Define and track organizational structure and internal processes ■ Define contractual policies and procedures ■ Align and implement customer business strategy ■ Manage customer relationship, service level, and cost structure ■ Monitor performance
Delivery director (Offshore)	■ Overall delivery management ■ Set strategic directions for effective delivery ■ Act as a point of escalation for the delivery leadership team ■ Align delivery processes to meet customer expectations ■ Monitor and control project costs ■ Chair project management review meetings ■ First point of contact from global service provider for the applicable center of excellence ■ Drive new project initiation and execution ■ Manage SLAs, financials, resources, and global service provider teams ■ Ensure compliance with visa regulations ■ Strategic business planning and execution ■ Customer satisfaction and relationship management ■ Engagement escalation management
Group manager (Onsite and Offshore)	■ First point of contact from global service provider for mid-level and senior company executive managers ■ Manage global service provider team, ramp-up of resource requirements ■ Ensures compliance with visa regulations ■ Owns delivery from global service provider ■ Handles the escalations from the global service provider IT managers and company group manager (GM) ■ Reports progress to company GM and partnership management
Project manager (Onsite and Offshore)	■ First point of contact from for IT managers ■ Accountable for delivery, schedules, project plans, and reporting to IT manager ■ Manages vendor team ■ Plans project activities, prioritizes and assigns tasks to teams, coordinates and tracks progress

continued

Table 4.2 (continued) Typical Roles and Responsibilities of the Global Service Provider or Supplier

Role	Responsibility
Project manager (Onsite and Offshore)	■ Facilitates on-boarding formalities for the vendor team members ■ Executes timely delivery from vendor ■ Handles the escalations from the team and company manager ■ Coordinates communication and knowledge flow between onsite and offshore teams ■ Plans and executes training programs on need basis
Team member (Onsite and Offshore)	■ Executes activities of the project, namely, requirement analysis, design, coding, documentation, testing, reviews, reporting ■ Collects metrics ■ Assists offshore in causal analysis and preparation of checklist ■ Prepares weekly status report ■ Reports to vendor Project manager

2. Internal Development Team Roles and Responsibilities

You may find it interesting *Managing Global Development Risk* has dedicated a section covering the roles and responsibilities of your internal team (see Table 4.3). Experience has proven that GDMs will tend to deal with a greater level of executive attention when executing a global development project. In addition, there will be a more significant network of internal stakeholders wanting to fully understand project developments. These individuals may or may not support the use of global resources and probably have no real knowledge of the implications.

In some respects, as GDM, in addition to executing the project, you will find yourself spending time communicating internally to a significant group of executives and managers. Surprises tend to have amplified impact when dealing with global development. Reduce this risk by over-communicating throughout the entire global development life cycle.

An additional benefit from this aggressive communications posture will be a heightened visibility for your project and the manner in which you have applied your global development skills.

H. Global Success Factors — Service Level Agreements and Metrics

Success in managing global development project boils down to three key factors and one dose of common sense:

Table 4.3 Typical Roles and Responsibilities — Internal Development Team Structure

Role	Responsibility
CIO	■ Executive sponsor for the engagement ■ Business strategy alignment ■ Directions for company directors ■ Focal point for global service provider executive team
IT director	■ First point of contact for global service provider COE directors and relationship managers ■ Performance monitoring ■ Owns new project initiation and setting directions ■ Financial management ■ Strategic business planning and execution ■ Relationship management ■ Engagement escalation management
IT group manager	■ First point of contact for global service provider general managers ■ Oversees ramp-up for new resources ■ Ensures compliance with visa regulations ■ Oversees delivery from global service provider ■ Handles the escalations from global service provider ■ Reports progress to company directors and global service provider management ■ Approves timesheet
IT manager	■ Planning and prioritizing of projects ■ Oversees delivery from global service provider ■ Handles the escalations between global service provider and IT manager ■ Approves timesheets
Partnership management	■ Contract management ■ Point of contact for issues resolution ■ Track global service provider using performance metrics ■ Coordinate with global service provider and PMO for sourcing and on-boarding of resources ■ Time tracking and billing and payables management ■ Document partnership management processes

■ Establishing and measuring SLAs
■ Establishing and measuring key metrics
■ Identifying and managing risks

SLAs and metric measurement can quickly become a cumbersome task for any global development project. Make certain you are measuring items that have true project impact. Do not assign SLAs and penalties to items that will unduly penalize your global service provider and ultimately force them into a losing proposition.

In each phase of a global development project, GDMs must clearly define and manage the "Big 3" and resist the temptation to pile on SLAs and metric documentation that burden managers and contributors alike. There will always be technical hurdles, logistic issues, communication barriers, and a myriad of other issues the GDM will need to manage, but if you excel in the Big 3, you will have the data, the relationship, and the mitigation strategy to successfully overcome these obstacles.

1. Service Level Agreements

Service levels are a critical aspect to successful software development projects. They provide all team members with a clear and defined target for success. Unfortunately, many internal development activities lack clear metrics and service levels as the concept seems to lack being a priority. In somewhat of an ironic twist, SLAs really gain traction among internal teams with the introduction of global resources.

GDMs deal with the area of SLAs during the project initiation phase of a global development project. Most likely, your global service provider has already committed to a general concept and risk-reward model in the MSA. It is now time for the GDM to determine if these SLAs are appropriate for the specific project and determine if metrics exist to form a baseline for measurements acceptable to your partner.

Service level management involves comparing actual performance with predefined expectations, determining appropriate actions, and producing meaningful reports. The most significant challenge encountered with global development is the lack of documented actual performance. Global service providers will have recommendations on how to establish a baseline, but GDMs need to be careful not to get locked into an SLA approach that does not support their project objectives. A common example is SLAs associated with productivity.

Many U.S. firms do not specifically measure productivity in terms of function points per day, lines of code per day, etc., but expect these productivity measurements from their offshore provider. In lieu of this information, suppliers will state they need to use a baseline number over a defined time period (six months to a year) before they can agree to specific productivity numbers. Suppliers typically won't agree to industry standards or internal measurements. They will want to use baseline numbers for the specific organization and develop these baselines during the least productive time in the project. That typically means that the GDM is agreeing to a very low productivity bar and won't see significant improvement for several years.

SLAs also define the responsibilities placed on all parties as well as the quality levels and metrics. The service levels carry incentives for the global service providers to exceed productivity targets, as well as penalties when they are in default. Additionally, service monitoring will allow weaknesses in existing global development processes to be identified and provide the opportunity for improved quality. Most SLA measurements are difficult to set. When building an SLA, include specific metrics, as well as related industry ranges and calculation criteria, on key measures such as availability and performance.

Good SLAs focus on desired results with only minimal attention to how the global service provider will achieve success. This allows the provider to leverage its own experience and bring its best practices to the table.

So what are the right SLAs for the initiation phase of a global development project? Clearly, GDMs will want to set agreements for future deliverables within the SOW. Most importantly, though, you should use the initiation phase to explain and document your general philosophy toward SLAs with the entire global development team. Use this as an opportunity to discuss risk-based SLAs and establish incentives for the global service providers to exceed SLAs. The SOW should contain a detailed SLA section that provides the following:

- A clear statement of purpose
- A description of the services and their duration
- Timetables
- Payment terms
- Termination conditions
- Legal issues (warranties, indemnities, and limitation of liability)

The initiation phase is also a good time to establish global staffing-related SLAs. Agreements should be established that measure the global service provider's ability to find quality individuals, to ramp up to meet both onsite and offshore staffing needs, and to retain key resources.

Another effective SLA to measure during the initiation phase is milestones delivered on time and budget and completion of one-time deliverables. This SLA measures how effectively your supplier meets its commitments. An effective way to establish this early in the project is to create a project plan with well-defined milestones, for example, completion of the global measure of success and one-time deliverables such as the policy and procedure manual.

For global development projects, *Managing Global Development Risk* suggests the establishment of SLAs that cover the following categories:

- Core development productivity
- Ability to deliver milestones to budget and schedule
- Ability to meet quality goals (i.e., number of defects and defect injection rate)
- Global infrastructure performance
- Global staffing dynamics:
  - Attrition
  - Onsite-offshore ratio
  - Project management certifications of key managers

Table 4.4   Initiation Phase Metrics

Metric	Definition	Target
On-time resource loading (Onsite)	Measure the effectiveness of the offshore vendor to meet onsite staffing needs within required timeframes	70%
On-time resource loading (Offshore)	Measure the effectiveness of the offshore vendor to meet onsite staffing needs within required timeframes	90%
Retention of key resources	Measure ability of offshore vendor to retain critical resources during life of project	90%
Retention of all resources	Measure ability of offshore vendor to retain all resources during life of project	75%
Time to resolution of issues	Measure effectiveness of offshore vendors to resolve issues noted during initiation within established timeframes	90%
On-time delivery	Measure effectiveness of offshore vendor to complete all specified deliverables within established timeframes	90%

2.   Metrics

Metrics will continue to play an integral role in measuring the success of global development projects. Metrics should be twofold. First, and most importantly, they should provide early warning signs. Second, metrics should validate the SLAs. If an SLA is established, a corresponding metric and tracking process should be established

Metrics for "metrics sake" is a waste of time and energy. Many quality theorists will argue with this perspective, but, in general, management will ignore metrics that do not directly contribute to the success of a project. This doesn't mean that all metrics without immediate use are meaningless. For example, time utilization, percentage of change, and defect density rates help fine-tune estimates, thus leading to future project success.

Table 4.4 suggests metrics for the initiation phase of SLAs that were defined earlier.

I.   Identification of Global Risks

To clearly understand the risk of executing a global development project, GDMs should assess the risks of doing it in house. Once you understand the in-house risks, double your risk variable and identify subsequent risks of executing the project with a global model. This will help you begin to identify the multitude of risks that offshore outsourcing will introduce. If the risks are too high or cannot be adequately mitigated, reconsider going offshore and find another project or establish a more conservative move to global sourcing.

There are several types of risks that should be identified in the initiation phase. What are the inherent risks that will need to be managed? These can be categorized in three categories: global risk, contractual risk, and project risk.

1. Global Risk

Global risks must be mitigated regardless of the selected supplier, location, or specific project you are executing. These risks are typically defined and mitigated during the contractor negotiation phase, but must be continuously monitored through the relationship. Global risks include:

a. Loss of Intellectual Property

Intellectual property (IP) is the sum of a corporation's patents, trademarks, designs, copyrights, and company confidential information. Protection of this information from counterfeiting, piracy, and bootlegging is a major concern when engaging global service providers. Software vendors are particularly concerned about the loss of IP when dealing with global sourcing because of the competitive advantage that can be lost if their IP is stolen.

The contract language should specifically address IP protections and appropriate recourse if IP is compromised. Non-competition and non-solicitation provisions should also be included in the agreement if needed to prevent the contractor from working for competitors of the business or soliciting its customers. It is also essential to understand the employment agreement the global service provider utilizes with its employees as it will ultimately be the governing document in the event legal recourse is pursued on an individual basis.

b. Loss of Internal Knowledge or Innovation

A major concern among CIOs is the loss of internal knowledge and innovations that potentially occur as more work is moved offshore. To some companies, the risk of losing their innovative spirit is as critical as the potential loss of IP. Management should protect innovativeness by outsourcing only non-critical applications. Systems or applications that provide a competitive advantage should be closely guarded and only outsourced when adequate protections are established. The challenge, though, is to identify those systems and applications that truly provide competitive advantage. All too often this is used as a reason not to outsource or increase offshore utilization.

c. Potential Breach of Security

Security and protection of data are also major concerns with offshore vendors. Recent regulatory changes, such as Gramm-Leach-Bliley (GLB), which requires clear disclosure by all financial institutions of their privacy policy regarding the sharing of non-public personal information with both affiliates and third parties, and the Sarbanes–Oxley Act, which aims to deter fraud in public companies by requiring stringent internal controls over significant financial transactions, including procurement of goods and services, highlight the importance of data security. The proposal process and contract must contain specific language on how data will be protected and appropriate recourses if the data is compromised.

d. Potential for Poorer Quality

Poor quality continues to be the number one concern voiced by offshore practitioners. Despite the emphasis on CMM and other quality initiatives, many offshore vendors continue to struggle with quality perception. Many of the concepts discussed throughout this book are designed to improve the quality of deliverables. The contract and individual statements of work should articulate clear quality goals, and SLAs should be established to measure quality standards.

e. Language and Cultural Barriers

Language and cultural barriers will be a reoccurring theme throughout this book and throughout the offshore relationship. Misunderstandings related to scope, schedule, or specific tasks will occur. Hopefully, we'll equip you with the necessary tools and techniques to successfully handle the communication and cultural barriers.

2. Contractual Risk

Contractual risks are associated with a new supplier agreement. These risks include:

- How financially viable is the global service provider?
- How will the client manage the relationship, and does it have the bandwidth to do so?
- How will it transfer expertise from the client organization to the global service provider?
- Will it need to expand or improve its communications links, and, if so, at what cost?

The above risks are common to many global development projects; thus offshore service providers have learned to address and mitigate these risks early in the process. Again, as the GDM, the time you spend familiarizing yourself with the overall MSA will help you effectively execute the project.

3. Project Risk

Project risks may not be fully understood during the initiation phase, so it may be difficult to identify and mitigate all potential risks. But there are several common risks (listed in Table 4.5) that impact a variety of global development projects.

J. Global Issue Management

In general, the larger your project, the more likely you will encounter significant issues. Large projects, for instance, may have a dedicated person that does nothing but help to identify, document, and expedite problem resolutions.

A formal process for managing issues will ensure that the problems are identified and resolved as quickly and effectively as possible. With a software development project leveraging global resources, the establishment of a clear, concise, and direct global issue management process is critical.

Having a defined global issue resolution process allows you to calmly and effectively work through a resolution process whenever issues arise. It serves equally well for internal issues and those associated with the global service provider. We suggest you engage the global service provider early in these discussions so they are equally aware and have the opportunity for input. Having buy-in at this time will prove incredibly valuable and will instill a true team dynamic.

K. Summary

As we conclude this section covering global development project initiation and prepare to enter the global development project planning phase, it is important to take a moment to fully understand the position a GDM finds himself or herself in.

You have taken the time to study the existing MSA between your company and the selected global service provider to understand how the basic terms support your unique needs. We have determined that it is feasible to execute your project in the global development model and engage the senior project representation for your offshore partner.

Throughout this important stage, you have continually sought the input of internal executives, stakeholders, and development team members, assessing the internal tolerance and real desire to leverage the global model. At the same time, you have established a strong line of communications with your global service provider, extending multiple opportunities to participate in the development of important project process decisions.

We have accomplished a great deal, building a strong foundation for your project and other subsequent projects.

Table 4.5　Initiation Phase Risks

Risk No.	Risk	Probability	Impact	Risk Exposure	Mitigation Plan
1	Executive commitment	H	H	9	■ Discuss project goals and strategic alignment with senior management
2	Organizational readiness	H	VH	12	■ Ensure open communication with project team. ■ Discuss impacts with senior management and garner support. ■ Encourage open dialogue and discussion of strategic objectives and goals
3	Employee backlash	H	H	9	■ Communicate rationale for global project. ■ Collaborate with human resources or senior management to develop policies to manage employee morale and attrition
4	Infrastructure challenges	M	H	6	■ Define infrastructure needs during project planning. ■ Coordinate with offshore team to minimize infrastructure issues (create and track plan once needs are determined)
5	Delays in creating and approving SOW	M	M	4	■ Ensure budget is approved, and work with supplier to ensure SOW addresses all requested work
6	Regulatory impacts due to visa changes (e.g., selected offshore vendor not having correct mix of visas to support needs).	L	M	2	■ Openly discuss with offshore supplier and have a backup plan established to move work offshore or have an onsite resource perform the functions
7	Qualified project manager (Onsite and offshore)	L	H	3	Interview supplier candidates and demand that supplier staff the project with talented resources. Threats of contract termination or "pulling the plug" will motivate the supplier to staff the project correctly

Table 4.6   Initiation Phase Checklist

Initiation Phase Checklist
■ Master service agreement (MSA) signed ■ Statement of work (SOW) created and signed ■ Measure of success (MOS) defined ■ Right project defined ■ Project evaluation C/L completed ■ Onsite-offshore resource goals defined ■ Offshore procedures manual and key processes defined ■ Roles and responsibilities ■ Service level agreements (SLAs) defined ■ Metrics defined ■ Risk defined and risk, issue, decision (RID) log initiated

Initiation Phase SLAs	*Initiation Phase Metrics*
■ Agreements for future deliverables ■ Document SLA philosophy ■ Initiation phase deliverables completed on time and budget ■ Staffing quality individuals — onsite and offshore staffing needs ■ Retain key resources	■ On-time resource loading; onsite ■ On-time resource loading; offshore ■ Retention of key resources ■ Retention of all resources ■ Issue resolution; time to resolution ■ On-time delivery

Initiation Phase Risks
■ Employee backlash ■ Executive commitment ■ Infrastructure challenges ■ Organizational readiness ■ Qualified project manager; onsite and offshore ■ Delays in creating and approving SOW ■ Regulatory impacts due to visa changes; selected offshore vendor not having correct mix of visas to support needs

Chapter 5

Planning the Global Development Project

A. Introduction

The old axiom "plan the work and work the plan" carries new meaning when planning a global development project. As a Global Development Manager (GDM), you will create or review plans for a myriad of details that will be thought through and discussed. The large number of tasks involved in global development project planning should not be misinterpreted as the primary phase of global development management. Instead, planning should be considered the foundation for executing and controlling the activities required to deliver positive results.

So what are the activities that need to go into the development of a global development project plan (GDPP)? Are there differences between planning a typical development project and those that incorporate global developers?

> **Section Key Concepts: PLANNING**
> ➤ Global Development Project Planning Activities
> ➤ Global Project Plan Components and Management

Figure 5.1 Section V Key Concepts

Managing Global Development Risk answers these important questions. We again suggest that at this point in planning a process, you engage the project manager (PM) of your service provider to gain their input, advice, and buy-in. They will have a very different perspective on project planning that may provide valuable insight into their processes and additional tasks that should be included in your plan. By doing so, you may be able to refine the final plan and have reinforced an open, communicative dynamic.

Global development project planning activities is segmented into eight core tasks (see Table 5.1).

Planning offshore engagements is a difficult process and can be overwhelming if you don't involve your offshore partner. Hopefully, your supplier will have done this before and have established templates, processes, and best practices to help you through the planning phase. There will be a host of issues that as a PM you probably haven't dealt with, but as a GDM will become part of your ongoing responsibilities. For example, you'll need to determine the best means to train the offshore team on your applications and internal processes. What training is required? What is the best way to facilitate this training? Where should the training be conducted? Most offshore firms have established processes for completing the training phase, as we will discuss later in this chapter. The key, though, is to engage your partner so you can plan and execute these activities.

B. Develop Statement of Work

The Statement of Work (SOW) is created during the initiation or planning phases of the project. The SOW compliments the master service agreement (MSA) by defining the specific deliverables, scope of work, and other important contractual items for the specified global development project. Because the global sourcing agreement is a legal contract between two corporations, the SOW must clearly state the terms associated with this specific work effort. Either party can initiate creation of the SOW. GDMs should check with internal procurement or contracting to see if an SOW or SOW template was included as an appendix or as an attachment to the MSA.

As global sourcing consultants, we often generate the first drafts of the SOW and meet with the client to review the details independent of the global service provider. We negotiate specific items and reach agreement on a final document internally before engaging the global providers. This approach works well when GDMs are unsure of the details that a global provider may need or are working with a vendor who has time-tested processes for developing these agreements. However, do not relinquish your control. The SOW represents what you want delivered. It is your project, and you must ensure that the expectations, tasks, and deliverables are well defined, clearly articulated, and understood.

We strongly suggest that as the customer, you "encourage" the global service provider to accept your SOW format, which the GDM completes.

Table 5.1   Global Development Project Planning Activities

Activity	Components
1. Develop statement of work	■ Contractual agreement ■ Project description ■ Scope of services ■ Roles and responsibilities ■ Deliverables (timetable and milestones) ■ Acceptance criteria ■ Pricing (fixed, T&M, other) ■ Signatures
2. Knowledge acquisition (KA)	■ Overview of business (provide details on core products, market space, etc.) ■ Project overview (review of requirements or project description, expectations) ■ Architecture, technologies, languages ■ Processes and methodologies of software development life cycle (SDLC) ■ Environment (tools, environment, configuration management, defect tracking, integrated development environment (IDE) ■ Application details and primary components (breakdown of core applications or process that will be supported offshore, review code) ■ Format and template for all KA deliverables
3. Knowledge transfer	■ Format and template of deliverables ■ Signoff on transition staffing dynamic ■ Review training capabilities, process, and schedule ■ Review training material refresh schedule
4. Estimate effort	■ Method used to estimate ■ Review estimates with global service provider PM and management team ■ Productivity level ■ Detailed estimates
5. Global development execution plan	■ Project overview ■ Project scope ■ Project organization ■ Key contact list ■ Key milestones ■ Assumptions ■ Processes ■ Scope and change in management process ■ Configuration of management process ■ Estimated size and effort

continued

Table 5.1 (continued)   Global Development Project Planning Activities

Activity	Components
	■ Schedule ■ Staffing plan (onsite-offshore mix) ■ Roles and responsibilities ■ Development environment ■ Hardware and software requirements ■ Tools ■ Training plan ■ Quality assurance plan ■ Risk management plan ■ Project tracking plan ■ Issue reporting ■ Communications plan ■ Escalation process
6. Global staffing	■ Review staffing plan by development activity and development life cycle ■ Review the staff dynamics, understanding the movement of onsite resources ■ Review visa strategy for onsite team
7. Develop project schedule (WBS)	■ Task list by phase ■ Baselined project schedule ■ Weekly milestones
8. Finalize SLAs, metrics, and risks	■ Service levels defined and tracking mechanisms established ■ Metrics established and baselined; tracking tools and processes defined ■ Risks and mitigation strategies defined and tracked

With global projects, the entire scope of the effort is often not understood until the onsite team is completely engaged and KA is complete. This is due to variants in estimates, schedules, deliverables, and processes that may be defined or negotiated later. To manage these issues and to minimize the impact of change requests, *Managing Global Development Risk* recommends the creation of two parallel SOWs when first engaging a global service provider.

1. Global Knowledge Acquisition and Knowledge Transfer Statement of Work

The first SOW addresses the deliverables and timeline for the knowledge acquisition and knowledge transfer (KA-KT) activities of the GDPP. We suggest using a time-boxed approach for these two critical phases, which means a specified amount of time and resources being allocated to both the KA-KT effort. Time-boxing originated with iterative development methodologies and has become a useful tool to manage short duration tasks as well as breaking global development projects into manageable components. The key to successful time-boxing is to establish mini-milestones through the full time-boxed period. GDMs should strive for weekly deliverables that provide real value and measure real progress. The advantage of this approach is that it focuses the entire global project team on deliverables, provides GDMs clear expectation of the cost for both KA-KT activities, and provides a timeline on when the "real" project can begin.

2. Global Development Project Statement of Work

The second SOW addresses the actual project. GDMs should initiate the second SOW toward the end of the planning phase when the scope is better understood and the delivery processes and procedures are defined. This SOW will define the entire scope of the project, the deliverables for each phase, the acceptance criteria for the deliverables, including the software code, global project plan, and the projected costs of the effort. The output from the planning process is used to create the signed agreement.

Again, the SOW is a legal document that specifies the specific agreements between two legal entities. As such, you must ensure that all deliverables and expectations are clearly defined. All suppliers will use the change control process to their advantage if the SOW is not clear on expectations; global service providers are no exception and, in fact, are quite gifted in this regard. Even with offshore rates, change requests can have a significant impact on the timing, cost, and quality of the project.

Let's take a closer look at the important sections of a SOW:

- **Contractual agreement.** Legalese that defines the effective date and the entities (vendor and company). This section usually references the MSA for specific terms and agreements. If an MSA does not exist, you should include the pertinent sections in the SOW and make reference to them at the beginning of the document. Pertinent sections may include warranties, standard rates, terms and conditions, payment terms, confidentiality, intellectual property, indemnification, limits of liability, insurance requirements, etc.
- **Project description.** Include project title, project tracking number (if applicable), and the name of the GDM. Also include the project overview or charter, which should be copied from the business case or the project request.
- **Scope of services.** Clearly identify what is in scope for the project. It is also helpful to identify what is not in scope.
- **Roles and responsibilities.** Define who is responsible for major activities.
- **Deliverables (timetable and milestones).** Including a template or sample table of contents is an excellent way to reduce confusion.

- **Acceptance criteria.** Define the required content of the deliverable. Who is authorized to accept? What is the time in which the customer must respond? What is the required action on the part of global service provider in the event the deliverable does not satisfy requirements?
- **Warranty.** If you are seeking additional or different clauses than what is stated in the MSA.
- **Staffing plan.** Defines the client and suppliers onsite and offshore resources. Should include the minimum experience level for supplier personnel and the estimated duration for supplier personnel.
- **Dependencies.** Defines dependencies that may impact supplier's ability to deliver services per the timeframe, for example, establishing the network between the onsite and offshore locations.
- **Assumptions.** Defines assumptions that may impact the supplier's ability to deliver services per the plan. Examples include the assumption that client personnel will be available, that the client will sign off on deliverables within a specified amount of time, etc.
- **Intellectual property (IP).** Defines what IP, if any, supplier plans to use to deliver the services specified in the SOW.
- **Payment terms.** If you are seeking additional or different clauses than what is stated in the MSA.
- **Pricing (fixed, T&M, other).** Include costs for labor, network, hardware and software. Budget for offshore visits and onsite visits from the offshore team (typical costs).
- **Signatures**

In general, the creation of parallel SOWs is a best practice in which you begin to appreciate how your global service provider and internal team will work together during the actual project. If GDMs have taken the advice described in the pages of *Managing Global Risk Development* up to this point, you have created multiple opportunities to have team members working side by side.

C. Knowledge Acquisition

KA is the process of understanding the business, applications, processes, and procedures of the organization. The KA phase is critical to global delivery projects to allow the offshore team to learn your business. The knowledge acquisition is similar to new hire training. What does a new hire need to know to be productive on a project? What tools? What methodologies? What is the project? In fact, a great way to meet the KA requirements is to send the global service provider's onsite team through any internal new hire classes that are offered. This could include classes on a company overview or specific product or application overviews.

The KA phase is not typically a part of IT solutions and delivery. KA prepares the global team for the project by providing relevant background information on the business, specific project, and technologies used on the project. The global service provider will typically have a defined process for completing the KA phase. This will involve formal and informal interviews, a review of project documentation, and detailed reviews of all deliverables and expectations. Most PMs have limited experience with the KA phase; therefore, let the global service provider take the leading role during this period, but remain active in both the planning and execution of the KA phase. The supplier is experienced and has the most to gain from a successful KA.

KA should be formulated around specific training goals with a mix of formal and informal training or based on analysis of the specific problem being solved. If focused on a specific problem, the onsite team should be an integral part of the project team.

In general, assume a six- to eight-week ramp-up time for KA and then another three to four months before the global development team is as productive as your current teams. For larger projects or outsourcing arrangements, you can estimate 12 to 15 months' ramp-up time before the offshore team is meeting your current productivity levels.

As with any project, the KA phase should be planned and managed. From a planning perspective, the GDM should identify expectations and deliverables for the KA phase. Because the core function of the phase is to prepare the offshore team, a good deliverable is the training and procedures document. This document should evolve over the course of the engagement and be reviewed weekly. Specific goals and deliverables should be identified, and progress should be tracked against these goals. Deliverables can include summaries of training that will be used to train the offshore team or first iteration of requirement-analysis documents — the key is to ensure knowledge transfer is successful by establishing incremental milestones.

In the early planning phases, work with the global service provider onsite PM to identify the core information the team will need to understand. This typically involves the following:

- Overview of business (provide details on core products, market space, etc.)
- Project overview (review of requirements or project description, expectations)
- Architecture, technologies, and languages
- Processes and methodologies (SDLC)
- Environment (tools, environment, configuration management, defect tracking) Integrated Development Environment (IDE) etc.)
- Application details, primary components (breakdown of core applications or process that will be supported offshore; review code)

The global development team should document each of these areas to ensure clear and concise understanding of the required work and environment. Again, the purpose of this phase is to train the offshore team, so you need to ensure that the onsite team "gets it." To facilitate this, it is often helpful to conduct scheduled training classes at least four hours, three days a week, throughout the KA period. These facilitated sessions should be scheduled and reviewed with the offshore PM.

From a cost perspective, the KA phase can add ten to fifteen percent to the total project costs. The KA phase typically occurs onsite, so the rates are higher. The phase also does not directly address the goals of the project, so additional ramp-up time is also required. Many offshore firms will offer the first two or three weeks of free labor — you will usually be expected to pay travel expenses. Although this is attractive from a financial perspective, it doesn't help get your project delivered on time. You will also need to allocate internal resources to "train" the offshore team on the project and products. This is additional cost and time that needs to be allocated. The key is to plan the phase as part of your overall engagement.

Many offshore firms have developed processes to further facilitate the KA process. They create a System Application Document (SAD), Application Reference Manual (ARM) or similar document "Induction Manual" for every application they support. This manual addresses core processes and procedures, and provides an overview of the systems they are supporting. What is nice about this process is that the offshore firms typically maintain these documents throughout the project, which makes it easy for new resources to come on board.

The initial KA-KT activities are designed to ensure the success of the global service provider. The service provider clearly has the most to gain, but the success and subsequent team dynamics that develop during these activities will ultimately determine the success of your global development project. Therefore, we strongly recommend that the GDM be actively involved in KA-KT phases. Your involvement will drive strategy to successfully influence the service provider through the KA-KT process and the longer-term project. You will gain a true, ground level understanding of how your global teams operate, and you will know exactly what's "under the hood."

Each time we have observed a GDM take ownership of this activity by truly participating, we have seen:

■ Smoother than normal transitions
■ Quicker achievement of targeted productivity
■ Stronger team interaction
■ Effective on-boarding of subsequent rounds of global resources

Do we have your interest? If so, let's take a look at the potential interaction with your offshore provider.

When you discuss KA-KT, your selected global service provider will take great pride in sharing with you the strength and effectiveness of their proprietary KA-KT process. Your goal is to be intimately involved throughout the KA-KT process, making this a truly integrated global team effort. If you want to be successful, don't sit back and wait to review and approve the compiled documentation. You need to develop the strategy during the global development project planning phase, and you need to get involved by actively participating in the KA process and by identifying a few select members of your senior development team to get actively involved in the process, assuming some of the contributing and production roles.

Unfortunately, many offshore service providers will be more than happy to let you kick back and approve documents. In fact, you will probably encounter resistance if you try to get more involved. The supplier may see this as a direct challenge to his or her PM, or may exhibit a more passive-aggressive style of non-conformity. But GDMs need to persist on this issue.

By executing this *Managing Global Development Risk* tactic, you will demonstrate to the global service provider that as GDM, you and your team are going to be actively engaged and involved. You have also engaged several strategic internal leaders into the global team that will be responsible for bringing the documentation back to the global development team. This will provide a positive team dynamic and great insight as to exactly how and why documentation is compiled across your internal team. Finally, you will have both internal champions and global resources able to prime the training pump as your project scales up.

D. Knowledge Transfer

The KT phase begins with the GDMs formal approval of the KA documentation. At this point, the global service provider begins the transitional process of rotating staff so that the actual KT can be conducted at the vendor's offshore facility. The purpose is to train the initial global development team, but GDMs need to have a longer-term vision and ensure the processes are established for maintaining the integrity of the documentation and training manuals so that resources of subsequent rounds can also be trained effectively. Typically the global service provider has one or several of the original onsite resources conduct the training, but we have also seen customers insert their own staff to be present for initial training and execute train-the-trainer sessions, using the material developed during KA.

This phase absolutely requires the GDM's proactive management. Specific training goals should be established and measured on a weekly basis. Deliverables should be established to ensure understanding and to start addressing the specific project goals, and GDMs should consider using tests and quizzes as an ongoing means to monitor effectiveness, not just code quality.

Many global service providers accelerate the KT phase. Although this may appear to be advantageous to the project, in reality in puts the project at somewhat higher risk by perhaps having untrained resources start design or coding activities. As we have already stated, it is important to plan the KA-KT activities and carefully monitor the progress. We wouldn't recommend accelerating the KA phase to get resources fully utilized unless there are clear metrics or other indicators that validate that the team is fully ready to start development.

Although everyone is eager to get started, it is best to ensure the global development team is ready to perform before launching the actual project. There are exceptions to this rule, which may include the following:

- Technologies are well understood.
- Business or application overviews are not necessary.
- Offshore team is "augmenting" the onsite team, and thus will be receiving day-to-day directions.

E. Estimating the Effort

Software estimating is both a science and an art. Although many processes exist for estimating projects, they are rarely standardized in the industry or even throughout an organization. Most U.S.-based PMs and development managers apply a "rule of thumb" when estimating projects. They typically have calculations that determine the effort per phase, but will usually rely on a senior developer's intuition to determine the size of the coding effort. This leads to inaccurate estimates that are often adjusted as the project progresses.

With global development projects, estimation tends to take on a new challenge: internal staff estimates compared with those of a CMM Level 5 estimation process. There will certainly be some significant differences.

We will discuss each of these in more detail, but there are essentially four processes that can be used to estimate a project:

- Expert judgment
- Analogous estimates
- Bottom up or top down
- Algorithmic or parametric

In addition, many U.S. and global firms use a two- or three-step process to estimate a project:

- **High-level estimate** — A high-level estimate is generally provided at the start of a project based on some high-level discussions with business users or review of a high-level project description. This estimate is often ±100 percent of the actual effort.
- **Mid-level estimate** — A mid-level estimate is usually completed after the requirements are baselined. A team of developers will review the requirements, determine the components required to support the requirements, and provide an estimate based on this functional decomposition. This estimate is typically ±30 to 50% of the actual effort.

■ **Detailed estimate** — The detailed estimate is provided after the design phase. The development group has had the opportunity to break down the functional components and provides a more accurate picture of the individual components. These estimates are typically ±10% of the actuals.

Global service providers, which are typically CMM Level 5 development organizations, have tighter control around the estimating processes. This is one area where the global service provider takes a great deal of pride. GDMs should allow their service providers to complete their estimations as it can help define the true cost of the project. Historically, estimates from a global service provider are 20 to 30% higher than U.S. estimates because of the factors we discussed earlier (productivity rates, CMM process, overhead, etc.). However, their process to determine the actual coding phase is very reliable.

Global service providers rarely provide a high-level estimate. They understand that these estimates are error-prone and subject to large fluctuations. They generally provide estimates after the requirements are baselined and the project is well understood. This allows them to identify and manage project risks and provides a more accurate estimate based on projects of similar scope. The bottom-up estimation approach is the preferred approach for most global service providers. This allows them to fully utilize data from past projects and provide a complete task list on which to base their estimate. The task approach allows the GDM to divide the project into components and classify each component as simple, medium, or complex, based on predefined criteria (number of screens, number of date elements, complexity of interface, etc.). For each classification the GDM is to define a standard effort for coding and unit testing the component.

When it comes to estimation of a global development project, we recommend you instruct your team to fully cooperate with your global partners' resources as they gather the necessary information to develop their estimates. This is a proven global sourcing best practice that facilitates a detailed estimate that will ultimately meet your project timelines and budget. Let's take a look at the various estimating techniques in more detail.

1. Estimating Techniques

The bottom-up approach provides a detailed list of tasks and a reliable estimate, but it is typically not used in global development projects because organizations usually require an estimate of the cost before releasing funds. With the bottom-up approach, the team needs to spend extensive time and cost in analysis and design to define the tasks. The more common approach is to use a top-down approach that is based on function point analysis (FPA) or use case analysis (UCA) techniques.

The top-down approach requires an estimate of productivity. The productivity levels are based on historical projects or agreed to according to global team productivity levels (see productivity SLAs). The productivity estimate is then used to calculate the overall estimate. Again, once the development effort is known, GDMs derive the subsequent phases by using percentage distributions.

a. Function Point Analysis

FPA is a technique that breaks complex problems into smaller components that can then be better analyzed. It provides a structured technique for estimating the effort and decomposing the problem into discrete components. Function points view the problem from the user's perspective, so the process counts the number of screens, reports, input files, output files, etc., that a user would interact with. From an estimation perspective, the process determines the effort required to develop each of these discrete components. This is similar to other bottom-up approaches, but the difference is that there have been significant work and industry benchmarks created to define function points and determine the average effort to develop an application based on the number of function points.

The challenge with function points has always been what and how to count them. It's easy to say that it is functionality from a user's perspective, but it is a bit harder in practice to get consistent counts. Function-point counting is the process of reviewing an application or a design for an application to determine the number of function points. Again, all activities of function-point counting are based on the user's view of the application — screens, reports, system input and output files, data stores, etc. Lines of code (LOCs) are not counted and are not considered in the estimation process.

The most common way that organizations desire to use function points for ongoing work is as a productivity measurement, usually expressed in function points per staff month. If a team can average more than the industry norm, they are productive. However, the work of most development teams can be broken up into three major areas: new development, enhancement, and maintenance or break-fix. Function-point counting, and associated metrics that go along with it, are not as equally effective for each of these.

■ **New development** — With new development, function points are a very effective measure of size, and can be used as inputs to the estimating process, understanding the size of the system delivered and understanding productivity (provided hours were tracked, etc.).

■ **Enhancement** — Function points are fairly good for enhancement as a size metric, provided that the enhancement can be experienced by the user. An example is a new report or screen. However, an enhancement such as runtime improvement will have no function points associated with it, so it cannot be used in any meaningful way. Function points can be used as an input to estimating for enhancements, again provided that the user can experience the enhancement.

■ **Maintenance or break-fix** — Function points are largely useless for maintenance work. Most maintenance efforts are based on the stability of the system (number of open tickets) and the degree of change (number of change requests) and a baseline of the effort required. Large systems of 10,000-plus function points may be very stable, whereas a system with no function points (i.e., a middleware interface) may require extensive efforts.

Because function-point counting has been established, many individuals and organizations have looked at ways to do a "quick and easy" count and circumvent the rigor (and time and expense) of doing a full count. The most common of these is known as a backfire count, done by counting lines of code and using generally understood multiplication and weighting factors to estimate the number of function points. Another method uses the system's data model to determine a quick count — it can literally be done in an hour or two if you have a subject matter expert (SME) who understands both the database and the system.

FPA has not been a focus area in most information technology (IT) organizations, but because of outsourcing, it is having a resurgence. This area of estimating and productivity management will be interesting to watch over the next several years. Major U.S. firms that are spending tremendous amounts of money counting and baselining function points still have not decided if the cost and time are worth the effort and if it truly improves the overall productivity of the supplier.

A final thought before we leave this section. When using function points as an estimation technique, you'll need to agree to the estimation parameters and fully understand the scope of the estimate. Does the estimate cover just the coding phase (which means you'll need to use the algorithmic or parametric estimation process to determine the overall effort)? Or does the estimate cover a subset of development activities, such technical design through unit testing? Your overall estimation model will be dramatically impacted if you don't have this defined. Unfortunately, there is not a defined standard, so you'll need to discuss and reach agreement with your service provider before completing the estimate.

b. Use Case Analysis

UCA is similar to FPA, but relies on use cases as defined by the rational unified process (RUP) instead of function points.

Use case modeling is an accepted and widespread technique to capture the business processes and requirements of a software application. Because use cases provide the functional scope of the application, analyzing their contents provides valuable insight into the effort and size needed to design and implement the application. In general, applications with large, complicated use cases take more effort to design and implement than small applications with less complicated use cases. Moreover, the effort is affected by:

- The number of steps to complete the use case
- The number and complexity of the actors
- The technical requirements of the use case such as concurrency, security, and performance
- Various environmental factors such as the development team's experience and knowledge

Use case points (UCPs) have the potential to produce reliable results because their estimates are produced from the actual business processes — the use cases — of a software application. Additionally, in many traditional estimation methods, influential technical and environmental factors are often not adequately given enough consideration. UCPs include and abstract these subjective factors into an equation. When tweaked, over time, UCPs can provide estimates that are reliable.

Because the basis of the UCP model is built on the premise that use cases can be classified by complexity (simple, medium, complex), several organizations have simplified the used case estimate process by determining the complexity of each use case and then applying historical estimates to calculate the overall effort per use case. Although this is not as accurate as the complete process, it does provide a high-level estimate based on historical estimates and has proven successful.

As with the function point approach, you'll need to clarify if the UCP estimate is for the coding phase or a subset of development activities. Once you know the scope of the estimate, you can apply other variables to determine the overall effort.

2. Evaluating Global Productivity

Estimating the size of an application is just the first step in the estimation process. Equally important in a global environment is estimating the productivity of your offshore team. Many people want to simplify this step by adding the additional effort required because of a less productive team to the overall estimation process. As sourcing advisors, we strongly recommend that you keep these as two separate variables. As your relationship with your offshore provider grows, both variables — estimation accuracy and productivity — will be subject to continuous improvement; the offshore productivity factor should be reduced to a 1:1 ratio, and the estimating parameters should be reduced.

It is well documented and understood that the global service partner will not initially be at the same technical level or productivity levels as your internal resources. In addition, the global development project introduces new phases that will impact the cost and schedule. Thus, project estimates, staffing profiles, timelines, etc., will be adjusted to allow for KA-KT, environment setup, and other project logistics.

In general, GDMs should assume a productivity factor of 1.5 to 1.8 during the first six months of a new global development engagement. This means that if you estimated a team of 10 offshore resources, you should staff it with 12 or 14 (assumes eight developers). If you estimated the project will take four months, GDMs should assume it will take six or seven months. This is an important concept to remember as you are setting expectations in the early phases of the global development project.

The productivity level will become more efficient over time; however, it will most likely take several projects before the global team is performing at the same level as your internal resources (1:1 ratio). Productivity levels will be a key metric that should be baselined and tracked through the performance of the project and the length of the contract.

The good news is that the successful integration of global resources can significantly boost overall productivity. The use of a capability maturity model (CMM), and metrics adds discipline and visibility to the global development process. You can also establish SLAs that mandate year-by-year productivity improvements. In addition, if the offshore development center is several time zones away, as is India, it enables "round the clock" development and testing, which can dramatically reduce the development cycle times and significantly improve the productivity of the team.

Productivity concerns can have an immediate negative impact on global projects if the expectations are not properly set and communicated. This is especially true if executive sponsors of the global agreement are not aware of the issues and are not realizing the savings that were "promised." Executive sponsorship, from the client and the supplier, of a global sourcing project is typically not a problem during the early stages because the sales cycle and negotiations usually occur at a senior level.

The challenge for the GDM, though, is setting expectations with the executive team early in the planning phase, once the champagne hangover has passed and the teams are on the ground working through these issues. As within any sales cycle, there is often major "hype" built around the cost savings and dramatic improvements that will be realized when global development is fully engaged. Many procurement officers, chief financial officers (CFOs), or IT executives may expect to see these cost savings out of the gate and are not fully aware of the additional startup costs or overall financial impact of the productivity differences. It is the responsibility of the GDM to clearly define the expectations for the initial projects.

3. Global Resource Ramp-Up Plan

Another important dimension to global development project estimation is the speed and extent of the global resource ramp-up. The global resource ramp-up measures the increase of headcount at the offshore facility over the life of the project. At times, the onsite-offshore ratio, KA-KT activities, and the global resource ramp-up strategy are defined within the MSA. If this is the case, the GDM needs to review the MSA to understand what is defined within the overall agreement and determine if it is sufficient for the global development project. Figure 5.2 provides two samples on how global resource ramp-up plans may be represented.

The goal of the ramp-up strategy is to achieve steady state as soon as possible without assuming unnecessary risk. During the estimation process, GDMs should collaborate with the onsite PM to drive the analysis below superficial levels so as to fully understand staff movement as well as the specific activities that will be executed as the team ramps up. The following model, which is included with the compact disk (CD), provides a simplified view of the ramp-up strategy. It allows the GDM to model various ramp-up strategies and measure the internal and supplier's abilities to meet the staffing needs. As you can see, even on a relatively small project, the number of resources joining the project on a monthly basis can be dramatic. You will have to balance your internal team's ability to accommodate this number of resources with the project goals.

Procurement may also have set expectations with the global service provider to achieve the ramp-up strategy on a project-by-project level. There may be penalties or awards associated with hitting these targets. The global service provider is also motivated to hit these targets: remember this is a business, and more billable resources equate to higher revenue, which hopefully leads to higher profits and margins. Unfortunately, many GDMs are not fully prepared to handle the initial complexities with quickly ramping up a global team.

So what can GDMs do? First, you need to fully understand the drivers for achieving the ramp-up. Were they realistic? Are there real factors (i.e., a major project initiating in six months that will require trained resources, significant market factors that require dramatic cost cuts, or a faster time to market for a new product)? When you understand the drivers, you can make better decisions based on the risk-reward of an aggressive ramp-up. If the drivers are not clear, reset management expectations. Articulate your concerns and the risks to the project. If possible, demonstrate the wasted cost of resources that are not fully utilized or are spending their time training and orienting newcomers to the project instead of working on the project and establishing solid procedures that will help accelerate growth.

4. Final Estimation

Once the global development effort is determined, the productivity levels are calculated, and the ramp-up strategy is finalized, the total effort required for the project, which includes all phases, is determined by calculating the coding effort as a percentage of the overall effort (algorithmic-parametric). Again, this is based on historical efforts on projects of similar scope and size.

See Figure 5.3 for an estimation worksheet that demonstrates how estimates are determined.

Projected Head Count	150
Increase Per Month	20%
Initial Team	15

Phase	Knowledge Acquisition		Knowledge Transfer		Ramp-up					Steady State		
Phase/ Month	Jan	Feb	Mar	Apr	May	Jun	Jul	Aug	Sep	Oct	Nov	Dec
Staff	15	15	30	36	43	52	62	74	89	107	128	150
Net Increase	15	0	15	6	7	9	10	12	15	18	21	22

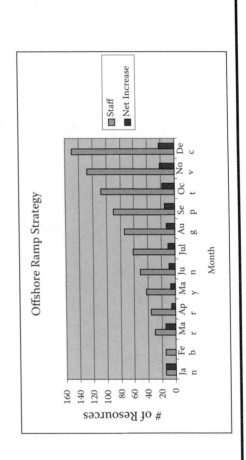

Figure 5.2   Sample Global Resource Roadmap

Coding Effort	6800	% Effort
PM Effort	1020.00	7.32%
Dev Effort	10880.00	78.05%
Test Effort	2040.00	14.63%
	3940.00	

	Request	Requirements	Design	Development	Acceptance	Implementation	Post Imp	Total Effort
PMs	5.00%	20.00%	20.00%	20.00%	20.00%	10.00%	5.00%	100.00%
Development	1.00%	5.00%	20.00%	40.00%	20.00%	10.00%	4.00%	100.00%
Test	1.00%	5.00%	10.00%	10.00%	60.00%	10.00%	4.00%	100.00%
PM Effort	51	204	204	204	204	102	51	1020.00
Dev Effort	68	340	1360	6800	1360	680	272	10880.00
Test Effort	20	102	204	204	1224	204	82	2040.00
Total	139	646	1768	7208	2788	986	405	13940

Figure 5.3   Estimation: Distribution of Effort

Let's assume that the total coding effort was estimated at 6800 hours. In this example, the total project would be 13,940 hours. The percentages we used are historic industry percentages based on a waterfall development methodology. We do caution, though, when using this method. Many offshore service providers include multiple phases in their estimations. For example, their function point estimates may include all activities from receipt of the specifications (requirements) through completion of system testing. You'll need to coordinate with your provider to understand the phases and deliverables that are included in their estimates.

Regardless of the estimation process used, it is important for the onsite and offshore teams to collaborate and agree on the final estimate. As you will read later in *Managing Global Development Risk*, we recommend the integration of the onsite team and your internal staff to reduce the "us versus them" potential when it comes to estimate differences. Once your entire global team is in agreement, the estimate will become the baseline for the rest of the planning activities.

GDMs should listen and evaluate the process utilized by the global development team to derive their numbers. Chances are it is based on a scientific method that is proven and time-tested. Although higher, it may be a truer reflection of the actual work.

F. Global Development Project Plan (GDPP)

The GDPP documents the results of the planning, negotiating, and strategy sessions. It is the baseline document, which will guide the execution and controlling phase of the project. The plan communicates critical information to management and the project team. Global development project planning is most successful when the GDM engages the service provider's PMs and technical leaders in the process. This iterative process will unite both domestic and global stakeholders and present yet another opportunity to integrate common goals. By sharing the project plans early in the process, GDMs build consensus, develop more thorough plans based on multiple inputs and reviews, and unite the team in their successful achievement.

The primary purpose of the planning documents is to help ensure the success of the projects by keeping all team members focused. One of our favorite mottos is "Plan a successful engagement." This motto sets the mind frame that you fully expect to be successful with the project and shows the team you are serious about success and serious about implementing the right process and procedures to guide the team through the various phases.

Central rallying themes such as this tend to be a great tool for global development projects; although we like the above statement, don't allow that to limit your creativity. Having all your team members regardless of location or role focused on the same goals has immeasurable impact to productivity. Like a high school coach who hangs inspirational sayings in the locker room, you have that same opportunity here to excite the team and have them focused: metrics, SLAs, project milestones, whatever you choose. Perhaps one of the reasons we have observed this type of treatment to be so successful is the natural desire of global development teams to exceed all possible expectations. They do this with large wall charts of metrics and other key project tracking. Add your unique flavor to these with your project-specific signage.

The GDPP must be well defined, but flexible. The key is to develop a plan that specifies key deliverables for every phase and to track progress to the plan using weekly deliverables (inch-pebble milestones). When milestones are missed or require more effort than expected to complete, evaluate the root cause and make mid-course corrections to the plan. This is the flexible part of the plan. You should ask yourself and the team tough questions to understand why the plan is not working:

- Is the plan overly optimistic?
- Are the right resources assigned?
- Are the goals and timelines well understood?
- Do all global teams understand expectations?
- Are the training or productivity assumptions wrong?
- Are there logistical issues that are impacting the plan (lack of hardware or software, communication lines, network bandwidth, tools, etc.)?
- What should we do to revise the plan or get back on course?

We recognize that the process of defining, tracking, and monitoring weekly deliverables can be daunting for GDMs. Your global development partner may not be used to this approach and will assume it is "micro-managing" their work. In some instances this may be true, but as the GDM, your job is to deliver the project within the defined scope, schedule, and budget. The process proposed here does exactly that. It provides the early warning signs so you can take action versus explaining why you missed the dates. If you have taken the time to engage the PM for the global service provider up to this point, he or she is already aware of your sincere desire to integrate the two separate teams into one through an open and ongoing communications channel.

To balance the oversight versus micro-management equation, focus on the deliverables, not the specific tasks individuals are working on. As we have repeatedly stressed, it is important for the teams to be integrated and that there be complete transparency between the onsite and offshore teams. With that being said, though, from a practical standpoint, the GDM cannot manage every aspect of a project. Once you have established a relationship with your onsite coordinator and the offshore leader, let them earn their money by managing many of the day-to-day activities, including selecting the offshore team members. Once the relationship is established, your focus should change to a deliverables-based approach: set clear expectations, measure quality, and track progress on a weekly basis.

Now that we've discussed the purpose of the global development plan, let's take a look at the major sections in a GDPP. You'll quickly notice that many sections of the plan are similar to those in the SOW. This is by design because the SOW is typically not shared with all project team members, but contains information that will drive the plan and influence project decisions. There are many sections, though, that are not included in the SOW that are critical as well. We briefly discuss each section and provide tips for including specific information. However, global projects are influenced by the type of work, technologies involved, and methodologies used; thus there may be other areas that are important to your individual plan. We would encourage you to collaborate with your offshore provider to ensure the plan adequately addresses all areas.

1. Global Development Project Overview

This section of the project plan provides an overview of the project. The intent of this section is to ensure that everyone on the team understands the overall project goals and not just their piece of the puzzle. This section can typically be copied directly from the overview information in the SOW or change request.

2. Project Scope

The project scope section defines the major items that are in scope and the items that are out of scope. This section will usually contain major subsections of functionality or phases for which the supplier is responsible. For example, the supplier may be responsible for design, development, and unit testing of several major components, which should be listed, but is not responsible for the requirements or the system testing. Define the major functions of the application that are in scope (i.e., user interface, electronic reports, interfaces), and list related components or projects that are not in the scope of this release (i.e., Web-based reporting).

3. Project Organization

A best practice with global development teams is to provide a detailed organization chart of the project team, including business users and global team members. The organization chart should indicate management responsibilities and escalation points for both organizations. As you will see later in this chapter, many offshore resources cannot report directly to a client because of visa regulations; thus you will need to be cautious and clearly articulate reporting responsibilities.

The organization chart should demonstrate who the key decision-makers are for both parties, as this will facilitate team communications and help the escalation process. Later in *Managing Global Development Risk,* we will cover techniques to validate that the governance and escalation process does in fact work and contain the right decision-makers for your project. Remember, with global service providers, titles and roles do not necessarily mean authority. GDMs need to understand this so they can assess appropriate escalation timing. Again, we'll provide some tips on this later.

4. Key Contact List

Provide a contact list of all global team members (onsite and offshore). Where appropriate include home, cell, or pager numbers.

5. Key Milestones

Identify all key project dates (design dates, code completion dates, testing, etc.) and milestones Many corporations follow release schedules with predefined dates for all deliverables. These dates should be clearly communicated in the global development plan. Major milestones, such as design review or Q-gate reviews, should also be included in the plan. From a global perspective, it may also be helpful to define the acceptance criteria for each milestone, assuming this was defined in the SOW and whatever is added to this section does not conflict with the SOW.

6. Assumptions

Assumptions should be added to the risk, assumption, issue, decision (RAID) log, and initial assumptions documented in the project plan. It is important to document all assumptions early on to prevent scope-creep and misunderstandings later. In addition to the tactical aspect of having the list of assumptions contained within the global development execution plan, we would recommend a direct discussion with your global service provider concerning project-specific assumptions. Although this may seem redundant, the goal here is to discuss these assumptions with multiple levels from your partner. As mentioned previously and as will again be covered in greater detail later in *Managing Global Development Risk*, it is important to reach multiple layers with your partner due to their hierarchical authority structure. Although unspoken, you will be in much better shape having a larger portion of the provider management team involved in the planning activities.

7. Processes

Defining the software development and project management processes that will be used on a global development engagement helps clarify expectations and firmly establishes the GDM role for all team members. The teams should agree on the

CMM maturity level and key process areas (KPAs) that will be enforced on the project. This is often difficult for many U.S. firms because the processes associated with the higher maturity levels are typically not performed. However, to maintain their certifications, many global providers will include the time and costs of the activities into their bids. This is another friction point that must be quickly understood and resolved by GDMs.

The preferred method is to discuss and document the software development process during the planning phase. If RUP and CMM are going to be used together, identify the deliverables for each iteration and the specific processes that will be followed.

Most global providers are flexible with their processes and will modify them to fit the customer's needs. It will be to your advantage to spend time during the planning phase discussing the benefits and costs associated with these processes and then determine if you want to modify or enhance the processes or require additional oversight. Keep in mind, though, that if you are working on a global project, you will still need to bridge and align processes with your internal software development process.

8. Scope and Change Management Process

A formal scope change process should also be established during the planning phase. This process should include a formal change request form and approval process that evaluates the impact of the request on the schedule and budget. We are certain your global provider will have a detailed template that he or she will suggest using for the project. However, we recommend GDMs first and foremost use your internal change control template and make certain to discuss your philosophy with your global provider's management team so you can establish an expectation baseline. As with all outsourcing projects, change control can become contentious. The scope can be better managed when you articulate your perspective and goals, which will help the service provider understand your challenges.

Change management is a CMM Level-2 activity that has been well defined by most global service providers. They understand the cost and customer perception impacts of a poor change management process. Most have established a robust change control process that ensures customer buy-in of all scope changes.

This process consists of the following:

- Change request — Formal documentation and acceptance of change. Change will typically be logged to a change control log where the approval and impacts will be tracked.
- Impact analysis — Determine impacted subsystems and deliverables.
- Estimate effort.
- Evaluate impact on delivery schedule; re-estimate if necessary.

- Review impacts with project management and senior management. The project plan should define cost or hour impacts and the approval levels if cost and hours exceed predefined thresholds.
- Formal sign-off and acceptance of change.

GDMs should also define acceptable change management metrics during the planning process. Key metrics will measure the total number of change requests, the total impact (cost and hours), and the degree of change introduced (total change requests per total project hours). Global development projects that exceed these predefined thresholds should be reviewed to understand why the changes are occurring and what should be done to curtail the degree of change.

9. Estimated Size and Effort

Summarize the estimation effort. This should include an overview of the methodology used to estimate the global development effort and any assumptions that were made relative to the estimate. Document the estimate for each phase, and emphasize onsite and offshore efforts.

10. Schedule and Project Tracking

When significant portions of the project work are performed at the global location, the importance of clear descriptive deliverables cannot be overstated. Tools such as a work breakdown structure (WBS), activity sequencing, and a complete set of constraints and assumptions enable the entire global team to know what is and is not part of the project's scope. This clear understanding helps to reduce the risk of cost overruns and misinterpreted requirements.

Create a detailed project schedule and WBS using Microsoft Project or a similar product. Communicate the name and location of the project schedule in the plan. In addition to documenting the location of the project schedule, you should also document your overall project tracking process. There are three primary activities that will need to be tracked and monitored:

1. Activity and schedule tracking (per project schedule)
2. Defect tracking (per phase)
3. Issue tracking (per phase)

The project plan should specify the approach and tools to support each of the above activities. If a shared repository is used, the plan should articulate the location of the files or the project file structure.

Scheduling with the offshore team can also be an interesting exercise. We have often seen offshore teams maintain their own schedules under the guise of CMM-5 or too much detail for a master schedule. Maintain one master schedule, which includes the offshore activities. On several projects we have managed, the global team wanted to own the project schedule or have their own version of the plan. The thought was that the client's plan was too high-level, and they needed a detailed plan to track the actual work. Without question, a detailed global project plan is required to track true progress across all areas, but we strongly suggest that GDMs neither relinquish responsibility for the plan to the offshore team nor establish separate plans. The GDM is responsible for the delivery of the project (not a portion of the project); thus you should have complete accountability and insight into all tasks being executed by the global development team. Having two separate plans makes it difficult to synchronize activities or measure the progress and makes it too easy to "hide" important details from the onsite team, such as the number of resources supporting the effort or the actual hours expended.

Again, use the global development team and the onsite coordinator to help plan the activities, project due dates, and incremental milestones. Get early and frequent buy-in from the global development team. Discuss ways to best use the integrated global team and processes (typically CMM Level 5) to help make the project a success.

11. Staffing Plan (Onsite and Offshore Mix)

The staffing plan should indicate the number of resources assigned to the project and the labor categories required to complete the project. Each labor category should specify the number of resources in the specific category and the expected experience level of the global resources.

With experience levels, GDMs need to avoid generic terms, such as senior, mid-level, or junior. These terms are arbitrary and have different meanings based on where the work is being performed. For example, a mid-level programmer in the United States or Europe will have a minimum of five years of experience. A mid-level programmer in India may have less than three years of experience. Global service providers often staff developers with less than two years of experience in positions offshore that a GDM would reasonably expect a more senior resource, primarily because there are fewer developers with five or more years experience still coding.

Global service providers continue to struggle with career paths for technical roles. The core reason for the lack of experienced developers is that they are promoted to project management, account management, or other non-technical roles as soon as they have a few years of experience. This is a highly desired career path as the reward is far greater than remaining a developer. Another cause for the lack of experienced developers actually working on projects is the explosion of staff augmentation as the preferred method of delivering global projects. Visa requirements mandate that developers be employed with the firm for one year prior to working in the United States. The demand for qualified onsite resources has forced global providers to transition qualified resources to U.S.-based projects and backfill with less experienced developers.

12. Roles and Responsibilities

GDMs need to be as specific as possible concerning responsibilities and experience levels. The matrix needs to include all global project roles as a means to demonstrate total effort. It is also useful when you are discussing skills and experience levels with the global service provider as it is an easy tool to demonstrate the capabilities of the internal team. The onsite PM will be very careful to field experienced resources to work side by side with your internal leaders.

The core global team provided by the global service provider will typically be made up of the onsite PM, onsite coordinator, offshore PM, and a development leader. This core team must understand the business drivers and global measure of success for the projects — what does success mean. Make sure your global partner understands that so they can make good decisions as they staff and begin working on the project.

As the GDM works with the global service provider to define the role and responsibilities for all contributors both onsite and offshore, it will be essential to integrate this information into the overall global project roles and responsibilities, including your internal staff.

Although this may seem quite logical and redundant to what was covered earlier in *Managing Global Development Risk*, GDMs need to clearly articulate the roles and responsibilities for the complete team. As you work to have your internal technical leaders take on more and more of the global coordination, a role the global service provider views as essential for their resources, you may meet some resistance. This may seem trivial to you, but the onsite coordinator or PM will need to explain to the project offshore PM at the global development facility the manner in which you as GDM want the project executed. Do not forget that the offshore PM is the individual that typically has control over the majority of your global team's activities wherever the resource may be based.

It is this reason that *Managing Global Development Risk* has recommended several previous times to include as many of the global service provider's management in your meetings covering expectation and execution.

13. Global Development Methodology

The majority of global service providers use the standard waterfall software development life cycle to complete software projects. This cycle, which includes requirements, design, coding, testing, and implementation, is often modified to meet customer-specific needs. The project plan should specify any customization or other development cycles that will be used, i.e., spiral or RUP.

We have been told by leading global service providers they support RUP, rapid application development, agile development, or extreme programming by "tailoring" the waterfall model to meet these more iterative development models.

However, the nature of these development methodologies makes them extremely difficult to support in a global model with an efficient onsite-offshore ratio. Each of these models relies on a high degree of interaction between the users of the systems and the developers of the system. The requirements and designs using these methodologies are also highly iterative, thus requiring extensive coordination to deliver. The goals of these methodologies are to deliver functional code every 90 to 100 days. This is achieved through a highly iterative process that requires extensive coordination, negotiation, and refactoring as the product is developed, all of which make it extremely difficult to complete with a high percentage of your development organization at a global location.

Managing Global Development Risk strongly discourages the use of extreme programming methodologies on your first global development project, or any global engagement unless the users are co-located with the global team, which is unlikely and again has a cost impact to the overall project. We are very leery of any offshore firm that attempts extreme methodologies on an offshore project, unless, of course, they own all aspects of the project. Our guess is if you truly dig into these projects, they may have applied a concept or two, but at the true execution level, you're looking at waterfall-executed development.

The number one challenge with global projects is communication. This communication issue is magnified tenfold in an XP environment. Even in a shared environment, the challenges of completing the global development project offshore far outweigh any benefits of an extreme methodology.

Managing Global Development Risk does recommend using some of the core concepts from these methodologies. For example, we are strong proponents of time-boxing techniques to drive functionality and limit scope. In addition, we are firm believers in weekly deliverables throughout the build phase, even in a mainframe or global development environment. The weekly build provides GDM's insight into key functionality and provides early indicators of problems. If weekly build targets can't be hit, there is something wrong with the project that needs to be corrected as soon as possible.

Oftentimes with global engagements, GDMs do not know the quality of the code until it is delivered to system or user acceptance testing. As we all know, this is often too late to effectively remediate or course correct. Time boxing and weekly deliverables reduce these risks by clearly defining working segments of code that are moved into a defined environment. Even if the code is refactored at some later point, it still shows true progress against baseline targets.

We recognize this is an easy technique to suggest, but can be much harder in practice to implement. As you have probably already determined, *Managing Global Development Risk* is not an academic exercise in global project management. We are offering what we believe to be practical advice that we have implemented on real projects. We have seen the value of the suggestions provided, including the weekly deliverables, and have designed templates and best practices to support them.

14. *Global Development Environment*

The development section of the project plan specifies the hardware, software, tools, and communications infrastructure required to complete the project. The hardware and software list should specify if the the hardware or software is required onsite or offshore. You will want to consider all the available tools and not make any assumptions regarding the availability of certain tools. For example, if your project calls for a specific Java Virtual Machine (JVM) or C++ compiler or a specific version of Microsoft Project, put it on the list.

For global development projects, GDMs need to plan the appropriate manner in which global resources will be connected. Having an environment with appropriate hardware, software, and tools is essential, but if it is in isolation and your global team members are having challenges connecting or gaining access, your productivity will take a significant hit. This may seem simple, but we have observed many projects get off to a slow start and produce unnecessary frustration as this simple, logistical need was not appropriately planned.

Through our experiences, we have identified a simple list of tasks that GDMs should complete prior to assigning development resources offshore. This simple list should help ensure your global team is productive from day one:

1. Establish communication links between offshore facility and client facility. Facilitate working sessions with your internal and the supplier's networking teams.
2. Provision hardware and software at offshore facility, including any licenses that may be required to support the development effort.
3. Establish coding standards.
4. Define clear roles and responsibility for development tasks.
5. Establish common templates and acceptance criteria for all deliverables.
6. Coordinate with security to provide appropriate access to required systems; see that physical and data security requirements are met and onsite resources are properly badged and have access to appropriate areas.

If this is the first global project, you may also need to document the communications infrastructure that will link the two sites. It is best to pull in the experts for this process and get the two groups talking. However, as a minimum, you will want to document the major hub and routers that connect the sites and indicate the redundant paths should a failover to the alternate path be required. You will absolutely need a secure means of communication between the onsite and offshore development facilities. This may be accomplished through a virtual private network (VPN), direct access to the mainframe environment, or distributed computing development tools and a central repository. Your communications infrastructure must also allow the free flow of information via e-mail, instant messaging, or intranet-based project Web sites.

15. Configuration Management Plan and Process

Configuration management of any software development project is a critical management function. Tools and processes must be established to ensure proper check-in and check-out and control of the software baseline. These activities are made even more difficult when managing a global project due to the necessity of synchronizing activities between multiple sites.

Configuration management (CM) or software configuration management (SCM) is a KPA for CMM Level-2 organizations. As such, global service providers have developed robust tools and processes to ensure CM is maintained through the life of the global project. *Managing Global Development Risk* will spend significant time in the execution and controlling sections discussing these processes. During the planning phase, GDMs should identify the CM tool (ChangeMan, Visual Source Save, CVS, PVCS, ClearCase, etc.) and the process that will be followed to check in and check out code from the applicable tool. The plan should clearly state the following:

- CM environment — Can also be included in development environment section
- Configuration items (CIs) — Deliverables that will be under change control (i.e., requirements, design elements, software components, test scripts, etc.)
- Version control process — Tools and processes for the number of versions that need to be saved
- Process to move items through the CM process
- Change request traceability process, i.e., how to determine who made the last change and mapping the requirements changed to all impacted components
- Access control process — Define who can modify files once they are checked into the change control system
- Naming conventions and organization of files

Many global service providers have also defined formal tracking mechanisms to report and track the state of a component at any given time. This is a recommended best practice that should be included in the plan. Typical states include:

- Under construction — in developer's private library
- Unit testing — Component developed and ready for unit testing
- System testing — Completed unit testing, with defects corrected, and ready for system testing
- Acceptance testing — Component passed system testing, with defects corrected, and ready for user acceptance testing
- Release — All testing completed and component ready to be included in release

16.   *Issue Reporting and Risk Management*

Issue tracking and risk management are the primary project functions of a GDM once the project gets rolling. There are numerous tools available that GDMs can use for issue tracking. Many of the commercial defect tracking tools can also be used for issue tracking and follow-up. During the planning phase you should evaluate several tools. *Managing Global Development Risk* has proposed the RAID log in other sections and find it to be a very valuable issue-tracking tool.

Regardless of the tool, GDMs need a plan and strategy for communicating issues that are focused on issue resolution, not hiding bad news. The entire global team will need to over-communicate to ensure all understand the impact of issues and have contingency plans in place to handle adverse scenarios.

Issue tracking ensures problems that have the potential to delay the project do not go undetected, unreported, or unmanaged. The planning document should address how issues and risks will be reported and managed.

Many global providers use the weekly status report to notify customers of risks and issues. We prefer using the weekly status report in conjunction with a weekly status meeting because it provides an opportunity for direct dialogue on many issues. This approach also places focus and emphasis on the importance of resolving issues. Many offshore firms deliver metrics and reports on a weekly basis, but, unless directly questioned, will often not proactively resolve these outstanding issues. The weekly status meeting highlights these issues and lets your offshore provider know that you are serious about resolving them before they impact your project.

The RAID log provides a great way to track and report the issues, but it also provides a summary page that indicates the overall impact of the issues and risks on the project. Unfortunately, this critical information is often missed when teams spend too much time reviewing the issues without seeing the larger picture. GDMs can use the summarized metrics to maintain the global perspective and see the true impact of the risks and issues.

The weekly status report, weekly status meeting, and RAID log are all means to communicate status and maintain open lines of communication between you and the supplier. There are several other effective methods as well, such as digital dashboards and project or program status sheets. Whichever method or process you use, select one that maximizes communications, document it, and adhere to it.

17.   *Global Communications Plan*

The GDPP should contain a global communications plan that details the escalation path, standard meetings, status reports, and other project-related communications. The communications matrix should clearly state the owner of each communications and the specifics to be executed for that specific communications effort.

Managing Global Development Risk recommends that global communications plans have two areas of focus: formal project communications and informal project communications.

The formal global communications plan is focused on standard software development best practices to ensure open, timely, and concise project communications. The informal global communications plan is dedicated to team integration and enhancing individual productivity.

Informal global communications plans look at:

- How do global team members interact dynamically: phone, video conference, instant messaging (IM)
- Communications interactions of an integrated onsite team: What are the meetings, discussions, activities that can be implemented to unify all onsite staff?
- Communications interactions of the global development team: What are the activities and staffing dynamics that will ensure the global development team is fully integrated and informed?
- Multi-level communications between the onsite team and the global development location: What are the activities a GDM can implement to remove the typical single channel of communications (onsite PM to offshore PM) that most global service providers prefer?

18. Estimated Costs

Estimated costs are an optional section of the GDPP. Some organizations and suppliers prefer the costs not be included in the GDPP because it is shared with many of the team members who may not need to understand the costs associated with the project.

If the cost section is included, it should address the following processes that are important to track and should verify costs on an ongoing basis:

- Weekly time reporting, if not included in the procedures manual
- Invoice submittal and verification process, if not included in the MSA, SOW, or procedures manual
- Summary of charges that may be included on an invoice (labor, network, hardware, software, etc.), if not included in MSA, SOW, or procedures manual
- Invoice dispute resolution process, if not previously defined
- Process to track costs on an ongoing basis
- Process to review costs and upcoming expenses on a monthly basis
- Key metrics that trigger action if costs exceed predetermined thresholds (percentage of budget or overall impact of X percent)

There are many factors other than labor arbitrage that will impact the costs. For example, productivity, management overhead, deliverables unique to offshore projects, CMM processes, and time zone differences will all impact the overall effort, and thus have some impact on the project budget.

- Productivity levels will directly impact the number of resources and project timelines.
- Offshore engagements require a high degree of management for both the onsite global resources and global development teams. If billable, this management overhead can increase the project costs by at least 20%.
- Additional phases, such as KA-KT, absorb another 10 to 15% of the budget.
- CMM Level 5 processes, which include rigorous software quality assurance practices, can also increase the project budget by 5 to 10%.

Managing Global Development Risk recommends budgeting travel for the key team members to travel to the global facility at least once per quarter. These trips will help resolve issues, enhance communications between the teams, and enhance overall productivity. Depending on the nature of your project, a substantial portion of the team will be based offshore. That team must know who you are. The absolute best way to do this is to be present with them for two or three weeks at a time to truly embrace them as a team. We will touch on this subject in greater detail later in *Managing Global Development Risk.*

GDMs should seriously consider walk-throughs, reviews, and testing at the global development location for three reasons. First, you'll be assured that any feedback is understood and incorporated accurately. Second, feedback can be incorporated in a timely manner; delayed feedback from your site will take longer to implement if the developers have moved on to other tasks or new projects. And third, your personal feedback will motivate the global team.

G. Global Staffing

GDMs must ensure the global service provider provides resources onsite to help manage the day-to-day activities and coordinate project deliverables with the global team. The offshore coordinator should be seen as a key member of the project-management team. Involve them in all key discussions, and use them as a resource to manage the success of the project.

As discussed earlier, it is important for GDMs to have their internal leaders closely aligned with the onsite resources of the global provider. A technique we have seen work very well is the actual intermingling of responsibilities of these individuals, giving the onsite coordinator some responsibility for internal, onsite activities and providing an internal team leader some active role with the offshore team. As long as GDMs clearly define the roles and responsibilities and you work with both parties to have a positive relationship, this type of alignment eliminates barriers and reduces potential blind spots for the overall project.

Skill alignment is also important when staffing global teams. This includes aligning the skills for both the onsite and offshore teams with your expectations. The sourcing or procurement team probably negotiated an exhibit to the agreement that defined the basic skills and years of experience required to support the project. This will be another document that you will want to familiarize yourself with as you begin staffing the global team.

Interviewing offshore team members is often a question that is asked when companies first set up offshore operations. Many companies continue to look at the offshore resources as an extension of their onsite team and thus want to review their resumes and interview them in the same manner that they do onsite. Though we strongly recommend that you interview onsite resources, especially for communication and cultural fit, we have seen mixed results with interviewing offshore resources. You may be able to determine if a developer is technically qualified to perform the necessary activities, but because of the communication challenges, time zone differences, and internal preparation for interviews, it is hard to determine the team fit. Our general recommendation is to hold the supplier accountable for deliverables, schedules, and budgets, and let them determine the right offshore staffing mix.

H.   Resource Management

Resource management of global resources is one of the more difficult tasks for a GDM to master. *Managing Global Development Risk* will cover this subject in great detail later in the book, but it is very important that the concept is introduced during the project planning stage of the global development project as it is the time you are establishing your capabilities with the global service provider. Suppliers need to be aware of your desire and plan to manage the onsite and offshore members of your global development team.

It is natural for GDMs and your technical leaders to want to understand what their resources are doing on a daily basis and to establish a line of communication with all relevant team members. This is often difficult with a global team because of time and distant constraints. In addition, recent changes in visa laws have also mandated that offshore resources cannot report directly to a corporation's management team.

Although *Managing Global Development Risk* does not recommend GDMs or your internal technical leaders manage global resources directly, it is essential you are aware of the resources' day-to-day activities and have an open line of communication that does not blur formal reporting and management responsibilities. GDMs can still effectively manage the project by using the MSA, SOW, and project schedule. These documents should address the following issues to guarantee the right resources are assigned to your global development project and that they stay engaged for the specified period:

■ Define required experience levels for each position in the SOW.
■ Specify that resources can't be reassigned without your approval.
■ Specify that no more than 15% of staff can be transitioned in a year.
■ Enforce penalties if the targets are exceeded.
■ Specify supplier overstaff project by 10 to 15% to account for attrition and lower productivity levels.
■ After you complete KA, allow time in the project schedule to transition tasks to the offshore team.
■ Don't micromanage resources. Stay focused on deliverables (inch pebble milestones and focus on weekly deliverables).

Managing Global Development Risk strongly recommends GDMs become resident experts in the area of visa management, visa requirements, and ongoing changes in visa laws. This is a far more complex issue than simply knowing the current federal government limit on the number of H1-Bs that can enter the country. There are some real issues over the direct "management" of a global resource. Table 5.4 provides guidance on current GDM visa management best practices. The unique contribution of an experienced GDM will be the ability to influence and integrate a true global team without assuming unnecessary project risk because of visa infractions.

Given the complexities of visa management, you may want the supplier to report the visa status on a monthly basis. This report should indicate the name of the person, the type of visa (L-1, B-1, H-1, etc.), the visa expirations or renewal date, and any pertinent comments, such as the return dates that are planned within the next 90 days.

I. Quality Plan

The quality plan is another important deliverable that should be completed during the planning phase. This document defines the overall goals and objectives of a quality program and at a high level defines the project's philosophical approach to quality. A quality plan does much more than just define the testing approach. In fact, a good quality plan will define processes to detect errors prior to testing, predict the number of defects detected in each testing phase (defect injection rates), define a process for root cause analysis, and include a feedback loop that hopefully prevents errors from recurring. A good plan will also define key processes to ensure the development process was correctly followed (i.e., all deliverables for a

Table 5.4 Visa Management Best Practices

Visa Change	Best Practice
L-1B	■ Create an organization chart for global resource teams separate from corporate team to document compliance with the control and supervision provisions ■ Educate managers on impact of new legislation ■ Define an operational model that clearly depicts reporting relationship with offshore vendor
H1-B	■ Develop an overall strategy for use of H1-Bs. Because costs are no longer at a reduced rate, many of the cost benefits may not be realized ■ Include validation of attestation clauses during the on-boarding process ■ Implement attestation process to be executed prior to bringing H1-B contractors on board
General practice	■ Allocate work to the supplier only through designated supplier's managers. Don't allocate work directly to a supplier's employee. You'll want to ensure the SOW or change requests clearly articulate the work you want accomplished and minimize day-to-day tasking that goes beyond clarifications ■ Involve supplier employee(s) and appropriate supervisors in project-related meetings, but don't include supplier employees in your internal company-related meetings ■ Provide project clarification or verification to supplier employees, but don't re-task them

phase were completed correctly) and lessons learned from one phase of a project are applied to the next phase.

The quality plan is the guiding document that will define the quality expectations for the entire project. It should define the following:

■ Overall goals of the quality assurance program
■ Processes that will be used to measure quality
■ Key metrics that will be collected and goals for them
■ Software tools that will be employed to support quality initiatives

1. Quality Goals

The most important aspect of the quality plan is defining the quality goals and agreeing to a definition of quality and a common approach to measure quality. As you have probably already seen in your career, quality can be highly subjective and certainly depends on an individual's unique perspective. From an industry perspective, quality is typically measured by the number of defects in the final product, or more commonly referred to as the defect density rate. We will discuss the defect density rate in more detail in Section VII, but during the planning process, you'll want to meet with your supplier to define the expected defect density rate using a standard process. Oftentimes, quality goals and expectations are defined with contractual service levels, so you may also want to review the MSA and the SOW for any agreements.

2. Quality Processes

When defining the quality processes, your offshore supplier will define much more than just a testing approach. The goal will be to define both review and testing processes to validate that the delivered product meets specifications and is "defect free," to measure the effectiveness of the overall quality program by defining key metrics, and to compare these predefined metrics to actual performance.

So what is the difference between reviews and testing? Reviews are scheduled activities to validate the process was followed, or formal inspections of deliverables (documents and code) to determine if standards were adhered to and, through visual inspection, determine if any notable logic errors or coding errors exist. Testing, on the other hand, executes the actual software code, or portions of the code, and compares the execution of output against predetermined criteria to determine if errors exist.

Thus, the quality plan addresses both review and testing processes and defines the comparison criteria to validate that quality expectations were met. As a minimum, the processes should:

- Define the procedures for completing peer reviews
- Define the checkpoints within the software development life cycle where quality will be verified
- Define the testing processes and phases employed (i.e., automated test scripts and support for unit, system, and user acceptance testing)
- Define continuous process improvement initiatives or goals

As you already realize, quality is an integral part of the global service provider's project execution. Their commitment to CMM and international standards are core to their delivery models. As the GDM, you'll want to clearly understand the quality assurance processes that are being proposed, your company's internal quality expectations, and the role of the supplier's software quality assurance (SQA) organization. Each of these must support the overall project's goals, but will come at a cost, either in real dollars or in time.

CMM Level-5 organizations have very defined quality assurance processes. Once you understand their capabilities, it will be easier to determine what you

Table 5.5   Defect Removal Rate Best Practices

Proposed Best Practice	*Defect Removal Goal*
Requirements and design formal review and sign-off	20%
Code reviews — peer reviews and formal code walk-through	20%
Unit testing — review of unit test scripts and validation of test results	40%
System and regression testing — review of system and regression test scripts and validation of test results	15%
User acceptance testing — review of user acceptance test scripts and validation of test results	4%
Post-implementation test and validation — review of post-implementation test scripts and validation of test results	1%
Total defect removal:	100%

are willing to pay for. In the planning phases, however, there are several important advantages to engaging the offshore supplier's SQA organization. The biggest advantage is the predictive powers of quantitative quality assurance, in other words predicting how many defects should be detected in each phase and using that prediction to manage the project.

Think of the advantage you would have if you knew that with a certain technology, development process, and development estimate you could actually predict the number of defects detected in each testing phase. You could make decisions on applying better processes up front (i.e., more peer reviews, audits, or code walk-through), increase or decrease the number of testers, or even set better expectations with your management and user community. This is the power of quantitative quality management. Most offshore firms have extensive research on both internal and industrywide defect injection rates and have a repository of actual findings from past projects that allows them to compute the projected number of defects based on the number of development hours and software processes.

An effective quality plan can identify the projected number of defects for a project and then identify specific process and defect removal goals. Table 5.5 provides examples of review and testing best practices, with an associated defect removal rate that could be included in the quality plan. In this example, which is based on industry data, 99 percent of the predicted defects can be removed prior to implementation, and the remaining 1 percent should be identified during a planned post-implementation validation process.

Once you and your team understand the power of predicting defects early in the process, it will be much easier to define the right defect removal processes and evaluate or justify any additional costs or schedule impacts that may result from the introduction of quality processes.

3. Metrics Collection and Evaluation

To track project performance, it is essential to identify indicators that measure both the overall quality of the delivered product as well as the quality of the overall process. To measure project performance it is essential to set target values for these indicators and compare them with their actual values gathered over a period of time. The goals for the metrics program are to:

- Improve project planning
- Increase defect containment
- Decrease software defect density
- Increase software productivity
- Optimize resource utilization
- Improve customer satisfaction

These metrics should be provided on a monthly basis or on a sufficient enough basis to measure quality on an ongoing basis to implement actions to improve quality before something impacts the overall project. If suppliers are being measured on their ability to hit quality targets, they may want to compare the targets to your internal numbers before baselining performance. They also may want to have a six-month stabilizing period to establish baselines. Though both of these are common industry practices, they are often a ruse for committing to quality goals. There are clearly client-specific practices and applications that impact the supplier's ability to meet quality goals. But a large percentage of processes and applications are "standard" or at least similar enough to other projects that suppliers should have a reasonable degree of confidence in their ability to hit the metrics.

Managing Global Development Risk places significant focus on metrics; thus we have defined key metrics throughout the book. We've also provided sample metrics in this section that may help you and your supplier brainstorm various metrics that will help drive project success. An important aspect with metrics that we often stress is to define what it is you want to measure and what behavior you expect when you define a metric. The behavior aspect of metrics is often overlooked, but it has a tremendous impact of the supplier's actions with regard to managing an engagement. When service levels or metrics are reported and follow-up actions required, then the supplier is motivated to ensure compliance with metrics. However, as with anything in life, suppliers can't be perfect with everything, so you really need to determine the critical metrics that will drive project success and focus your efforts on achieving them. With that said, Table 5.6 is a laundry list of metrics that could be considered, but we would strongly recommend selecting only those that will make a difference.

Table 5.6 Sample Project Metrics

Goal	Metric	Metric Definition	Corrective Action
Deliver projects per schedule	Percentage of deliverables completed per schedule, delivered within five days of due date	Measures ability to complete deliverables per the project plan. Deliverables are defined in the project plan and tracked against actual completion dates	If over a defined period the supplier fails to complete 90 percent of the deliverables within five days of the deliverable due date, then the team will conduct a root cause analysis to determine if the schedule should be adjusted, resources transitioned, additional resources added, or another course of action should be taken.
Deliver projects per schedule	Percentage of milestones achieved per schedule, completed within five days of milestone date	Measures ability to achieve critical project milestones, such as tollgate reviews or completion of phases	If over a defined period the supplier fails to meet 90 percent of the milestones within five days of the milestone date, then the team will conduct a root cause analysis to determine if the schedule should be adjusted, resources transitioned, additional resources added, or another course of action should be taken.
Deliver projects per budget	Percentage of deliverables completed within ±10 percent of budget	Measure ability to accurately estimate the cost of deliverables and complete the deliverable within ±10 percent of the estimate	If over a defined period the supplier fails to complete 90 percent of the deliverables within ±10 percent of the estimated budget, then the team will conduct a root cause analysis to determine if the budget or schedule should be adjusted, resources transitioned, additional resources added, or another course of action should be taken.

continued

Table 5.6 (continued) Sample Project Metrics

Goal	Metric	Metric Definition	Corrective Action
Network utilization and network bandwidth	Daily link usage	Average daily link usage over 15-minute periods	If during any month 70 percent of samples exceed 70 percent utilization, then the teams will discuss and agree on link upgrade plans.
Network utilization and network bandwidth	Network uptime: 95 percent availability during scheduled hours	Measures the availability of the network link during core development hours	In a month if the network availability (number of hours unavailable per total number of hours scheduled) is less than 98 percent, then the teams will conduct a root cause analysis and agree to corrective actions to stabilize the link.
Productivity: function points or UCPs	Defined as functions points per person per month, UCPs per person per month, or other industry standard of measurement	Measures overall productivity of supplier personnel	If over a defined period the supplier's productivity is less than 90 percent of expected productivity, then the teams will conduct a root cause analysis and implement actions to improve productivity.
Productivity: re-work and percentage of bad fixes	Percentage of re-work required to resolve problems	Measures the effectiveness of maintenance. (Number of bad fixes) per (total number of fixes) × 100	If during a month the number of bad fixes is less than 90 percent, then teams will conduct a root cause analysis to define and correct process breakdowns.
Productivity: backlog management	Percentage of items resolved in a month	Measures ability to manage the backlog queue. (Number of requests closed during a month) per (opening balance for the month + number of requests received in the month)	If during a month the percentage of backlog items is less than 90 percent of the projected target, then the supplier will provide an action to plan to reduce the backlog queue and conduct a root cause analysis to maintain the queue numbers on an ongoing basis.

Quality	Number of defects detected per phase compared with the projected defect injection rate	Measures the overall quality of the release by computing the projected defect injection rate and comparing the actual number of defects to the projected rate	If in a defined period the number of defects detected in a phase is ±10 percent of the projected defect rate for the phase, then the teams shall conduct a root cause analysis to determine if additional testing is required and what actions are required to address quality concerns.
Quality	Percentage of phases that successfully complete SQA audits	Measures adherence to SQA standards (failed SQA audits per number of SQA audits)	If in a defined period the number of failed SQA audits is greater than 10 percent, then teams shall conduct a root cause analysis to determine the corrective actions.
Staffing: ability to staff the KT Team or other teams that require offshore resources on site	Number of days activities delayed pending supplier resources	Measures suppliers ability to staff and manage visas for resources required to perform activities on site	If the number of days that an activity is delayed due to availability of offshore resources onsite exceeds five days, then the teams will review the staffing plan to determine corrective actions.
Staffing: ability to staff qualified personnel	Percentage of positions that supplier has filled with qualified candidates	Measure supplier's ability to meet the project's staffing needs. (Number of staffed positions per total number of positions)	If in a defined period the supplier fails to staff 95 percent of the positions or a single position requires three or more candidates (interviews) before acceptance, then teams shall review the staffing plan to determine appropriate actions.

continued

Table 5.6 (continued)   Sample Project Metrics

Goal	Metric	Metric Definition	Corrective Action
Staffing: ability to complete KA	Percentage of resources that have completed KA per the plan	Measure the supplier's ability to appropriately plan, staff, and execute KA activities (number completed per number planned)	If upon completion of KA, 95 percent of the planned resources are not trained, then the teams will review status to determine appropriate actions.
Change management	Percentage of hours added through change control	Measures the supplier's ability to accurately estimate the work and effort required to complete a project by measuring the amount of change introduced as a percentage of hours that are added to a project through change control (total hours per original estimate)	If the amount of change exceeds 10 percent of the original estimate, then the teams will review the approved changes to determine why the original SOW did not identify the scope and will take corrective actions to reduce the degree of change.

J. Global Risk Management

Risk management and risk assessment is a must do when managing global development projects. A goal of *Managing Global Development Risk* is to provide GDMs with the framework and tools to succeed in executing global development projects, which means effectively managing the inherent risks introduced by global development.

Given the risks identified with global development, a strong risk management program is paramount to success. In general, risk management is the measure of the probability of an unsatisfactory outcome times the impact occurring from such an outcome. One of the key tasks in risk management is identifying and prioritizing the events that could negatively impact your project. This exercise of calculating the risk exposure calculates the product of the probability of the risk occurring and the impact if it does occur. The risk exposure should drive your risk prioritization and risk mitigation activities.

Risk management is a core process for CMM and ISO certifications; thus GDMs can be assured that the global service provider will have a detailed global risk management process. This program will typically consist of two phases: risk assessment and risk control.

1. Risk Assessment

Risk assessment is the process of identifying and prioritizing risks. As we have already seen, the prioritization is based on the product of the probability and the impact. Identifying risks, especially those associated with global development projects, can be difficult. PMs by nature are usually optimistic, so it is even more difficult to discover and analyze the various risks. A great approach is to work with your global team to brainstorm potential risks. GDMs should see if the global service provider has developed standardized processes for global risk assessment. Methods that can aid risk identification include:

- Checklists of possible risks to consider for every project
- Client or technical surveys
- Brainstorming session
- Facilitated risk management meetings
- Detailed review of plans, process, and work products to identify potential gaps and risks
- CMM and SEI tools
- Surveys and lessons learned from previous projects or previously encountered risks

2. Risk Control

Risk control is the process of determining what to do about the risk. Although it may be helpful to understand the potential risks, it is much more powerful to have thought through mitigation steps to either prevent the risk from occurring or minimize its impact should it occur. This is an interesting concept because it looks at risk from two perspectives.

The first perspective recognizes that challenges will occur throughout the project, and effective management should proactively identify the obstacles and set a course to avoid them. For example, it is well known that attrition is a major issue with global development projects. Instead of just knowing that, though, what if, as GDM, you took specific actions, such as overstaffing the project by 15 percent to absorb the attrition when it occurs? This could be a negotiation point with your global service provider so that costs are contained but the risk is managed.

The second perspective is to allow GDMs to think through difficult scenarios before they are in the battle and need to make quick and timely decisions. This "role playing" aspect of risk control is a powerful tool. For example, let's assume your project plan required a server to be installed at the offshore facility on a specific date. You have meticulously planned the pickup, delivery, and availability of resources to install the hardware when it arrives. You have also developed mitigation plans that allow a three-week schedule slip should the hardware be delayed in customs. But what if the hardware never arrives? What actions can you take to complete the project without a development environment? It will probably be too costly to ship multiple machines for a just-in-case scenario, and you may not want to absorb the communication costs of installing a dedicated line to your environment if everything goes according to plan. But a good GDM will consider these alternatives and devise strategies to minimize the risk should it occur. By the way, this isn't just a fictional exercise. It occurred on a project we managed several years ago and required that we implement our mitigation steps, which happened to be sharing an environment off hours with another global team. Suffice it to say that Indian Customs authorities can, at times, be a challenge!

The last aspect of risk management is risk monitoring and tracking. GDMs should review risk and mitigation steps for each risk during weekly global team meetings. This provides a high degree of focus on the risks and ensures the entire team is properly managing these risks. Because risks are probabilistic events, the threat due to risks may change over time. It is also comforting to downgrade a risk throughout a project because you actively took steps to mitigate its impact. If your mitigation steps are intended to prevent the risk from occurring, then it should be actionable.

The heart of the risk management program is the RAID log. This log or database contains all identified risks, the probability of the risk occurring, the impact if it does occur, and the mitigation steps to both prevent the risk from occurring and address it head on should it occur. RAID is a means of tracking key project items in a single deliverable. This living document should be reviewed during all team meetings and updated by both the offshore PM and the onsite PM. The RAID log provides details of each risk, assumption, issue, and decision, but more importantly, it provides a summary page that quantifies the status of a project based on the number and criticality of risks and issues and items pending decision. This extremely valuable tool provides yet another insight into the overall status of a project.

K. Summary

This section focused on the global activities that should be completed in the planning phase of a global project. The core activities are completion of SOW, KA-KT, estimation, and development of the various planning documents (project plan, project schedule, global staffing plan, quality assurance plan, and risk plan). Each of these activities requires close coordination with your offshore supplier and an overall view of your project goals and objectives.

1. Deliverables from the Planning Phase

- SOW
- GDPP
- Detailed project schedule
- KAs, plan and schedule
- KT, plan and schedule
- Estimation for development effort
- Global staffing plan
- Quality assurance p
- Risk plan and RAID log

2. Planning Phase Service Levels

The service levels measured in the planning phase should focus on the timely completion and quality of the planning documents. Although many of the key service levels and metrics used to monitor and control the project will be defined in the planning phase, many of them won't be measurable until development and testing are underway. Sample service levels to measure in the planning phase include:

- Percentage of deliverables completed on time
- Percentage of deliverables completed to budget
- Percentage of milestone completed per plan
- Percentage of supplier resources staffed compared with the percentage that complete KA per the plan
- SQA results, overall score for phase greater than 90%

3. *Planning Phase Metrics*

The overall metrics program should be defined during the planning phase with specific metrics, goals, and metric collection mechanisms defined. Specific metrics collected during the planning phase should validate the selected service levels and validate that planning activities are completed ontime and with the expected quality.

Sample metrics for the planning phase are highlighted in Table 5.7.

4. *Planning Phase Risks and Issues*

The risk management plan and the RAID log are critical deliverables during the planning phase. These documents define the ongoing process to resolve project risks and provide a means to capture project issues, assumptions, and decisions. The RAID log can be used, in conjunction with other project metrics, to provide an overall view of the project.

Although the RAID log is started in the initiation phase, we suggest a subsequent brainstorming session with your offshore supplier during the planning phase to further define the key project risks and issues and specific mitigation steps. We also recommend that you identify the risks and issues specific to the planning phase and establish a weekly process to discuss the risks and issues and if necessary, implement your mitigation plans. Although there are many project-specific risks that you will need to consider, we have identified in Table 5.8 some of the generic planning-phase risks that we have seen with other global projects.

Table 5.7 Planning Phase Metrics

Metric	Definition	Target
Percentage of weekly deliverables completed on time	On a weekly basis, measure percentage of deliverables completed per the number of deliverables planned for completion	90%
Weekly staffing profile	On a weekly basis, measures supplier's ability to meet staffing needs. (Number staffed for week per number planned) and number staffed to date per number planned)	Weekly: 85% To date: 90%
Milestone completion	On a weekly basis, measures: ■ Number of milestones completed in week per total milestones planned for week ■ Total number of milestones met to date per total milestones planned to date ■ Total number of milestones met per total number of milestones	Weekly: 85% To date: 90% Project dependent on plan (goal is 95%)
Compliance to SLAs	For planning phase, measures number of SLAs achieved per total number of SLAs	90%
Percentage of deliverables accepted (no major issues)	On a weekly basis, measures the total numbers of deliverables that are delivered and accepted with no major issues (deliverable does not require re-work) ■ Number of deliverables accepted for week per number of deliverables submitted for week ■ Number of deliverables accepted to date per number of deliverables submitted to date	Weekly: 85% To date: 90%
Earned value (CPI per SPI) or estimates to complete	On a weekly basis, measures the actual effort expended to date (time reporting) compared with estimated effort to date and compares the actual work completed compared to work scheduled to be completed	Effort: within ±10 of estimate for week or SPI between 0.9 and 1.1 Work: 90% of work scheduled to date is completed

continued

Table 5.7 (continued) Planning Phase Metrics

Metric	Definition	Target
Onsite-offshore ratio	On a monthly basis, measures the actual onsite-offshore ratio and compares the projected onsite-offshore ratio	95%
Issue resolution: time to resolution	Measure effectiveness of offshore vendors to resolve issues within established timeframes	90%

Table 5.8 Planning Phase Risks and Issues

Global Risk or Issue	Mitigation Strategy
Development estimates exceed (greater than 20% of effort or 10 percent of budget) internal estimates or budget to complete effort	Review estimation process, including CMM processes that are proposed (i.e., peer reviews and SQA). Discuss with supplier and internal organization to reset budget expectations, reduce scope, etc.
Cost overruns or saving expectations not achieved or plan indicates that savings goals are not attainable within expected timeframe	Review factors that are impacting costs (KA-KT, CMM, management overhead, facilities, network, etc.). Determine if costs can be reduced and discuss additional costs with internal management. Once costs and savings targets are adjusted, calculate baseline costs and track actual costs on a monthly basis
Supplier accelerates KA-KT activities to get project team ramped up and fully billable faster	Define deliverables, milestones, and number of personnel that are required to be trained at start of KA-KT. If these metrics are consistently met, then evaluate overall project impact, including cost impacts, if KA-KT is accelerated. If metrics are not met, discuss with supplier and remain on schedule

Table 5.8 (continued)   Planning Phase Risks and Issues

Global Risk or Issue	Mitigation Strategy
Supplier's ramp-up strategy is too aggressive; internal organization or project team cannot absorb the number of resources as quickly as planned	Define the ramp-up strategy in the planning phase, and establish metrics to measure it weekly. If metrics are not met (too fast or too slow), coordinate with supplier to resolve the issue
Limited insight into offshore team's activities, including deliverables, expended effort, and expenses	Define weekly deliverables to measure progress against plan. Establish weekly status reporting and meetings that include the offshore team that reviews offshore activities in detail
Supplier is not meeting staffing obligations; resources do not have expected experience or are not available per the project plan	Clearly define staffing plan and expectations in planning phase and track staffing on a weekly basis. Discuss and revise plans with supplier. If staffing continues to be a problem, add staffing to service levels, and define financial penalties for missing
Staffing: offshore team is inexperienced or does not have requisite business knowledge or experience with tool, processes, methodologies, etc.	Ensure KT plan addresses additional weakness, add peer reviews to deliverables, and coordinate with offshore supplier to increase overall team experience
Visa management issues: no insight into types of visa or work being performed	Request monthly report with relevant visa information. Ensure project organization chart clearly delineates responsibilities. Discuss concerns with supplier, human resources, or legal counsel.

Table 5.9   Planning Phase Checklist

Planning Phase Checklist	
■ Complete SOW ■ Plan and execute KA ■ Plan and execute KT ■ Estimate remaining effort ■ Develop staffing plan (skills and ramp-up strategy) ■ Establish visa management process ■ Develop configuration management process ■ Complete GDPP ■ Develop quality assurance plan ■ Develop risk mitigation plan ■ Update RAID log ■ Define project metrics	
Planning Phase SLAs	*Planning Phase Metrics*
■ Percentage of deliverables completed on time ■ Percentage of deliverables completed to budget ■ Percentage of milestone completed per plan ■ Percentage of supplier resources staffed as compared to the percentage that complete KA per the plan ■ SQA results: overall score for phase greater than 90%	■ Percentage of deliverables completed on time ■ Milestones delivered on time ■ Weekly staffing profile ■ Compliance to service levels ■ Percentage of deliverables accepted ■ Estimates to complete ■ Onsite-offshore ratios ■ Issue resolution
Planning Phase Risks	*Planning Phase Deliverables*
■ Estimates exceed budget ■ Cost overruns or savings not achieved ■ KA-KT accelerated ■ Ramp-up strategy too aggressive ■ Limited insight into offshore activities ■ Staffing obligations not met ■ Offshore team is inexperienced ■ Visa management	■ SOW ■ GDPP ■ Detailed project schedule ■ KAs: plan and schedule ■ KT: plan and schedule ■ Estimation for development effort ■ Global staffing plan ■ Quality assurance plan ■ Risk plan and RAID log

Chapter 6

Executing a Global Development Project

A. Introduction

Congratulations! You've reached a critical phase in the life cycle of a global development project. You've completed the arduous planning that is required to initiate and plan a global engagement, incorporating the best of software development practices and the fine nuances necessary for global development managers (GDMs) to truly integrate and form one cohesive global team. At this point in your global project plan, you hopefully have completed the knowledge acquisition (KA) and knowledge transfer (KT) phases so you have a fully performing team ready to support your project. So now what? How do you transition from a planning mode to a doing mode? In this section, *Managing Global Development Risk* will define the key activities that should be performed during the execution phase and provide some best practices for keeping global development projects like yours on task during this phase.

> Section Key Concepts: EXECUTION
> ➤ Global Communications Strategy
> ➤ Global Communications Tools
> ➤ Dynamic Meeting Tactics
> ➤ Metric and SLA Monitoring

Figure 6.1   Section VI Key Concepts

Table 6.1 Global Communication Checklist

Global Communications Checklist
1. Use weekly status meetings to discuss status issues, plans for next build, etc.
2. Use the earned value tracking tools and other tools, such as a digital dashboard, to provide easy indicators of progress and insight on your progress
3. Invest in collaboration tools
4. Share documents on a common server. Ensure only one set of project plans, schedules, requirements, and designs
5. Set up project folders that everyone uses (standards on what goes in what folders) and guidelines for version control of documents
6. Take advantage of the time zone differences with "round the clock" testing and bug fixing by using a common test bed and shared defect-tracking tools
7. Alternate meeting times every month or so. The offshore team typically stays later, so early morning meetings work great, but also be accommodating to later night meetings when appropriate
8. Establish a common bridge number that people can use anytime to work through issues
9. Take advantage of instant messaging (IM), e-mail, and video-conferencing to further enhance communication
10. Visit the global development facility. Make it your own by bringing things that highlight your corporate culture, marketing image, or personalize the space. This helps your global resources feel part of the team

There will be many new ideas and discussions over the following pages. But the number one item to walk away with is the importance of communication in a global environment and the tools and techniques that can improve communication. The philosophy behind this section is communicate, communicate, communicate. Use all the mechanisms at your disposal to communicate status, requirements, changes, designs, etc., to both teams.

See Table 6.1 for a Global "Top 10" checklist that will help you with communications. For your first couple of projects, we would even suggest you make a similar "Top 10" list, or feel free to copy ours, and place it in a prominent place in your office. Forward copies to your onsite and offshore partner, letting them know you want to hear their ideas as well as to facilitate better communication between the teams.

We started the previous section on global project planning with the important GDM mantra, "plan the work and work the plan." The executing phase involves performing all the activities so carefully planned out in the previous phase. Execution includes assuring the quality of every deliverable to provide confidence that the work will satisfy all the project stakeholders.

Developing a sense of teamwork between offshore and domestic staff, with different reporting structures and goals, is difficult. But good team dynamics is one way to improve overall communication, identify issues, and resolve problems. Team meetings, training, performance reports, staff biographies, and travel all work to develop a sense of unity despite the distance and cultural differences. Tools at the heart of the execution phase involve improving communication. The growth of network technologies has made it easier to share documents and communicate directly with individuals around the world. This is one area in which technology can provide advancements for offshore projects. Some of the tools available today include networked applications, version control, document repository tools, e-mail, video conferencing, Internet chat, and wireless communication. Let's quickly review the tools of choice and how they can be effectively used to manage offshore activities.

1. Conference Calls

It is important to have regularly scheduled conference calls with the entire global project team. The calls should be conducted by the onsite and offsite project leaders, although everyone should have an opportunity to participate. Calls should be carefully managed to ensure they start and end on time. Detailed issues should be assigned to individuals to be followed-up offline. Issues and tasks should be documented and entered into a tool that can be accessed by the entire project team at any time. It might be necessary to have a variety of project conference calls for different teams based on the size of the project (some involving the business owner and customer and others with only the project participants).

GDMs need to recognize that this important mode of communication is somewhat formal and will lack the full team dynamic that you are striving for. No matter what you try, it will be challenging to get the actual contributor-level developers at the global location to speak up consistently. Do not get frustrated as this is very typical due to cultural issues and hesitation to speak out when the manager is present. As noted several times in *Managing Global Development Risk*, we suggest GDMs work through these issues with a number of proactive activities designed to break down normal communications barriers.

2. Chat Tools

Tools like AOL Instant Messenger, MSN Messenger, and Yahoo are indispensable to managing offshore projects and enhancing communications across all levels of your global team. However, it is important that everyone has an assigned identification (ID), that these IDs are communicated throughout the team, and that project members follow some form of "etiquette" (because not all issues can be resolved by instant messages).

3. Video Conferencing

If you have access to good video conferencing facilities, we would recommend using them. However, video conferencing due to its cost and the challenges of setting it up is probably best for formal status updates.

4. Application Sharing

One area that can greatly aid collaborative development with a global development team is exploring some of the application sharing tools that are available. These tools allow teams to "whiteboard" different solutions and to work on a common document together (such as a use case or architecture diagram). These tools are useful in place of the brainstorming that onsite teams often are involved in.

5. E-Mail Usage

E-mail is an important mechanism for sharing information between onsite and offsite teams. However, it should not be used to replace other components of your communication strategy, particular a document repository. All too often, e-mail is used as a mechanism to share artifacts; the risk is that these artifacts can be difficult to track and manage. It can also be difficult to ensure that everyone has the most current version of an artifact. For global development projects this becomes a critical risk. To address this, GDMs need to draft guidelines for the project where documents are transmitted via e-mail only in unique circumstances. Otherwise, all documents should be placed in a repository and notifications of these deposits provided through e-mail with a link back to the repository. Using e-mail for short, focused forms of documented communication is the best way to use this technology for project communication purposes.

6. Document Repository

A commonly accessible document repository is an important tool for facilitating communication within a global development project. A good document repository should be accessible 24/7 (remember your offshore team will need access to information primarily during the night). It should also support versioning of artifacts and provide a check-in-check-out feature (all things that a configuration manager will be familiar with). We also encourage GDMs to keep the interface and any document property fields as simple as possible. Many document repositories have rich interfaces that can cause unnecessary delays in loading pages, particularly from offsite locations if there are any bottlenecks in network speed. Also adding too much detail about the properties of a document being uploaded to a repository (such as document class, sub-class, status, etc.) can be needlessly demanding for the real needs that a repository serves (namely, providing a common location for all project-related material).

Tools are an important mechanism to support your global team's communication needs, but they can also be important in managing more discrete elements of a global development project, such as requirements management, source code, and defect tracking. Selecting the appropriate tools for your global development project should align with your enterprise tool requirements, but the tools you use are an important component of your global development strategy. Regardless of the tools you select, validate that there are no barriers for their use in your environment. Tools need to have the ability to synchronize easily through either the Internet, dedicated lines (T1, T3, etc.) or a virtual private network (VPN). Ensure that there are no barriers to using the tools like operating system or browser differences between your onsite and offsite locations. Agree on the use of tools before the project, and test them to make sure they work as required. If you don't have any tools to manage your development effort, you might want to consider this before embarking on a global development project. During the planning phase, we recommended that you identify the tools required to support all phases of the project. During the execution phase, you should review that list and acquire the necessary licenses required to support the project. Table 6.2 provides a "laundry list" of tools that you may want to consider.

These same tools, which provide improved communication, can also lead to problems if not kept in check. For example: e-mailing requirement changes between staff may seem quick and effective but can leave projects at risk for scope creep and cost overruns if configuration management and change control procedures are not followed. GDMs need to keep in mind project communication appropriate for the task and the overall project goals when building and executing the project's plan.

It is obvious that there will be issues with language that can complicate communications. If you are working with China, Russia, or other areas where English is not prevalent, you will need an onsite coordinator who can act as an interpreter with the global team. This can lead to problems because of misunderstandings or simple bottlenecks in the communications; developers may not be able to achieve the necessary communication dynamic with their offshore peers.

However, there are just as many problems when using offshore service providers in countries where English is the primary language, for example, India or the Philippines. Differences in the use and comprehension of the language exist because of accents; dialects, colloquialisms, or use of local references can also lead to misunderstandings. Even simple day-to-day communication among project members can be hampered by a global delivery model due to geographic dispersion and time zone differences.

Managing Global Development Risk strongly encourages GDMs to define a communication strategy for your global development project. This should document a number of important communication techniques such as the frequency of scheduled

Table 6.2   Global Tool Roster

Phase	Tools	Purpose
All	Collaboration tools	Tools to enhance communications, such as Microsoft SharePoint, IBM Lotus SameTime, Microsoft NetMeeting, WebEx, etc.
All	Issue management	A tool that tracks issues, who they are assigned to, possible impacts on the project, and resolutions. This book recommends the risk, assumption, issue, decision (RAID) log, but there are many excellent issue management tools on the market, such as IBM's Rational ClearCase, Mercury's IT Governance (ITG) suite, or PVCS Tracker.
All	Project planning	Tools, such as Microsoft Project or large-scale project management tools such as PlanView or Primavera, that track at a task level for duration, actual effort, percentage complete, resource assignment, predecessor, and provide critical path planning
All	Scope control	Tracks and reports recommend scope changes. Maintains description of the scope change, impacts, cost, and benefits, etc.
All	Time reporting	Tools, such as PlanView or ITG, that capture and approve time worked on a project by phase
All	Version control	Ensures correct version of a controlled item and also allows developer to revert to an earlier version of the item if the circumstances so demand. Version control tools include PVCS, CVS, Microsoft SourceSave
Design and build	Configuration management	Allows the migration of configurations automatically from one environment to another
Design and build	Database modeling tools	Tools, such as ERWIN, that allow DBAs to manage the database, create database schemas, and manage the data dictionary
Design and build	Database design tools	Tools, such as IBM'S Rational Suite, that enable complex modeling of software applications
Design and build	Development tools, including IDE	Integrated development environment (IDE), SQL generation, or other software authoring tools
Design and build	ETL/Data conversion and data cleansing tools	Extraction, transformation, and load (ETL) tools, such as *Ab Initio*, to support conversion and data cleansing activities

Table 6.2 (continued)   Global Tool Roster

Phase	Tools	Purpose
Test	Regression testing	Provides an integrated functional testing product, which captures, verifies, and replays user interactions automatically so that defects can be identified quickly. Used primarily for regression testing to ensure that the entire business process works correctly after any change is made to the system. Tools include Mercury, QSC, and IBM's Rational suites
Test	Test problem reporting	Records and monitors test problems and change requests for every phase of testing
Test	Test script authoring	Provides a standard approach and method for capturing test scripts that can be leveraged repeatedly in support of testing activities
Test	Volume testing	Testing tools such as LoadRunner that test and predict system behavior and performance. It exercises the entire enterprise infrastructure by emulating thousands of users and employs performance monitors to identify and isolate problems

conference calls with the entire team, the use of chat tools, whether or not video conferencing will be supported, application sharing tools, how to use e-mail, and the use of a repository to manage project artifacts.

The first rule in enhancing global communications is to document everything. We have already discussed the importance of a well-documented planning phase with deliverables, milestones, and roles and responsibilities clearly articulated. This same level of documentation is required on all deliverables in the execution phase as well. Document the design, test plans, unit test scripts, code reviews, issues, action items, and even decisions. All processes and procedures should also be documented using standard templates that are easily accessible to all team members.

If communication barriers are impeding progress on the project or the longer-term relationship, *Managing Global Development Risk* recommends the following:

1. GDMs need to insist that the global supplier invest in an English immersion program or other training mechanisms to improve the language capabilities of the team. Be prepared for some pushback on the part of the global supplier as he or she will say this is redundant with existing training, but it is the need to improve comprehension and conversational use that is critical.

2. GDMs should overlap shifts during critical phases of the project. This will allow teams to communicate via the phone or e-mail to work through issues more quickly. Check the contract language, though, before proposing

off-hours work. Some offshore suppliers are beginning to add shift differential rates to their contract terms, so it could cost you more to work within similar time zones. In lieu of same shift scheduling, face-to-face trips and more frequent calls can also help to close the communication gap.

3. As already discussed in *Managing Global Development Risk*, another great way to help close the communication gap is to send one or more of your key project leaders to work at the global facility for an extended period. This is actually a great opportunity for foreign-born employees who may have joined your organization during the Y2K or dot.com boom and are seeking other challenges. We used this approach on a major conversion effort and it turned out to be a great decision. The individual spent almost a year in India working with the global team. He kept his U.S.-based salary, which helped him financially, but more importantly he bridged the knowledge gap between the global teams. He was able to work directly with developers and help them understand the core business applications. This same technique was used on similar projects with similar results.

   A word of caution, though. It will be important for GDMs to have this concept well understood by the global supplier as it could be viewed as an attempt by the customer to undermine the authority of the offshore project manager (PM). This is another example of why global roles and responsibilities developed for your global project also incorporate the dimension of resource location so as to reduce possible conflicts that could impact productivity.

4. Of course, you don't always have the opportunity to send someone to the offshore facility to help manage the engagement. The most consistent way to overcome the communication challenges, however, is through standardized processes and well-organized meetings. At the beginning of an engagement, insist on standard templates for all project deliverables. Also establish and document a common set of terms that apply to your industry or project.

5. Insist that during business hours, the global development team speak only English. This might seem like a given, but is not necessarily the case. Work with the offshore PM to ensure this is executed.

Effective meetings are the weapon of choice for fixing global communication challenges and delivering successful projects. If your meetings are disorganized, non-productive, and a general waste of your time, then the process is broken, and you had better fix it quickly before the entire project fails. Your weekly status meetings and other meetings should always be focused on a specific agenda. Remember, meetings are tools for accomplishing work and thus become even more critical as you manage global resources. If you want a successful project, run a successful meeting. So what are the rules for meetings?

■ **Ensure you have the right people in attendance.** If the offshore PM is responsible for the project schedule and the meeting is designed to review the schedule, he or she must be in attendance. This also applies to people who do not need to attend the meetings. Don't ask every developer or tester to attend the project status meeting. They probably don't want to attend, have more pressing things to do, and will likely contribute little to the discussion items. Invite only those who can contribute to achieving your goals for the meeting. Crowds of observers and supporters bog down progress in a meeting.

■ **Pick a productive time.** This can be difficult when a 12-hour time difference is involved. But be flexible and select times that can be accommodated by all parties. Global sourcing requires compromise, and as the PM you will often be in the position of negotiating meeting times between end users, onsite developers, and the offshore team. Try to be fair to all parties, but focus on selecting times that are productive (3 a.m. Eastern Standard Time, which is 12:30 p.m. India Standard Time, may be great for the offshore team, but I doubt that your brain will be firing on all cylinders).

■ **Set and communicate the agenda in advance.** *Managing Global Development Risk* presented a proposed agenda for your weekly status meeting in the previous section. Use a similar approach for all meetings. It is also beneficial to rotate responsibility for setting the agenda and facilitating the meeting between the entire global team. This bolsters participation and helps drive home that the offshore team is a central contributor to the global team.

■ **Allow time to finish, but finish on time.** If you want productive meetings you need to plan enough time to complete the agenda but also finish on time. Nobody likes meetings that drag on and on (especially when one of the parties is already tired from a long day). If you are stuck on a particular topic, move on and agree to address it in a separate conversation.

■ **Parking lots.** Parking lots are a place to put items that need to be discussed, but aren't really appropriate for the specific meeting. Parking lots are very effective tools for global meetings because they keep the team focused without losing important ideas. Parking lot items should be documented with the meeting minutes and, if appropriate, included on the record identifier (RID) log.

■ **Distribute items before the meeting.** If you plan on reviewing the project schedule during your meeting, ensure that everyone who needs it has a copy before the meeting and quickly address issues.

■ **Maximize participation.** Everyone attending a meeting should have a purpose for being there. By assigning specific actions items to them, they will be more accountable and participative in the meeting. I've shared the facilitation role in many meetings by requesting or assigning different tasks. For example, you may want the offshore PM to review the project schedule, the onsite coordinator to review the issue list, and the development or test leader to review the current defect rates.

■ **Maximize information sharing.** Another useful tool, especially with status and team meetings is the "question game." With the question game, set aside 15 minutes in the agenda to go around the room and every person (or you can mix it up and use the one-skip rule) must ask a project-related question. It can be directed to anyone in the room. The benefits of the question game are that it gets to issues that are concerning the team that may not be addressed in other environments. A simple thing, such as when is this due or where do I move the code to, are often asked and answered during the question period. It is also fun to watch as you see people thinking through their questions. It became such a habit on one project that people actually prepared questions before the meeting and were disappointed if we didn't use the question period.

Over the past several years, we have managed a diverse group of PMs who manage virtual teams. Their inability to get full participation in meetings frustrated many of them. As you well know, it is difficult to execute a successful conference call if the group is not actively engaged in the conversation. This is a common concern for GDMs. So what can be done? Let's take a quick look at Table 6.3 to see common problems.

On a final note, it is important for GDMs to remember that communication is a two-way street. Corporations that are engaged in a global delivery model should invest in their employees to ensure they are able to adapt and work effectively with other cultures. Cultural immersion programs should be introduced that raise awareness of the cultural differences and celebrate the diversity of the global team. The immersion program should support communication classes that discuss how disagreements are raised and resolved in various cultures. *Managing Global Development Risk* recommends culture-based team-building events to help celebrate the team diversity and learn more of each other's cultures. This can involve an afternoon of "good ole" American bowling and another afternoon of cricket.

B. Integrating the Global Team through the Software Development Life Cycle

As mentioned earlier, the number one question we are asked by information technology (IT) executives is, "What type of projects can be done offshore?" The number one question asked by PMs and people responsible for delivering projects is, "How do I get it done, and what work can I complete offshore?"

Your delivery model will drive the activities that can be completed offshore. If your organization is outsourcing the entire project, the offshore team may be involved in requirements through deployment. However, most organizations share responsibilities with their global sourcing partner; thus the question of what should be sent offshore becomes more pertinent.

In a "typical" engagement, a business analyst (BA), in collaboration with the business and development teams, generates the software requirements. Development

Table 6.3 Dynamic Meeting Tactics

Challenge	Solution
Members do not contribute to the discussion	Encourage members who have not contributed by asking them directly, "Raj, what do you think?" Make a general statement, "I'd like to hear other perspectives on this issue. What are some other thoughts?" Another effective solution is to rotate responsibility for the meeting to various team members. Make the entire team accountable for the success of the meeting, not just the GDM or onsite coordinator
A few members monopolize the discussion	This can be especially troublesome in some cultures and with younger teams. Oftentimes, younger team members will not voice an opinion because they do not want to be seen as disagreeing with their supervisor. Culturally, it is important that you are aware of this dynamic, but from a project perspective, you need to let the team know that you genuinely respect everyone's opinion and that it is important for you to hear diverse and even conflicting opinions to make the best possible decision for the project and the team
Members do not have information or knowledge about the issue or topic	Ensure that members receive information prior to the meeting (it's difficult to discuss an issue when the information is received at the meeting). Also, hold people accountable for reviewing information prior to the meeting so they are prepared to review and discuss. Summarize the issue at the beginning of the meeting
The discussion wanders away from the agenda and issues	Stay focused on the agenda. "I am not sure I understand. Can you explain how this relates to the topic or issues?"
An issue is being discussed for too long, and members are getting restless	Summarize frequently, and ask members if they have any additional comments. Watch and listen for signs that the group is in agreement to end the discussion. This can be difficult on conference calls because you can't pick up the non-verbal clues, unless you hear snoring on the line. You may need to use your own internal clock or simply ask the group if this is a parking lot item or an item that should be discussed with a smaller group. Be careful, though, that you don't suppress the conversation too soon. Enhancing the communication between team members is a critical goal, and you don't want to be seen as always squashing these conversations

continued

Table 6.3 (continued)   Dynamic Meeting Tactics

Challenge	Solution
The discussion is very heated and tense	Use neutral language to reframe a participant's suggestion or comment When a member makes claims about an issue, ask her or him to back up the claims — "Do you have evidence of that?" Ask how many other members feel "this way" Suggest a break, or table the issue for another meeting

teams will analyze the requirements to determine the sizing effort and begin their designs. Once the designs are baselined, the work is allocated to the teams. Testing then ramps up to create scripts, and once the code is delivered, executing the scripts begins. Finally, testing is complete, and the project is implemented. In each of these phases there are appropriate and inappropriate roles for the offshore team. You and your team must jointly decide what works best in your environment and how to effectively delegate the tasks to maximize the value and productivity of the offshore team.

In the following subsections, *Managing Global Development Risk* offers observations on completing global development projects. Fortunately, there are many different models, so when you begin working with your global sourcing supplier, discuss their experiences as well to determine what is best for your team.

1.   Definition (Scope and Requirements)

Some of the most interesting books we have read are on the development of software requirements (we know, we really need to get a life). Whether taking a waterfall approach or an iterative approach, the requirements or goals of the project are often the hardest to understand and explain. We are often challenged in our ability to state what we want in terms that others can understand. The proposed solution to "finding the right words" is "drawing the right picture," hence the development of the numerous modeling tools on the market today.

Once a decision is made to use global resources, GDMs should begin evaluating the requirements, or your approach to generating requirements, to ensure they accurately portray what the development project is intended to accomplish. You will probably find that your requirements are highly dependent on a general understanding of the current application or business model and are not in a form that can be handed to a third-party vendor. Any ambiguity is magnified when the project is developed offshore. Cultural or business understanding may be different, which can lead to a design or product that far exceeds or does not meet your needs. Beware of comparative terms such as small, large, costly, inexpensive, etc., that often require cultural judgments. This is a concern, but you need not despair.

Global firms have dealt with this issue for a long time and have developed processes to help re-engineer your requirements. One of the techniques they will use is visual modeling. The visual modeling tools enable you to draw the process flows, data flows, and screen designs, etc., that will help articulate the proposed end state.

If technical requirements are completed offshore, GDMs need to insist on models that visually demonstrate an understanding of the requirements. Requirements should be written in use-case format with detailed requirements that end users can understand or as functional requirements ("the system shall") to ensure traceability through all phases of the global development project. These standards should be followed even if the onsite portion of your global team writes the requirements. The offshore team will need a complete understanding of your needs to deliver the required functionality.

Process flows or maps are a common means of showing flow between major components of an application. The most important quality of the process flow is that everyone can understand it. Regardless of the symbols used, developers, testers, and users onsite and offshore must all be able to interpret and comprehend the flow.

It is often helpful to start with a high-level flow of the business process being modeled. These diagrams, known as business context diagrams, show the users or applications that interact with the primary process.

Unified modeling language (UML) has established a common language for developers and requirements analysts. Many end users may not understand the language, but when properly facilitated the language lends itself to a solid understanding of the requirements. Use case scenarios bridge the end-user and developer knowledge gap by providing a building block approach to the requirements. We have used use case scenarios on mainframe, Internet, and infrastructure projects, all with a high degree of success in articulating the requirements. In each of these environments the scenarios were shared with the global team to help drive the understanding of the project.

If a graphic user interface is required, propose a prototype or detailed screen layouts. A data dictionary is also valuable to ensure the teams understand each data element and any calculations that may be required. The number one rule with user interface requirements is DON'T ASSUME ANYTHING! Document everything you need, including field edits, tab orders, colors, fonts, etc., that may be important. Requirements such as "an intuitive user interface" must be avoided when working with offshore resources. A global sourcing partner probably will lack an overall understanding of your core business; thus the vagueness of "intuitiveness" will lead to frustration and missed expectations. Even simple calculations, such as determining the interest rate, will need to be spelled out.

The offshore team should review the requirements for completeness. *Managing Global Development Risk* recommends a complete walkthrough of the requirements document with the offshore team as part of the KA phase. We recommend

GDMs set aside several days to explore the details of the requirements so they are internalized by the offshore PM and onsite coordinator. It may even make sense for the GDM to visit the global location and meet face to face with the offshore PM at this time to ensure an accurate understanding of the requirements. We've learned over the years that there will always be questions about the requirements, and new requirements will "pop up" as the project progresses. The offshore PM will be required to make many decisions over the coming months. If he or she has a firm understanding of what you are trying to accomplish, these decisions are more apt to be in line with your needs.

2. Design

The design phase of a project offers multiple options for integrating the global team. The common approach in an IT organization is to have the lead developers onsite document the design in excruciating detail and ship it to the offshore team. The design is then further decomposed, discussed, and allocated to individual developers at the global facility. Although this has become a de facto model, it is far from ideal and fails to adequately involve all team members in key design discussions and more importantly fails to internalize the design with the offshore team. So just like requirements: when you hand a design over to an offshore team, you get exactly what you ask for, whether it is right or wrong.

This is where *Managing Global Development Risk* diverges from the majority of management books and takes a page from the agile development crowd. Success of a global development project should not be measured by its software engineering techniques, process improvement initiatives, or even the effectiveness of the communication. It should be measured as every project is measured: did you deliver the expected results? From an end-user perspective, they only want what they asked for, a system that meets their needs. They rarely care about the process to get there or the interim deliverables that help the global development team achieve those goals. Just like buying electronics that are stamped "Made in China," we need a level of transparency in the design phase of a global development project. GDMs need to be able to better tap into the well-educated minds that are often supporting their global development engagements.

Without a doubt there are major challenges with integrating the offshore team into the design phases of a project, in particular if this is the first global development project. But GDMs need to understand the returns are well worth the risk if they are focused and execute plans efficiently. As the GDM, you need to understand you are expanding the base of knowledge that can help resolve complex problems for this and future projects. You are relying on the experience gained by your offshore vendor on similar projects that you may not have. And most importantly, it fully engages the offshore teams and keeps everyone focused on what you are trying to achieve.

a. The Global Design Phase

There are several challenges that occur when GDMs integrate the offshore team into the design phase, forming a global design team. First and foremost is the communication challenge. Although *Managing Global Development Risk* provides a number of approaches to facilitate overall team communication, design is an iterative process that takes coordination with business and end users to ensure all aspects are concerned. A good global development method is to have a small team create the high-level design and architecture and then parse components to the broader global team. Design activities should also be time-boxed. There are three benefits of time-boxing that will help keep the design phase on-track:

1. Time-boxing forces trade-off decisions. Design is a thinking process that can lead a team down many paths. The more we learn about a process or a requirement, the more we can explore and design software to better meet the needs. This exploration often leads to expanded scope or "gold-plating" and puts the project dates at risks.
2. Time-boxing sets specific, realistic timeframes for the design (that is usually measured in weekly design deliverables) that forces trade-off decisions through all phases. Trade-off encourages all parties to make good business and technical decisions.
3. Time-boxing forces these decisions throughout the project instead of pushing them to the end when the options are limited.

The most productive model to integrate global resources into the design phase is to jointly design applications with your global sourcing partner. But how do you collaborate on designs? The best means is through the extensive use of collaboration tools and modeling. The rational unified process (RUP) is one example, but with today's advances in intranets and network capacity, you can even use Visio with NetMeeting to collaborate on a design. The use of a common repository and formal change control procedures (with check in and check out) allow documents to be shared, and the internet-based collaboration tools allow real-time updates.

Managing Global Development Risk also recommends iterative joint design reviews with the onsite and offshore members of the global design team at least twice a week to measure progress and ensure design decisions are not delayed. Joint walkthroughs should follow a formal inspection process that ensures the design is traceable to the requirements, meets corporate standards, and can be implemented in the "real world."

At the end of the design phase or completion of design for a specific component, GDMs need to conduct a joint review of the entire document and review any prototypes or proof of concepts. Mandate sign-off on the design from key stakeholders on both the onsite and offshore members of the global team.

As the global sourcing relationship grows and global resources begin to take on a greater role in the maintenance of certain modules, it is a natural evolution to have them create the design specifications. Even on major projects that require extensive integration with other groups, the global team will eventually be in a better position to design the interfaces to the applications they maintain than an onsite architecture or designer who is no longer involved in the coding.

Product development companies have more firmly embraced the need to integrate global resource teams into the product design phase. Once the work is allocated to global resources, it becomes quickly apparent that it is more productive if the offshore team takes full responsibility for the components or modules they maintain, which includes design, development, testing, and integrating the changes back into the product baseline.

Open source is also a topic that is getting significant press in the global development market lately. Many companies do not have defined standards for the use of open source in the development environment or integration of open source components into the solution. The GDM will want to work with the architectural group or standards committee to clearly define the open source rules before completing the project offshore. Many offshore firms use various open source components in the development environment and may integrate open source components into their solution. Once you have defined the standard, it should be included in the design and coding standards and added to peer review checklists to ensure compliance.

3. Code and Unit Test

Whew, finally the coding phase. This has to be the easy part, right? After all, this is why your organization made the decision to engage a global sourcing partner. This is how a company can take advantage of the economies of scale, improve quality, get products to market faster, and generally solve all of life's issues. What could go wrong in coding? This is the global sourcing company's bread and butter, right?

Well, think again. There are as many challenges introduced in the coding phase as any other phase of a project. Coding is where you will have your first real opportunity to apply the Earned Value Analysis (EVA) and weekly deliverable processes we have discussed. Coding, though, is also where you will first realize that global delivery is not a silver bullet.

For those of you who are just beginning a relationship with a global service provider, you may face a bit of an internal challenge managing expectations. Throughout the negotiation of the MSA, a customer and supplier will talk about the savings their development organization will realize. Unfortunately, typically a development manager is not part of the negotiations. It is these individuals who will communicate to company executives the impact of the agreement they just signed. If a project does not achieve these targeted levels, it must not have been managed properly, right?

The coding phase will introduce you to the realities of global development very quickly. If this is your first experience, you'll witness the communication frustrations and attrition issues that we have discussed. You or your senior developers will review code that will make you question almost every aspect of the deal. It will be common to have a team of ten or more developers with an average experience of perhaps two or three years. That means an offshore project manager with about five years of experience, a "senior developer" with three to five years of experience, and the rest of the team with less than two years of experience.

The "senior developer" is expected to coach and guide the inexperienced staff to meet the deliverables. Many of the junior developers are usually unable to make sound technical decisions and, in some of the worst examples, may have only a rudimentary knowledge of the technology they are working with. This can lead to poor quality and extended lead times.

Hence, *Managing Global Development Risk* focuses on weekly deliverables and measurable milestones. As GDM, you want to know as soon as possible if your team can deliver. Your best probability of success lies with early identification and resolution of issues. The more you know and the sooner you know it, the better you will be able to manage the issues.

Luckily, there are several tools at your disposal and when confronted with hard facts, your global sourcing partner will move to deliver on commitments, even if that means increasing the overall experience level of the project team. So let's take a look at some of the tools:

- Embrace coding standards.
- Enforce weekly builds.
- Enforce peer reviews of all deliverables.
- Conduct integrated code walkthroughs. Use a standard template for code walkthroughs. Recommend review of all new components of significance and random review of others. Document all issues noted during the walkthroughs in a formal defect-tracking tool. Require that your offshore vendor measure and report improvements in the defect density.
- Take advantage of regression test beds. The outsourcing partner should develop a test bed of regression test cases that ensures your build did not break existing functionality. The regression test bed should be run every time a new build is delivered.

Many global sourcing companies are now embracing a more iterative approach to the coding phase. Onsite and offshore members of the global team collaborate on a daily basis and make extensive use of proof-of-concepts and pilot releases. These releases are used to solicit feedback, try new ideas, and validate design assumptions. As the team experiences grow, there will be fewer issues noted during the coding phase, and you will begin to see productivity improvements. Until the global resources become familiar with the applications, though, expect a high degree of errors in the coding and testing phase, and be sure to allot sufficient time in the schedule to address these errors.

GDMs also need to introduce SLAs with teeth in the coding phase. Any SLA that is tied to payments (either paying when milestones are hit or withholding when productivity or defect rates miss targets) is going to get attention from the global supplier account manager. GDMs can use this relationship and this "trigger" to their advantage by accurately capturing and reporting the SLAs. Even if SLAs were not negotiated during the formal contract phase, we recommend you establish SLAs or key project metrics during this phase to focus the supplier on quality and on-time delivery.

Again, as the GDM, you are responsible for the successful delivery of the global development project. If the global sourcing partner has not staffed the team to be successful, use this as leverage to get better-qualified resources assigned to the project. Table 6.4 identifies some of the metrics and SLAs tracked during the coding phase.

4. Verification (System Test and User Acceptance)

Global testing is truly one of the silver bullets that can be quickly implemented in a global delivery model. Unlike other phases that demand a high degree of collaboration, testing, by its very nature, is an independent activity. A well-executed global test program allows you to shorten the test and development cycles by taking advantage of time zone differences between major global sourcing centers and the United States. This strategy is commonly referred to as "follow the sun." The follow-the-sun philosophy maximizes the productive hours in a given day by sharing the work between the onsite and offshore members of the global team. Testing is the ideal candidate for applying this philosophy. Let's look at how follow the sun really works.

During the build phase, testing can begin to integrate components into the baseline and conduct ongoing regression testing and system testing. Once the offshore team has completed unit testing the component, they check it into the baseline. The offshore test team then runs an automated regression script against the baseline to ensure the newly checked-in code has not broken anything else. Once the regression test completes, the offshore test organization pushes the code to the system test environment and sends an e-mail to the onsite test team that the new baseline is ready for system test, and they go home. When the onsite test team comes in, they open their e-mail, see that the code is ready, and begin executing their system test scripts. Defects that are noted are written up in the defect tracking system. At the end of the day, the onsite test leader sends an e-mail to the offshore test leader, development leader, and PM stating the progress that was made and the number of defects that were opened, and then they go home. When the offshore team arrives,

Table 6.4   Key Metrics and SLAs Monitored During Coding Phase

Metric	Definition	Target
On time delivery	Measures the percentage of deliverables provided on time. Use the EVA project schedule to track	85%
Productivity	Measures overall productivity of the global team. Measured as a percentage of components that are delivered within ±10% of the productivity estimate (function point, use case point, other estimation model) or as ratio of actual hours expended for development compared with estimate (±10%)	90% of components delivered within +10% or overall effort delivered within +10%
Quality	Measures percentage of deliverables provided error free, based on unit test and code reviews	90%
Defect removal rates	Measures ability to detect and resolve errors early in the process. In the planning phase the team identified the estimated number of defects for the project based on the development estimates and industry defect rejection. Approximately 60% of the errors should be detected and removed during the design and coding phase	90% of predicted errors that are removed
Error correction	Measure the percentage of errors that are corrected within the established timelines. This can be errors noted in production (trouble tickets) or errors noted during code walkthroughs, unit testing, or acceptance testing. Errors and time to resolve are generally classified as follows: (production errors divided by test issues minus production times divided by test timeline). Sev 1 = Showstopper (24 hours/4 hours); Sev 2 = High (5 days/24 hours); Sev 3 = Low (30 days/undetermined)	90%

they have immediate feedback on outstanding issues that can be resolved, and the new cycle begins.

The above scenario can easily be switched so the offshore team is executing the test scripts and the onsite team is doing the development. The same process would apply. The model is even adaptable to allow sharing of test or development responsibilities between the onsite and offshore teams. An added benefit is that the offshore team could create and maintain the regression test baselines that are executed on site. This is typically a time-intensive task that can easily be supported offshore.

This process also works great during the user acceptance phase. One of the common complaints between development and test is that testing doesn't identify defects early enough and development does not fix issues quickly enough. The follow-the-sun and weekly deliverable approach address both the concerns by testing and developing around the clock. It takes communications, a shared testing-development environment, and disciplined processes, but the rewards and productivity improvements are significant and well worth the investment.

There are challenges, however. Some problems are difficult to document and not well understood. To address these, *Managing Global Development Risk* recommends daily conference calls between the development and the test organizations during the test period to discuss any outstanding issues. We also recommend that screen prints, debug messages, and the specific test conditions and scripts be included with the defect when it is posted. It is also beneficial to summarize the daily testing results in an e-mail or on a common repository, so that progress can be measured.

a.   Common Test Bed

Establishing a common test bed is another great way to further reduce the risk of global development. Use a VPN, dedicated network, file transfer protocol (FTP), e-mail, and anything else to help move files between the global development environment and the test environment (or vice versa if testing is being outsourced first). Again, GDMs want early indicators that the team is progressing with your goals. A common approach is to do 90% of the testing offshore, but once a week or once every two weeks cut a baseline and conduct a series of tests onsite. This helps ensure that progress is being made and that errors are being identified and corrected. It also provides GDMs important data points to demonstrate to users and senior management that the project is meeting the defined goals. In our experience, the offshore projects that have failed have not had adequate oversight and attempted the "throw the code over the wall" approach.

The build schedule needs to be well understood by the entire team, developers, and testers. The test group will need to schedule script execution based on the build schedule and will also need to re-run tests once all components are delivered. This is yet another reason to focus on automated test scripts that allow you to add new scripts as new functionality is delivered. Ensure the test team understands the build schedules, and have a suite of regression tests built that can validate each build and specific functional test ready that can validate the new features in the build. A best practice is to post the weekly build schedule on the project Web site or collaboration tool. If one isn't available, send a weekly e-mail with the build schedule updated. The build schedule should state the specific modules or components that are included and the progress to date.

Many U.S. corporations understand the benefit of a set of regression test scripts and regression test files. We have spent millions of dollars on test automation tools such as Mercury WinRunner. The initial development of these baselines and ongoing maintenance is expensive and time consuming; thus oftentimes the scripts are out of date and do not accurately test the needed functionality. Using the offshore team to maintain these scripts is a great use of their skill, and the lower labor rate helps justify the test automation risk on investment (ROI). To keep the scripts current, the GDM should meet with the offshore test team after each release to define the new script requirements. Document these new test case requirements, and specify the details on what needs to be validated. Include time in your planning to validate the scripts before they are executed.

When using a global delivery model, testing in general must be more rigorous than usual to compensate for the increased likelihood that requirements were missed or misunderstood or that the system integration will be buggy due to incomplete specifications. Let's review some global best practices that help ensure the testing phase effectively mitigates:

- Define acceptance tests as early as possible in the process that capture the end-to-end user processes, replicate the complete system environment, and verify required results under as complete a range of scenarios as possible.
- Update test conditions whenever the requirements are clarified or extended.
- Set up test environments and procedures at the beginning of the project, and practice running and evaluating tests together.

You'll be surprised how much tweaking it takes to establish a testing process that is both smooth and complete and includes making product design and project plan changes based on the results.

As highlighted in Table 6.5, there are core metrics and SLAs that should be tracked and measured during the test phase. The two most important metrics to monitor during this phase are the defect density rate and the percentage of test conditions complete. Both of these metrics are critical because they both indicate the quality of the testing effort (is it tracking to plan? and are you finding the bugs?).

Measuring the project defect density can be a misleading statistic. This is a case where a low number does not always mean that things are OK. One of the advantages of inch pebble milestone and measuring things weekly is that GDMs gain small snapshots as the project progresses. If the defect density number is consistently below your target numbers (i.e., below 7 percent if measuring defect rate per scripts executed), you should dig deeper into the numbers to understand why. It could be that the product is simple, critical test cases have yet to be executed, or that the product is of high quality. However, it could also mean that your global test team is inexperienced and has not identified tests that will adequately detect defects. If it is the latter, it is better to know this early so you can ask tough questions or have your onsite team more involved in the testing instead of waiting until it goes to production and your users find the errors. Conversely, if the defect rate is greater than the norm, you should quickly evaluate the defects to determine patterns. Was the code

Table 6.5 Testing — Key Metrics and SLAs

Metric	Definition	Target
Defect density or defect ratio	Measures the number of defects per unit size or the percentage of defects per lines of code, function points, size of project, scripts executed, or other measurements. The most consistent measurement in-process is defects per number of executed scripts. This measurement provides a fairly reliable indicator of the software quality, assuming that detailed scripts are developed that are traceable to the requirements. Many offshore firms use percentage defect per person hour. A common percentage is 0.05 defect per person hour (a 10,000 hour project should identify 500 defects)	Dependent on method used, 7% is common rate for defects per executed scripts
Test completion	Measures percentage of test cases executed on time per test plan. Recommend a formal tracking tool that identifies all test cases and a plan to complete 100 percent of test cases with the specified timeframe. On a weekly basis, measure the actual number completed per the expected number completed	90%
Error correction	Measures the percentage of errors that are corrected and retested within the established timelines	90%
Test coverage	Measures the percentage of requirements that are tested	90%
Test automation	Measures the percentage of test conditions that are executed via automated test scripts	30%

too complex? Were the developers too inexperienced? If the team is finding a significant number of defects, are they missing others because of the constant rework? In these instances, you may need to delay the project or apply additional resources to ensure the quality meets the customer's expectations before it is released.

This section provided a very high-level overview of the key testing activities and some methods to better integrate the offshore team into your test efforts. Your global sourcing partner has probably invested thousands of hours into a software quality assurance (SQA) organization that can help you create a powerful test organization.

This is a tremendous opportunity for GDMs to tap into test advancements that can be realized through the introduction of test automation, quantitative measurements, statistical process control, and other formal measurement processes. The ROI on an extensive global test environment is significant and clearly worth investigating with the global sourcing partner.

5. Implementation

Implementation tasks are primarily completed by the onsite team. It may be beneficial to bring a few of the key global developers onsite for 30 to 60 days to support the implementation tasks. This will provide your team with the necessary technical expertise that understands the code and helps reinforce that it was a true global team implementation.

We also recommend that a contingent of offshore resources support the post-implementation tasks. As with any large-scale implementation, there are bound to be issues that need to be addressed. The offshore team can resolve issues, support implementation test activities, and support the longer-term sustainment tasks.

C. Impact of Cultural Issues on Execution

Cultural issues can impact the success of a global development engagement in many ways. Depending on the region you are outsourcing to, various cultural differences will exist that, if not understood, will lead to greater levels of frustration. The Asian and Indian cultures, for example, are hesitant to contradict others, push back, or deliver bad news. These cultures tend to have a fundamental deference to, and respect for, authority figures that can cause some people from these cultures to not question work assignments in the same way that we have come to expect from U.S. employees. Whereas U.S. personnel will commonly ask questions and make recommendations as to better or more effective ways of achieving results, personnel from certain Indian and Asian cultures will have a tendency to simply go and do the work, deferring to the judgment of senior personnel. When working with team members from such cultures, it is very important to realize that you will probably get exactly what you ask for, without question, even if what you ask for isn't the best possible solution. This situation places a premium on (1) being very certain that your requirements, specifications, etc., are very well defined and thoroughly vetted, and (2) actively cultivating lines of communication that will entice and facilitate feedback.

Unfortunately, delivering bad news, pushing back, and questioning decisions when you don't agree are fundamental to the U.S. culture and absolutely critical in our perspective to delivering solid projects. It is important, then, to build a culture of trust and teamwork, making it clear that open, direct communication is essential and that bad news is preferable than delaying issues or concerns. The cultural and communication challenges introduced with offshore outsourcing are by no means insurmountable. *Managing Global Development Risk* provides multiple tools and strategies to reduce the impact of these challenges. *Managing Global Development Risk* preaches the development of shared goals and a true global vision, coupled with a strong commitment to utilize sound project management principles at both the onsite and offshore facilities, such as EVA tracking and weekly deliverables. Once cultural issues are understood and addressed, teams can begin freely sharing information through ongoing dialogue and a disciplined approach.

One of our favorite cultural integration techniques is the potluck. We certainly enjoy eating and introduced theme-based potlucks to our teams early in our management careers. The potlucks provide an opportunity to share experiences and taste the foods from various parts of the world. The variety is incredible and without exception my co-workers were excited to share recipes from their native lands. One of the funniest themed lunches was a "tailgate party" to celebrate the opening of the American football season. We literally brought in a tailgate and set it on the conference table as the centerpiece. It brought a few stares of disbelief, but quickly started conversations about sports in various cultures and how they celebrate their sports heroes.

D. Summary

We started and finished this section discussing the importance of communication. Execution is truly where the "rubber meets the road," and success is most often influenced by the team's ability to effectively communicate. From the GDM perspective, the execution phase has the fewest deliverables and new tasks that the GDM is directly responsible for. The execution phase focuses on the core development activities, many of which will be completed by multiple teams.

GDMs are also typically more familiar with the execution phase; thus we focused on the unique activities introduced by the global delivery model. The focus on the core development activities identified the tasks that are completed offshore in a global project. Ideally, the global team is fully integrated with the onsite client team and participates in most development activities. To successfully complete the development activities, the GDM will need to enhance the communication between the team and establish key metrics to measure progress.

1. *Execution Phase Deliverables*

- Requirements: Requirements and functional specifications
- Design: Design specifications
- Development: Unit test scripts, code, unit test results

- Test: Acceptance test scripts and test results, user acceptance test scripts and results, automated test scripts
- Implementation: Deployment scripts, deployment test conditions
- Updated risk plan and RAID log

2. Execution Phase Service Levels

The service levels measured in the execution phase should measure each of the primary development phases. In addition to service levels, GDMs should establish a weekly build process and use key metrics to measure the development and test progress on a weekly basis. SLAs measured during execution include:

- Percentage of deliverables completed on time
- Percentage of deliverables completed to budget
- Percentage of milestone completed per plan
- Percentage of development activities completed within productivity estimates
- Defect removal rates
- Defect density rates
- Overall quality
- Supplier attrition rates
- SQA results; overall score for each phase greater than 90%

3. Execution Phase Metrics

Execution phase metrics are highlighted in Table 6.6.

4. Execution Phase Risks and Issues

The execution phase is where the majority of the work is completed; thus it is also the phase where it is most important to identify and mitigate risks. Many of the risks identified during earlier phases will occur during the execution phase. The GDM must continue to work with his or her global partner to brainstorm and resolve these risks. Typical execution phase risks and issues are outlined Table 6.7.

Table 6.6 Execution Phase Metrics

Development Phase	Metric	Definition	Target
All	Percentage of deliverables accepted (no major issues)	On a weekly basis, measures the total numbers of deliverables that are delivered and accepted with no major issues (deliverable does not require re-work) ■ Number of deliverables accepted for week per number of deliverables submitted for week ■ Number of deliverables accepted to date per number of deliverables submitted to date	Weekly, 85% To date 90%
All	Percentage of weekly deliverables completed on time	Measure percentage of deliverables completed per number of deliverables planned for completion	90%
All	Compliance to SLAs	For planning phase, measures number of SLAs achieved per total number of SLAs	90%
All	Error correction	Measure the percentage of errors that are corrected within the established timelines. This can be errors noted in production (trouble tickets) or errors noted during code walkthroughs, unit testing, or acceptance testing. Errors and time to resolve are generally classified as follows (production errors per test issues minus production times per test timeline). Sev 1 = showstopper (24 hours/4 hours); Sev 2 = high (5 days/24 hours); Sev 3 = low (30 days/undetermined)	90%

All	Milestone completion	On a weekly basis, measures ■ Number of milestones completed in week per total milestones planned for week ■ Total number of milestones met to date per total milestones planned to date ■ Total number of milestones met per total number of milestones	Weekly: 85% To date: 90% Project: dependent on plan (goal is 95%)
All	On time delivery	Measures the percentage of deliverables provided on time; use the EVA project schedule to track.	85%
All	Quality	Measure percentage of deliverables provided error free, based on unit test and code reviews	90%
Requirements	Requirements coverage	Measures ability of team to accurately capture requirements. Typically measured as requirements defect injection rate. Defects associated with requirements should be less than 20% of total, and 90% of all requirements should be identified	Percentage of requirements identified: 90% Injection rate <20%
Requirements	Degree of change	Measures team's ability to properly scope the project. Effectiveness is measured by dividing the original estimate by the (sum of the change requests [change requests for impacted project] plus the original hours)	Less than 15%
Code and unit test	Defect density or defect ratio	Measures the number of defects per unit size or the percentage of defects per line of code, function points, size of project, scripts executed, or other measurements. The most consistent measurement I have found is defects per number of executed scripts. This measurement provides a fairly reliable indicator of the software quality, assuming that detailed scripts are developed that are traceable to the requirements	Dependent on method used; 7% is common rate for defects per executed scripts

continued

Table 6.6 (continued)   Execution Phase Metrics

Development Phase	Metric	Definition	Target
Code and unit test	Defect density or defect ratio	Many offshore firms use percentage defects per person hour. A common percentage is 0.05 defects per person hour (a 10,000 hour project should identify 500 defects)	
Code and unit test	Defect removal rates	Measures ability to detect and resolve errors early in the process. In the planning phase the team identified the estimated number of defects for the project based on the development estimates and industry defect injection. Approximately 60% of the errors should be detected and removed during the design and coding phase	90% of predicted errors that are removed
Test	Error correction	Measures the percentage of errors that are corrected and retested within the established timelines	90%
Test	Test automation	Measures the percentage of test conditions that are executed via automated test scripts	30%
Test	Test completion	Measures the percentage of test cases executed on time per test plan. Recommend a formal tracking tool that identifies all test cases and a plan to complete 100% of the test cases with the specified timeframe. On a weekly basis, measure the actual number completed per the expected number completed	90%
Test	Test coverage	Measures the percentage of requirements that are tested	90%

Table 6.7   Execution Phase Risks and Issues

Development Phase	Risk	Mitigation Strategy
All	No change control. Requirements and design changes are tracked on e-mail	Implement formal change control process that includes a formal document repository with check-in and check-out capabilities
Requirement	Requirements are not understood by offshore team. May lead to "scope creep" or "gold-plating"	Review requirements with offshore PM and potentially travel to offshore location to ensure key team members fully understand requirements and core business processes
Design	Offshore team is supporting design, which causes delays, or team not familiar with design tools	Implement time-boxing principles to complete design activities. Standardize design tools, and provide training for all team members
Development	High defect rates, behind schedule, quality expectations not met	Implement weekly builds to monitor progress. Develop automated test cases to verify quality on weekly basis. Hold supplier accountable to quality goals and schedule commitments
Testing	Inadequate testing, poor quality, defects significantly exceed estimates	Monitor testing completion and defect rates on a weekly basis. Hold supplier accountable to quality goals and schedule commitments

Table 6.8   Execution Phase Checklist

Execution Phase Checklist	
■ Focus on communication ■ Establish rules for staff meetings and status reports ■ Integrate offshore team into all phases, but clearly define expectations ■ Use weekly builds to monitor progress ■ Automate test cases ■ Update RAID log ■ Track project metrics	
Execution Phase SLAs	*Execution Phase Metrics*
■ Percentage of deliverables completed on time ■ Percentage of deliverables completed to budget ■ Percentage of milestone completed per plan ■ Degree of change ■ Requirements coverage ■ Defect demoval rates ■ Defect density rates ■ Overall quality ■ Supplier attrition rates ■ SQA results; overall score for each phase greater than 90%	■ Percentage of deliverables completed on time ■ Milestones delivered on time ■ Defect injection per density rate ■ Percentage of test cases automated ■ Requirements coverage ■ Compliance to service levels ■ Percentage of deliverables accepted ■ Estimates to complete ■ Onsite-offshore ratios ■ Issue resolution
Execution Phase Risks	*Execution Phase Deliverables*
■ No change control ■ Requirements are not understood by offshore team ■ Offshore team supporting design ■ High defect rates, behind schedule, quality expectations not metInadequate testing, poor quality, defects significantly exceed estimates, cost overruns or savings not achieved ■ Limited insight into offshore activities ■ Staffing obligations not met ■ Offshore team is inexperienced	■ Requirements: requirements and functional specifications ■ Design: design specifications ■ Development: unit test scripts, code, unit test results ■ Test: acceptance test scripts and test results, user acceptance test scripts and results, automated test scripts ■ Implementation: deployment scripts, deployment test conditions

Chapter 7

Controlling a Global Delivery Project

A. Introduction

Executing and controlling offshore projects are complementary tasks. The control phase involves a series of tasks that ensure the offshore supplier adheres to contractual agreements and that the project moves forward per the project plan. Primary tasks in the controlling phase include performance reporting, performance management, change control, configuration management, and scope control and verification.

There are multiple means to exercise control. Control can be exercised through contract governance, sourcing management, and day-to-day management of project activities. Control exercised through contract management and sourcing management typically focuses on adherence to contractual obligations, such as performance management, financial management, and general contract administration functions. These activities are important, but are not the focus of this section. Our focus will continue to be the primary activities of the global development manager (GDM) that can help assure success at the project level.

> **Section VII Key Concepts – CONTROLLING**
> ➤ Common Global Metrics
> ➤ Earned Value to Manage Global Productivity

Figure 7.1   Section VII Key Concepts

Almost without exception, you will find the work ethic of experienced offshore outsourcing providers outstanding, and their team and project management disciplined. But it would be a mistake to conclude the offshore provider will manage the schedule and budget and complete all activities with little to no interaction with the onsite team. In fact, just the opposite is true. The best offshore firms will strive for a balanced relationship with the client that provides ongoing feedback and monitoring of project goals.

The best offshore providers understand that to be successful, they need client involvement and oversight. Although it is not necessary to micro-manage the offshore team, it is important to maintain a complete and accurate awareness of progress and issues, to be there when decisions get made, and to course-correct the plan as things evolve. Because you're managing from a distance, you'll need to overcompensate.

GDMs exercise control primarily through effective project communications, well-defined processes, established metrics, project plans, and proactively identifying and resolving project-related issues. As a GDM, you will often share control with the offshore manager and the supplier's onsite coordinator. These roles are typically required to ensure the correct level of oversight and control of the offshore activities and to ensure the smooth flow of communication between the teams. Your control activities will consist of summarizing issues and status from multiple teams and ensuring all teams are performing at an optimal level. We have identified several key areas that, if properly monitored and controlled, will significantly improve the probability of successfully delivering global projects on schedule and within the budget.

Project managers (PMs) must have visibility into the actual status of a project. Software metrics are designed to provide this visibility. Unfortunately, many PMs ignore the importance of these metrics and use their "gut instincts" to determine if a project is on track. Although "gut instincts" are beneficial in certain situations, they are no substitute for true metrics that measure the health of a project over a longer period.

Metrics must also be interpreted correctly. It is important for GDMs to update schedules, track and report issues and key decisions, and conduct weekly status reports, but it is even more critical for GDMs to interpret the metrics and take appropriate actions when a project is in trouble. GDMs must be skilled in identifying the critical metrics, monitoring these metrics, and taking decisive action when the data indicates trouble ahead. This is the essence of control.

Global projects require the GDM to understand and monitor the onsite and offshore ratios and manage these ratios to balance the risk and financial advantages of global development. Oftentimes, contractual and pricing structures will drive offshore providers to move more work offshore than what is reasonable or acceptable from a risk perspective. Conversely, project teams often feel more comfortable with a higher onsite ratio. As we have already seen, it is easier to complete many project tasks when the teams are co-located. However, if the budget estimates were built with the assumption that 70 or 80% of the effort would be completed offshore, then the additional costs associated with onsite resources may significantly impact the project budget.

As the GDM responsible for the delivery of the project, you should consistently monitor the onsite-offshore ratio (typically measured in hours or full-time equivalents [FTEs]). You'll not only want to monitor the ratio, but also ensure you understand the targeted ratios for each phase. As we discussed in the planning phase, it is important to plan the expected ratio and during the controlling phase, manage the ratio to the budget and risk tolerance. Many contracts now include a clause that requires suppliers to manage the ratio to within ±5 percent of the planned ratio. If the ratio is exceeded, suppliers are often contractually obligated to provide a plan to bring the ratio back in line with expectations.

Accurate time reporting is also an important component of the control phase. Time reporting is often misunderstood because global PMs attempt to reconcile weekly time reporting with invoices. Many offshore contracts are written with the concept of a "professional day," which limits billing to 8 or 8.5 hours per day and usually 160 to 175 hours per month. Unfortunately, many of us know all too well that we will work many more than 8 hours per day. From a project-tracking perspective, it is important to not lose these additional hours. You'll still want an invoice reconciliation process, but unless you are paying for every hour worked, don't worry if the actual hours recorded are greater than the hours invoiced.

Time reporting also lets you validate estimates on a weekly basis and monitor the time spent on each project phase. The schedule performance indicator (SPI), which is a fundamental function of the earned value analysis (EVA), provides the means to monitor the time spent on the project compared with work completed. Weekly time reporting and monitoring the SPI can indicate schedule overruns, which may lead to cost overruns, even if the weekly deliverables are being met. This is another example of how important it is for GDMs to understand project metrics and how those metrics collectively affect project performance.

B. Quality Assurance

Metrics are at the heart of an effective monitoring and control system. The balance, though, in the software development world is to define those metrics that impact quality, productivity, and on-time delivery and not get "bogged down" in a metrics program that doesn't improve the software quality.

Offshore suppliers have a host of metrics and organizations designed to track and monitor them. The challenge of the GDM is to both comprehend the importance of these metrics, choose those that drive project success, and use them appropriately. Table 7.1 lists some of the metrics that are used to measure an individual's productivity, the team's performance, and the overall development organization. We use this list to visually depict the number of metrics that can be included, not as a

Table 7.1 Common Development Metrics

Individual Developers	Project Teams	Development Organization
■ Work effort distribution ■ Estimated versus actual task duration and effort ■ Code covered by unit testing ■ Number of defects found by unit testing ■ Code and design complexity	■ Percentage of test cases passed ■ Estimated versus actual duration between major milestones ■ Number of defects found by integration and system testing ■ Number of defects found by inspections ■ Defect status ■ Number of tasks planned and completed	■ Released defect levels ■ Product development cycle time ■ Schedule and effort estimating accuracy ■ Reuse effectiveness ■ Planned and actual cost

recommendation to include them all. Your offshore supplier will recommend others, and you should collectively determine which metrics are appropriate for the project.

In addition to defining the metrics, one of the important goals of the quality assurance program is to define a process that will detect and remove a high percentage of the defects that will be introduced through each phase of the development life cycle. The most common processes include the following:

- Requirement reviews
- Design reviews
- Code inspections
- Unit testing
- Testing (functional, system, regression, integration, stress or performance, User Acceptance Testing (UAT), etc.)
- Independent verification and validation
- Audits
- Quality assurance reviews (process adherence)

The number and efficiency of defect removal operations have major impacts on schedules, costs, effort, quality, and downstream maintenance. Estimating quality and defect removal are so important that a case can be made that accurate software cost and schedule estimates are not possible unless quality is part of the estimate.

Monitoring and controlling defects is therefore a key aspect of the control phase. GDMs need to establish quality goals during the planning phase and consistently monitor them. The defect density rate is a key metric that should be monitored during the controlling phase.

Software Assessments, Benchmarks, and Best Practices by Caper Jones is an excellent reference to gain an understanding of industry benchmarks for defect injection

Table 7.2   Calculation for Defect Injection Rate

Defect Variables/Calculations	
Average person month of effort	176
Average percentage of development-related effort	50.00%
Estimated function points per person month	16
UAT defect injection rate (defect per person month)	1.68
UAT defect removal rate	90.00%
Percentage of UAT defects that occur in production	15.00%
Production defect injection rate	0.252
Percentage of production defects that are Sev 1	10.00%
Percentage of production defects that are Sev 2	20.00%
Sev 1 defect injection rate	0.0252
Sev 2 defect injection rate	0.0504

rates. The averages presented in his findings are based on the CMM level of the organization and in our experiences have accurately predicted the number of defects associated with a project. Table 7.2 provides a sample tool, which is based on these findings and which we have used on multiple engagements to accurately estimate the defect injection rates, and more importantly, the estimated number of production defects.

Quality control is also an important component of quality monitoring. In many cases, the offshore supplier is CMM Level 5 and will have defined quality control or software quality assurance standards. Most of the suppliers will have defined peer review process and form monitoring processes that validate the correctness of the work through sampling and formal review of key deliverables throughout the project life cycle. Many offshore firms used a series of charts to graphically represent their progress. Most offshore project teams proudly display many of the following charts within their project area. Examples of charts include:

- Statistical process control (SPC) charts: graphic display of the results over time of a process. They are used to determine if the process is "in control."
- Pareto diagrams: histogram ordered by frequency of occurrence that shows how many results were generated by type or category of identified cause. Rank ordering is used to guide corrective active, or fix the problems that cause the greatest number of defects. The 80:20 rule: 80% of problems are caused by 20% of the causes.
- Trend analysis: how many errors or defects have been found.
- Activities completed and tracking of SPI.

Quality programs enable GDMs to clearly define acceptance criteria for deliverables and fully expect the offshore suppliers will meet or exceed the acceptance criteria. In fact, global development requires GDMs to establish contractual processes for accepting all deliverables. The acceptance process should be defined during the contract negotiation phase, but the GDM will need to understand it and adhere to it throughout the life of the project.

There are three key concepts in the acceptance process. First is the concept of defining acceptance criteria at the beginning of each phase and clearly documenting the acceptance criteria in a contractual document, such as a statement of work (SOW), or a project plan that is updated at the beginning of each phase. In a global development environment, you will not have the opportunity to interact on every deliverable or use an iterative process to continually improve the deliverable. If you want quality deliverables and to keep the project on track, spend the time up front to clearly articulate the expectations and clear acceptance criteria from the beginning. This will dramatically improve the deliverables and minimize some of the communication challenges.

The second is the notion of categorizing errors with a deliverable such as Level 1, 2, and 3. This concept allows the supplier and the client to focus on the important aspects of a deliverable and not arbitrarily add criteria later or reject deliverables for unknown reasons. If the deliverable does not meet the Level 1 acceptance criteria, the offshore suppliers are on the hook for resolving them at their expense. This will motivate them to clearly understand the criteria and thoroughly review it internally before it is released, which results in a higher quality product. Level 2 and 3 errors that are noted often require change control, which means management can decide if the change is worth the additional costs or schedule impacts.

The final concept is the escalation process if the deliverable is not accepted within the specified timeframe. This is a "gotcha" on many projects because suppliers attempt to implement "automatic approval" if the deliverable is not accepted by the timeframe. This means that any subsequent issues or problems with the deliverables will potentially result in conflict if the parties argue cost or impacts on subsequent deliverables. For example, if the design document is automatically approved after five days and the design document is wrong, which impacts the development of a critical component, the warranty, liabilities, or service levels could all be impacted by the error. The best way to manage this is to escalate to management and use change control if the schedule or subsequent activities are delayed because the acceptance of the deliverable was delayed.

C. Risk Management

Risk tracking is probably the most common task that PMs associate with the controlling phase. Over the years, we have developed a system that significantly enhances the standard issue tracking process. The process known as the risks, assumptions, issues, and decisions (RAID) log tracks the four key areas and applies a scoring method to determine the overall project status based on the number of outstanding issues, critical assumptions, open issues, and pending decisions. The RAID log also provides a great tool for GDMs to reference throughout the project. The tool consists of five tabs in a Microsoft Excel Workbook, one tab for each major area and a summary tab that provides an overall view of the project. We have worked with several offshore suppliers that have automated this by providing a Web interface and a digital dashboard to the key areas. Regardless of the tool used to capture the data, the critical component is to use the RAID log to drive key decisions.

Project tracking is important, but there is more to tracking a project than just ensuring specific tasks are completed. Successful projects also have key milestones defined, and significant effort is expended to ensure these milestones are met. A common payment term in offshore contracts is to associate payments with the achievement of key milestones and to hold back a percentage of the amount due until the project is formally accepted. This milestone-based payment approach motivates the supplier's management team to achieve the milestones to bill the client for the services.

As an example, let's assume you are managing a project that is expected to cost $1 million U.S. dollars. The project is set up on a time and material basis, meaning that you pay for every hour worked; however, you've also set the project up with payment-based milestones and a holdback of 20 percent. In this example, over $200,000 would be held by the client until the entire project is accepted. The $200,000 is usually sufficient motivation for the supplier's management team to stay very involved with the project and help the onsite or offshore managers mitigate project risks. Figure 7.2, included with the GDM Toolkit, provides a simple means of tracking the payments and holdback amount.

D. Performance Reporting

Status reporting or performance reporting involves collecting and disseminating information to provide stakeholders with information about how resources are being used to achieve project objectives. Key activities in the reporting phase include the following:

- Status reporting describes where the project stands.
- Progress reporting describes what the project team has accomplished: - percentage complete, completed versus in progress, etc.
- Forecasting is predicting future project status and progress.
- Performance reviews: deep dives.
- Trend analysis: track key metrics, such as defects.
- EVA: report CPI/SPI.

The weekly status report (Figure 7.3) and the weekly status meeting are the primary control mechanisms used to manage offshore projects.

Holdback %:	20.00%

Phase	Deliverable	Estimated Cost	Actual Cost	Hold Amount	Amount Due
Requirements	Requirements Document	$125,000	$123,000	$24,600	$98,400
Design	Technical Design	$250,000	$257,500	$51,500	$206,000
Development	Unit Tested Code	$425,000	$425,000	$85,000	$340,000
Test	System Test Results	$200,000	$200,000	$40,000	$160,000
	Release Holdback:	$0	$0	$0	$201,100
	Total:	$1,000,000	$1,005,500	$201,100	$1,005,500

Figure 7.2   Global Project Holdback Methodology

Project:
Date:

Issue Reporting

Number Opened	Number Closed	Total Open

Top 3 Issues

Issue	Action Required

Major Accomplishments This Week

Earned Value

SPI	CPI	Comments

Test Status

Completion Ratio	Defect Ratio	Defect Count	
		Sev 1	
		Sev 2	
		Sev 3	
		Total	0

Milestones

Milestones Completed this Week

Milestones Scheduled but not Completed

Milestones Scheduled Next Week

Figure 7.3 Weekly Status Report

The weekly status meeting is the primary communication vehicle for global projects. Ideally, you should allocate at least two hours for these weekly meetings, and plan the meetings to ensure maximum participation from all parties. When we worked with a team in Chennai, India, we arranged the meetings for Thursdays, 6 a.m. MT, which was 6:30 p.m. India time. This time worked well for both of us. We would also have a meeting at 10 p.m. MT (10:30 a.m. India) because getting into the office earlier than 10 a.m. was difficult for the offshore team due to traffic.

Thursdays were important because of our dedication to weekly deliverables. We set Friday as the day code would be moved to the onsite development environment, so this gave us time to evaluate our progress to date, take corrective actions if necessary, and set good expectations with the customer.

A standard agenda is a must for effective offshore meetings and should include the following elements:

- Project-specific agenda items. Ensure agenda is set out at least 24 hours in advance and that you have input from offshore teams on any items.
- Review project schedule. Use EVA schedule and look at CPI/SPI and any tasks that are scheduled to be complete that week. Require the offshore project leader to explain deviations from plan, and plan actions to complete tasks. If CPI/SPI are impacted, collaborate with the offshore leader to identify overall impact to schedule and corrective actions.
- Review schedule for following week.
- Review outstanding change requests.
- Review RAID log. Discuss all open items and medium and high risks.
- Review key metrics and SLAs.
  - Attrition rates, staffing plans, onsite-offshore ratio
  - Current defect rate
  - Current change rate
  - Current estimate to complete (ETC)
- Review upcoming milestones.
- Open discussion. Encourage offshore participation by asking open-ended questions directly to GDM and project leaders.

The GDM needs to lead the weekly meetings and encourage participation from the team. As a minimum, ensure all onsite and offshore project managers or team leaders attend meetings and are in the loop on all issues and tracking progress. Don't let the onsite or offshore coordinator filter good news or bad news. Establish the tracking milestones and get involved in the issues, risks, and decisions. At the end-of-the-day, it is still your project. You need to be part of the ownership and solution.

A well-run weekly status meeting will identify many of the challenging issues that need to be addressed. However, weekly status meetings tend to be transaction-focused; thus they may not provide the best indication of any underlying issues or provide insight into how the team is performing. The deep dive is a mechanism for performing this more detailed analysis of the project.

We would conduct a deep dive of each offshore project at least once a quarter. This half-day or all-day meeting (some even take a week) focuses on costs, schedules, and overall health of the project. The numbers and issues are scrutinized. We dissect specific issues to identify longer-term solutions.

The deep dives also provide an opportunity to evaluate the team's effectiveness. You can use them as coaching opportunities for the GDM, onshore coordinator, and key offshore resources. The deep dives strengthen the relationship between key individuals because being in a problem-solving mode improves the overall relationship.

At the end of the deep dive sessions, you'll know where you stand and where your challenges are. As a team, you can walk away with a prioritized list of actions to tackle and a renewed sense of your outsourcing goals.

E. Change Control

Change control can be particularly challenging with offshore suppliers. Because you have limited insight into day-to-day tasks and because some cultures do not make it clear that they are reliant on information from you or your peers before proceeding, you can often be hit with change requests or schedule slippages and not even realize that the project was in danger. Change control also involves managing the change in scope once it is approved. It requires maintaining the integrity of the performance measurement baseline, ensuring changes to scope are reflected in the product, and coordinating changes across knowledge areas.

A common global practice is to request that the supplier document their proposed change control process within the first several weeks of contract award. This initial deliverable will become the baseline for the ongoing change control process. The change control process should include a description of the change, rationale for the change, number of additional hours required to implement the change, and any impacts to schedule or key milestones if a change is approved. The process should also identify the approval process and, where practical, the authorized approvers of the change request.

With global projects, the GDM needs to be very cautious with initiating and approving changes without thoroughly discussing the change with the offshore team. Often small changes that would be approved if the team is on site can cause significant issues with the offshore team because the change is not thoroughly documented and the impacts are not fully known.

You should also establish metrics to measure the degree of change. The metric should focus on the degree of change introduced by the supplier and the business. When approving change requests, document if the request was generated because of a new requirement or business need or a missed requirement or business need.

A simple measurement can be the estimated number of project hours divided by the estimated number of project hours plus the sum of all change requests.

The "death by a 1000 bites" syndrome, which is a common phrase for projects that fail because of lots of small changes or lots of small defects, is more prevalent when operating in a global development environment. An effective technique is to review submitted changes on a weekly basis only after they have been analyzed by the team and high-level impacts are understood. The goal is to understand the full impact of the change and the overall impact of all approved changes. If the current change ratio is already close to ten percent or the changes are impacting the scheduled completion date, then you should be more conservative in your approval of changes. Because the change will generally mean more revenue for suppliers, they will typically not be as motivated to decline the change; thus the task of asking the tough questions and validating that the change is a true necessity will often be the GDM's responsibility.

In most large and complex application development, integration, or outsourcing deals, "scope creep" is almost certain. Although this is an issue with outsourcing in general, it becomes critical in an offshore initiative for the key reason that the success of an offshore engagement where a significant number of resources are offshore depends on stability of the process. In fact, the upper levels of the SEI CMM Certification demand a process rigor that becomes difficult to maintain on a project in flux.

The primary mitigation technique for managing scope lies in the structure of the offshore initiatives. It is important that where the plan requires significant offshore resources, projects be mature and well documented. Often the client-side teams may not have a mature development process and may allow a more fluid scope and expect the offshore vendors to work seamlessly in their environment. This is a recipe for trouble. Costs will increase, and the probability of success will dramatically decrease.

F. Version Control

Software version control is an absolute necessity on any offshore project. There are multiple ways to conduct software version control, depending on if you share an environment or have duplicate environments at the onsite and offshore faculties. Many product vendors and information technology (IT) organizations have strict security guidelines that restrict outside access to their development environments. Many of these companies have established offshore development centers that parallel their own onsite development environments. The teams use a multi-site project repository outside the firewall that is set up with an automated version control system that automatically synchronizes the parallel environments.

A best practice in software version control is to back up the version control system on a nightly basis and always keep the latest source code and latest versions of project documentation in the version control system, not on individual developer's hard drives. The version control process and tool should be configured to require code to be checked in before developers log off for the day.

As we have already discussed, many global projects are completed with resources in multiple geographic locations. This makes it paramount to select and use a version control system that supports shared libraries and well-defined procedures that are rigidly followed to ensure the latest code is checked into the correct libraries.

Another best practice is to keep the most current version on a system at the client's site. The source code and technical documentation is vital to the project's success — presumably even the company's long-term success. Strong version control practices, which include an updated version control system, will protect your intellectual property (IP) and software assets. It may not be easy, but if the contract turns sour or an unexpected event occurs that impacts the offshore facility, you'll at least have the latest code and documentation that can be used to complete the project.

G. Managing Productivity

A significant portion of the outsourcing research over the past several years has been focused on offshore productivity. Many offshore suppliers have created expectations within the community that not only will you get higher quality code for less money (the cost savings and quality arguments), but also the use of standardized processes will result in a more productive workforce, which means you can even get more accomplished for the dollar. The debate in the IT community, though, has been focused on a few areas:

- How do you measure this perceived productivity gain?
- Should I measure productivity, or is this the service provider's responsibility?
- What data should be collected to permit accurate measurement?

The productivity argument generally comes down to your perception of the relationship with your offshore vendor. If you manage your IT organization or project through a set budget (i.e., operating budget for maintenance and support activities) or through estimation of larger projects, which may be capitalized, then your focus on productivity may be as simple as did I get what I wanted within the established timeframes. In these scenarios, you may measure productivity as a function of your estimation model, thus measuring how effective your offshore supplier is completing projects within the defined budget.

However, many offshore relationships are complex, multi-year arrangements with detailed service level agreements (SLAs) and productivity targets built into the contract. In these scenarios, the ability to agree on productivity measurements is important to adhere to contract terms and realize the cost savings. In these situations you may have to consider productivity improvements in terms of source lines of code (SLOCs), function points, or other metric-based approaches. We have seen the following measurements used with varying degrees of success.

1. Function Point Analysis

A function point is equated to business functionality (inputs, processes, outputs) developed or supported. Function points have become the accepted method for determining the work effort (output) for application development. The typical metric is number of function points per developer in a specified timeframe. For example, an industry standard for a COBOL programmer is ten function points per developer per month or the standard for a Visual Basic developer is 40 function points per developer per month.

For well-established software departments, function points work well. Unfortunately, many of us work in traditional IT departments where function points are neither well understood nor accurately measured. In these departments, it is very difficult to establish a function point baseline from which to measure improvement. Your supplier could help, but as we have already seen, the supplier may be less productive than your internal resources for many months. So a baseline established by the supplier may well be at their least productive point.

Function point analysis has been seen to work, and function points are currently considered to be the de facto standard as a base from which to measure productivity. Benefits include the accumulation of units of output measures from which comparisons and analysis can be performed and allowing the client or supplier to identify changes from one set of activities to another over time. This can permit a somewhat accurate assessment of estimates and productivity.

2. Estimating Models

In the planning section we discussed the numerous tools that are used to estimate the size of a project. When controlling projects and attempting to manage the team's productivity, you can use these models to validate their accuracy and measure the team's productivity. With the exception of function points and use-case points, there are few standards in the development community to measure productivity. However, competitive pressures and a focus on process improvements driven by CMMi and Six Sigma have introduced estimation models that allow suppliers to more accurately estimate the development effort. Unfortunately, many of these models are proprietary; thus have not been independently verified.

The models are effective, though, for measuring productivity if you require the supplier to deliver the project within ±10 percent of the estimates and you apply year-over-year or project-over-project productivity improvements.

Let's look at an example of an estimation model that accurately estimates the size of the project and allows for continuous improvement. Let's assume that you are managing an enterprise resource planning (ERP) initiative and have decided to complete the development of customized ERP offshore. The offshore supplier's model calculates the estimated time required to complete different types of components. This model defines each component as simple, medium, or complex using an algorithm that bases the complexity on the number of Structured Query Language (SQL) statements and defines an average development time for each component. The total effort is determined by multiplying the number of components in each category by the estimated number of hours and then summing the results. This estimation model was discussed in the planning section and is more commonly used than function points or use case points.

To monitor and improve the productivity with this estimation model, the GDM can define metrics and SLAs that report how effectively the supplier meets or exceeds the estimates, within some predefined tolerance levels (±10 percent) and then define a productivity measurement that reduces the estimated effort for each component, thus reducing the overall estimate for the project. Once the estimation model and year-over-year improvement goals are defined, an estimation model is built that is then used to calculate the effort for future projects. See Figure 7.4 for an example.

Estimating models can be extremely useful because they are straightforward to validate over time. The goal should be to consistently deliver projects with ±10% of the estimates. By establishing control charts with upper and lower control limits, you can measure the supplier's ability to consistently meet these targets. Presumably, the estimates are valid and agreed to; thus meeting them assumes a specific level of productivity.

H. Resource Management

Resource management may be the most influential GDM activity. Resource management in an offshore model typically does not involve performance reviews or annual salary adjustments. It does, however, include interviewing and selecting the right team, identifying and retaining critical resources, motivating the team to achieve project success, providing ongoing feedback, and monitoring several key metrics.

As the GDM, you should help select the key resources from the offshore provider that will support your project. This includes the onsite coordinator, offshore leader, and any other critical project positions (e.g., architect, lead developer, and tester).

If the majority of the resources are offshore, though, your primary responsibility is to monitor key metrics and ensure your offshore provider manages these metrics within acceptable limits. The two key metrics are attrition rate and required years of experience.

The attrition rate continues to be a major focus area for offshore providers. It is not uncommon to have attrition rates above 20%. As the offshore market grows, competition for staff remains fierce, and many organizations struggle to retain their

Activity	Baselined Expected Productivity (Effort in Hours per Activity)		
	Simple	Medium	Complex
Report	30	60	180
Interface	40	70	200
Conversion	60	140	220
Extension	70	160	240
Workflow	40	70	200
Forms	70	160	260

Productivity Improvements

% Improvement per Year	Simple				Medium				Complex			
	2.00%	3.00%	2.00%	2.00%								
	Year 2	Year 3	Year 4	Year 5	Year 2	Year 3	Year 4	Year 5	Year 2	Year 3	Year 4	Year 5
Report	29.40	28.52	27.95	27.39	58.80	57.04	55.90	54.78	176.4	171.11	167.69	164.33
Interface	39.20	38.02	37.26	36.52	68.60	66.54	65.21	63.91	196	190.12	186.32	182.59
Conversion	58.80	57.04	55.90	54.78	137.20	133.08	130.42	127.81	215.6	209.13	204.95	200.85
Extension	68.60	66.54	65.21	63.91	156.80	152.10	149.05	146.07	235.2	228.14	223.58	219.11
Workflow	39.20	38.02	37.26	36.52	68.60	66.54	65.21	63.91	196	190.12	186.32	182.59
Forms	68.60	66.54	65.21	63.91	156.80	152.10	149.05	146.07	254.8	247.16	242.21	237.37

Figure 7.4 Estimation Model with Productivity Improvements

best and brightest. The attrition rate should be reported and tracked on a monthly basis. Report the attrition rate for the month and for the year to date. During monthly reviews, discuss the project attrition rate and key individuals who may be at risk. Work with the supplier to define ways to retain these individuals: will another role help? additional responsibility? travel to onsite or rotation to offshore? If they are your top performers, you'll want to be creative and flexible to ensure they stay with the project.

Another resource issue with many offshore suppliers is the years of experience. As we have already discussed, offshore suppliers have a difficult time finding mid-level developers with five or more years of experience. Service levels can be written to require higher levels of experience and require suppliers to provide ongoing training to improve the overall experience level of the team. If the service levels aren't defined, use an average range of experience metric for similar roles, and drive the supplier to increase the average as the project progresses. Even without an SLA, the monthly visibility and reporting will help the offshore PM lobby for more experienced resources. Also, don't be shy about asking the offshore PM to replace individuals who aren't performing.

I. Earned Value Analysis (EVA)

Offshore outsourcing may no longer be in its infancy, but to ensure its growth offshore suppliers will have to improve two key areas of operations. When asked what has proved challenging in offshore outsourcing, companies report difficulty in getting their vendors to deliver projects on time and within budget. Considering that cost and speed are important drivers behind most offshore partnering, that's troubling for future outsourcing relationships.

So the core question is, "What can be done to increase the probability that offshore projects will be completed on time and within budget?" The best tool we have found is Earned Value Analysis (EVA). EVA is an objective method to measure project performance in terms of scope, schedule, and budget — the triple constraints of Project Management. It uses quantitative metrics that are obtained from the project schedule to track the actual cost of the work performed and compares the baseline plan to the actual plan. EVA, when combined with weekly deliverables and a weekly project status meeting, provides unbiased insight into the actual health of the project.

We have implemented EVA principles on multiple offshore projects, small month-long projects, and projects with budgets that exceeded $30 million and 350,000 development hours. Its utility has been a lifesaver on these projects because it quickly identifies when the project is behind schedule — when there is still time to take corrective actions.

Earned value analysis is an excellent technique to assess project health and apply metrics to manage your project. It is also an effective way to communicate to the team the overall budget and schedule performance of the project. In many projects, once the scope and schedule are baselined, the GDM is locked in to the "triple constraints" of scope, schedule, and budget. The scope is driven by the requirements documents and technical specifications. The schedule is driven by the release date or target implementation date. The budget is usually the estimated effort multiplied by an hourly rate, plus any additional costs that may be allocated to the project (e.g., network costs, travel, or miscellaneous expenses).

The process we use is able to monitor and control each of the triple constraints on a weekly basis and predict the impacts to schedule or costs at any point in the project. Scope is monitored through the weekly deliverables and project plan and controlled through a formal Change Control process. The schedule is monitored through the project plan and the combination of the three earned value metrics (Schedule Variance, Schedule Performance Indicator, and Estimate to Complete) and controlled through SLAs and Change Control. The costs are monitored through four earned value metrics (Actual Costs, Cost Variance, Cost Performance Indicator, and Estimate At Completion) and controlled through SLAs and Change Control.

Earned Value is effective only if you have created and baselined a detailed project plan. The core concept is to measure the actual work and budget expended to complete the work to the estimated effort and budget for the same work. GDMs must understand when the project is over and what work is in the baselined scope. Both of these concepts are important, because they are also the basis for offshore outsourcing – the offshore Statement of Work must also clearly define the scope and the estimated completion dates or milestones.

Earned Value Analysis is not complicated, but it does require a strong understanding of project planning principles and a general understanding of the algorithms used to calculate the important metrics. Since our focus is on the tools GDMs can employ to manage offshore risks, we'll briefly discuss the core EVA concepts and introduce the important terms. This is an in-depth subject though that we won't be able to fully cover in the following pages, so we would recommend researching EVA further. A personal recommendation is *Earned Value Project Management, Second Edition* by Quentin W. Fleming and Joel M. Koppelman.

From a project schedule and budget perspective, there are a few basic questions you need to consistently ask yourself when managing a global project:

■ When it the project going to be done? (Schedule)
■ How much is it going to cost? (Budget at Completion (BAC) or Estimate at Completion (EAC))
■ How far along are we? (Percent Complete and Estimate to Complete (ETC))
■ How well are we meeting the plan? (Schedule Variance (SV/SPI) and Cost Variance (CV/CPI))

Each of the above questions is answered through the Earned Value process by understanding the interrelationships between three metrics – Planned Value (PV),

Earned Value (EV) and Actual Cost (AC). These metrics individually provide important information about the project:

- Planned Value (PV) - represents the budgeted cost of the tasks planned to start and finish at any given point in time
- Earned Value (EV) - represents the sum of the budgeted costs of completed tasks at a given point in time. EV is based on the original project budget
- Actual Costs (AC) - the actual costs associated with the completed tasks

Microsoft Projects and other project management tools provide views of the EVA metrics, but we have found the simple tool, Figure 7.6 and included on the CD, to be extremely valuable when taking a "snapshot" of the project health. This tool prompts the GDM for basic project information, which should be available on the weekly status report and then calculates the core EVA metrics and displays the health of the project from an EVA perspective.

Now let's look at Figure 7.5 and Table 7.3 for a very simple example of how the PV, EV, and AC are calculated and used to drive project success.

Assume a small four-week software enhancement is budgeted for $10,000. The project is in its 3rd week and the team has completed 50% of the scheduled activities. Based on the project schedule though, the team was supposed to be 75% complete. The team has spent $9,000 of the budget. What is the overall health of the project?

By reviewing these calculations, the GDM can quickly determine that the project had spent 90% of its budget only to complete 50% of the work. The project is behind schedule and will be over budget at the end of the project. The GDM will likely need to reduce scope, extend the project schedule or obtain more funding to deliver the original software enhancement. What is more interesting though is the cumulative effects of the SV and CV. The project has used 90% of the budget to complete 50% of the work, so it will require another $9,000 dollars (ETC) to complete the remaining 50% of the effort.

The SPI and CPI should be included on the project status report and used to determine the overall status or color of the project. However, unlike the subjective traffic light reporting systems that are often used, the SPI and CPI provide a quantitative means to objectively report status. If either the CPI or SPI is less than .85, the project is 15% over budget or behind schedule and should be reported as Red. If either the CPI or SPI is between .85 and .95, the project is within acceptable limits,

---

EVA Example

Assume a small four-week software enhancement is budgeted for $10,000. The project is in its 3rd week and the team has completed 50% of the scheduled activities. Based on the project schedule though, the team was supposed to be 75% complete. The team has spent $9,000 of the budget. What is the overall health of the project?

Figure 7.5 Earned Value Analysis (EVA) Example

Table 7.3   Earned Value Terms and Calculations

EVA Term	Definition	Formula
Planned Value (PV)	Indicates how much work or how many activities were planned for completion. The Planned Value is calculated by multiplying the planned percent complete by the total project budget	PV = Planned % Complete × Project Budget (BAC) = 75% × $10,000 = $7,500
Earned Value (EV)	Indicates how much work or how many activities were actually completed or the amount of value that has been delivered to the project to date. The Earned Value is determined by multiplying the actual percent complete by the project budget	EV = Actual % Complete × Project Budget (BAC) = 50% × $10,000 = $5,000
Actual Costs (AC)	Actual expenditures against the project budget to date. Generally, it is calculated as the number of hours expended multiplied by the blended hourly rate plus any miscellaneous project expenses	AC = (Labor Costs + Miscellaneous Project Costs) = $9,000
Schedule Variance (SV)	Represents the difference between the planned work or activities and the actual completed work or activities. The SV is a measure of the actual progress to the project schedule. It is the difference between the EV and the PV	SV = EV − PV = $5000 - $7,500 = ($2,500)
Cost Variance (CV)	Represents the difference between the planned budget for the project and the actual budget expended to date. The CV indicates if the project is on budget from a cost perspective. It measures the difference between the actual costs of work performed to the project budget	CV = EV − AC = $5,000 − $9,000 = ($4,000)

Schedule Performance Indicator (SPI)	Represents the ratio of planned work or activities compared to the actual completed work or activities. It is a measure of actual progress to the project's schedule. The ratio should be as close to 1.00 as possible, meaning that the actual percent of activities completed is almost 100% of the activities planned to be completed. If the SPI is less than 1.00 then fewer activities have been completed than planned and the project is behind schedule. If the SPI is greater than 1.00, the project is ahead of schedule.	SPI = EV/PV = \$5,000/\$7,500 = .67
Cost Performance Indicator (CPI)	Represents the ratio of planned costs compared to the actual costs for the activities completed. The CPI is a is a measure of a project's earned value compared to the actual costs incurred, or the ratio of the costs expended to date compared to the costs planned to expend to date. Again, the CPI should be as close to 1.00 as possible. If the ratio is less than 1.00, the project is over budget. If the ratio is greater than 1.00, the project is under budget	CPI = EV / AC = \$5,000/\$9,000 = .56
Estimate At Completion (EAC)	Represents the total estimated costs and effort to complete the project based on the current status. The EAC is calculated by dividing the project budget, or BAC, by the CPI.	EAC = BAC/CPI = \$10,000/.56 = \$18,000 (rounding – actual CPI =.555556)

MGDR

Global EVA Calculation Worksheet

Planned % Complete:		75.00%
Actual % Complete:		50.00%
Budget at Completion (BAC):	$	10,000.00

Blended Hourly Rate:	$	25.00
Budgeted Hours:		400
Hours Expended to Date:		360
Labor Costs to Date:	$	9,000.00
Miscellaneous Costs to Date:	$	-

		Costs	Effort
Planned Value (PV):	$	7,500.00	300.00
Earned Value (EV):	$	5,000.00	200.00
Actual Costs (AC):	$	9,000.00	360.00

		Costs	Additional Effort	Additional % of Effort
Schedule Variance (SV):	$	(2,500.00)	60	16.67%
Cost Variance (CV):	$	(4,000.00)	160	44.44%
Schedule Performance Indicator (SPI):		0.667	SPI Warning	
Cost Performance Indicator (CPI):		0.556	CPI Warning	
Estimate At Completion (EAC):	$	18,000.00	720.00	80.00%
Estimate to Complete (ETC):	$	9,000.00	360.00	50.00%

Reference

PV = Planned % Complete * Project Budget
EV = Actual % Complete * Project Budget
AC = (Labor Costs + Miscellaneous Project Costs)

SV = EV – PV
CV = EV – AC

CPI = EV / AC
SPI = EV / PV
EAC = BAC/CPI

Figure 7.6 Earned Value Calculation Worksheet

Table 7.4 SPI/CPI Concerns

SPI	CPI	Possible Concerns/Actions
G/Y	Y/R	Review budgeted onsite/offshore ratios. Is project on schedule because more work is being completed onshore than planned? Can additional work be moved offshore?
Y/R	G/Y	Are schedule slippages due to communication issues with offshore? Is the offshore productivity lower than expected? Will adding additional offshore resources or onsite resources help schedule without negatively impacting costs? Can the scope be adjusted?
R	R	Project will likely be delivered late and over-budget. Recommend deep-dive review to understand core issues. Communicate schedule and budget to impacts, Develop improvement plan with Supplier. Review Service Level Agreements and Supplier contractual responsibilities

but needs monitoring and thus should be reported Amber or Yellow. If both the CPI and SPI are greater than .95, the project is tracking well and assuming risks, defects rates and other factors are in line with expectations, the project should be reported Green.

The SPI and CPI are the key factors that help determine the status of a project. Often times, one indicator may be red and the other yellow or green. For example, with offshore projects the costs (CPI) may be Green because more work has moved offshore at a lower labor rate, but the project is behind schedule (SPI) because the team is not working effectively. From experience, each project will have unique reasons for a poor SPI or CPI. Table 7.4 SPI/CPI Concerns, provides some general guidance for interpreting the EVA values.

J. Summary

Control is exercised at both the contractual level and project level. The focus of this chapter was on project level controls. Contractual controls, such as contractual management, governance, relationship management, SLA management, and financial control are critical to the success of the relationship, but are often outside the sphere of influence of the GDM. The GDM exercises control through communication and a focus on status and metrics.

Weekly status reports and weekly status meetings are the primary communications vehicle. GDMs should create a template to standardize reporting and facilitate the weekly meetings. The template should include key measurements such as the attrition rate, defect rate, and earned value measurements.

1. Deliverables from the Controlling Phase

- Weekly status reports
- Earned value calculations
- Updated risk plan and RAID log

2. Control Phase Service Levels

The service levels measured in the control phase should measure timeliness of reporting and the SPI/CPI. SLAs measured during execution include:

- Defect injection rates below industry average
- Defect detection greater than 90%
- Change rate less than 10%
- Supplier attrition rates less than 15%
- Supplier buffer pool greater than 10%
- Software quality assurance (SQA) results: overall score for each phase greater than 90%
- Schedule performance indicator (SPI) greater than 0.90
- Cost performance indicator (CPI) greater than 0.90

3. Control Phase Metrics

Many of the metrics defined and measured during the execution phase are monitored in the control phase. During the control phase, the focus is on ensuring the metrics are within acceptable limits and actively managing tasks that exceed limits. Control phase metrics are listed in Table 7.5.

4. Control Phase Risks and Issues

The control phase is primarily a monitoring and reporting phase. The majority of the project risks and issues are identified in the planning and execution phases and tracked in the control phase. The GDM must continue to work with his or her global partner to brainstorm and resolve these risks. Additional risks identified in the control phase are given in Table 7.6.

Table 7.5   Control Phase Metrics

Development Phase	Metric	Definition	Target
All	Percentage of deliverables accepted	On a weekly basis, measures the total numbers of deliverables that are delivered and accepted with no major issues (deliverable does not require re-work) ■ Number of deliverables accepted for week per number of deliverables submitted for week ■ Number of deliverables accepted to date per number of deliverables submitted to date	Weekly: 85 percent To date: 90%
All	Percentage of weekly deliverables completed on time	On a weekly basis, measure percentage of deliverables completed per number of deliverables planned for completion	90%
All	Degree of change	Measures team's ability to properly scope the project. Effectiveness is measured by dividing the original estimate by the (sum of the change requests [change requests for impacted project] plus the original hours)	Less than 10%
All	Attrition	Measures supplier's ability to retain key individuals and manage the overall attrition rate	Less than 15% year to date; less than 5% in a month
All	Buffer pool	Additional resources in non-billable roles available to support project if productivity dips or attrition impacts project	Buffer pool ~10% of estimated offshore FTEs
All	Experience level	Measures supplier's ability to staff project with experienced personnel. Can report average experience rate or set experience goals.	75% of supplier's project team greater than 3 years of experience

continued

Table 7.5 (continued)   Control Phase Metrics

Development Phase	Metric	Definition	Target
All	Schedule performance indicator (SPI)	Measures supplier's ability to deliver projects within the baseline project plan. Uses EVA to calculate the SPI on a weekly basis.	SPI >0.90
All	Cost performance indicator (CPI)	Measures supplier's ability to deliver projects within the baseline budget. Uses EVA to calculate the CPI on a weekly basis.	CPI >0.90

Table 7.6   Control Phase Risks and Issues

Development Phase	Risk	Mitigation Strategy
All	Change rate greater than 10 percent or number of approved changes impacting quality of delivery	Validated changes are required and limit future approvals
QA	Defect injection rate or defect density rates not monitored or exceed expectations	Include the estimated and actual defect injection rates and defect density rates on the weekly status report. If ratios exceed ±10 percent of estimate, conduct deep dive with development and QA team
All	Lack of project visibility; risks, issues, and key activities not discussed in weekly status report or weekly status meetings	Set expectations for accurate and timely completion of status reports. Discuss best times and process to facilitate an interactive, effective project status meeting
All	EVA; project is behind schedule or over budget	Report SPI and CPI on a weekly basis and adjust staffing, scope, or onsite-offshore ratios to manage schedule and costs impacts

Table 7.7   Controlling Phase Checklist

Controlling Phase Checklist	
▪ Focus on communications ▪ Establish rules for staff meetings and status reports ▪ Monitor defect injection and defect density rates ▪ Monitor earned value ▪ Monitor degree of change ▪ Update RAID log ▪ Track project metrics	
Controlling Phase SLAs	*Controlling Phase Metrics*
▪ Defect injection rates below industry average ▪ Defect detection greater than 90% ▪ Change rate less than 10% ▪ Supplier attrition rates less than 15% ▪ Supplier buffer pool greater than 10% ▪ SQA results; overall score for each phase greater than 90% ▪ Schedule performance indicator (SPI) greater than 0.90 ▪ Cost performance indicator (CPI) greater than 0.90	▪ Percentage of deliverables accepted ▪ Percentage of deliverables on time ▪ Degree of change ▪ Attrition ▪ Buffer pool ▪ Experience level ▪ Schedule performance indicator (SPI) ▪ Cost performance indicator (CPI) ▪ Estimates to complete ▪ Onsite-offshore ratios ▪ Issue resolution
Controlling Phase Risks	*Controlling Phase Deliverables*
▪ Change rate too high ▪ Defect injection or defect detection don't meet expectations ▪ Lack of project visibility ▪ EVA; project behind schedule or over budget	▪ Weekly status reports ▪ Earned value calculations ▪ Updated risk plan and RAID log

Chapter 8

Closing a Global Delivery Project

A.   Closing a Global Delivery Project

The unfortunate reality on many projects is that by the time a project gets to the closing phase, the project manager (PM) and executive sponsors have moved on, and there is little interest in "rehashing" the project. Completion of an offshore project, though, requires a thorough analysis to determine what went right and what needs to be fixed before starting the next project. Because offshore development tends to grow within an organization, it is critical to conduct a thorough post-mortem and ensure project successes can be repeated. Fortunately, most offshore firms have well-defined processes that support the closing process that help ensure the valuable lessons learned during the project can be applied to future projects.

The closing process is designed to gain final customer sign-off, finalize project deliverables, capture required artifacts and metrics in a project repository, and, most importantly, review the project with 20/20 hindsight to capture key lessons or

> **Section VIII Core Concepts: CLOSING**
> ➤ **Customer Satisfaction**
> ➤ **SLA Sign-Off**
> ➤ **Capturing Lessons Learned**

Figure 8.1   Section VIII Key Concepts

risks that can be applied to future projects. There are three primary tasks typically completed during the closing phase:

- Customer acceptance
- Service level agreement (SLA) sign-off
- Lessons learned

B. Customer Acceptance

In a global development environment there are often multiple customers. To the offshore provider, the "customer" is often the information technology (IT) manager, performance manager, or contract procurement officer who signs off on the deliverables and releases final payment, all critical functions from a supplier business perspective, but not necessarily the core reason to obtain customer acceptance of the project. From an internal IT perspective, the "customer" is viewed as the business or user group or the executive sponsor of the project. Presumably, the project was tied to a fundamental business issue that is now being met through implementation of your project. Let's take a look at both of these scenarios to understand how the customer acceptance process differs and identify the key steps in the customer acceptance process.

When offshore suppliers seek customer acceptance, it is usually because final payments and closeout of the statement of work (SOW) are directly tied to customer acceptance. As we discussed in Planning and Execution (Sections V and VI), a best practice is to align supplier payments with achievement of specific milestones for both time and material and fixed-price contracts. So, from the supplier's and contract officer's perspectives, the final acceptance "closes the books" on the project. The supplier will submit final invoices, which will include a checklist or inventory of all deliverables.

Often during this process, the supplier will perform an audit of the project deliverables that may identify required deliverables that were not formally accepted by the client, or at least proof of the acceptance can't be found in the thousands of e-mails or files that were generated during the project. In these instances, the supplier project manager may coordinate with the global development manager (GDM) or client sponsor to obtain sign-off of these artifacts. Normally, this is a simple oversight, and the e-mail approval is quickly found and re-sent or the artifact is re-reviewed and sign-off is provided.

However, in some situations, the supplier may have not completed the deliverable or even realized it was required to obtain payment. In these situations, you should be careful not to sign off on an artifact just because of supplier pressure to get paid. If the artifact is required, then apply the same rigor to the approval process, including requiring the supplier to correct identified defects, etc., as you would if the artifact was delivered in the context of the project. If the artifact was truly forgotten or somehow not required by the project, then request the supplier to submit a change request, which formally documents the artifact is not required.

Never approve a deliverable that is being presented during the closing phase that hasn't been fully vetted. It's a bad habit, can lead to future issues, potential Sarbanes-Oxley Act of 2002 (SoX) compliancy problems, or ultimately may invalidate future contract terms, such as warranty clauses.

Final sign-off often means acceptance of the final product, which in most cases is software code. If the supplier has committed to resolving all defects within the first 30 to 90 days of implementation, then you shouldn't accept the code until this period is complete. Acceptance implies you acknowledge and accept any known defects, which may also invalidate contract terms. The best advice is to check the SOW or contract language and not sign off on final acceptance of code until the warranty period expires.

The end-user or business customer acceptance process is focused on obtaining user feedback and agreement that the project met intended goals. This process typically does not involve sign-off of formal test results or production issues — these tasks are completed in the execution and controlling phases. Ideally, the customer acceptance activities in the closing phase validate that customer expectations were met and are used to plan future work.

Validating customer expectations is a tricky endeavor. From an engineering process perspective, the client's "expectations" were captured in the requirements, designed and coded in the development phase, and validated and accepted in the testing phases. However, these quantitative acceptance processes do not validate that the business drivers, such as reduction in call-handling time due to a more user-friendly graphical user interface, were met. The testing may validate that the screens were designed per the specifications and that the data was displayed and processed correctly. But did it make a difference? Were the business objectives achieved? If not, why not?

These questions can't be answered until the application has been used in the production and teams are using the software as designed. Unfortunately, once user training is completed, there is rarely follow-up with users to verify that specifications were met. A formal closing process that includes a customer feedback session through scheduled interviews, surveys, questionnaires, etc., and maybe even validation of the financial business case (i.e., could 10 resources be re-deployed because a process was automated?) is an excellent means to answer these questions.

Over the past several years, most of the major suppliers have developed "value realization" or similarly coined practices that are focused on clearly articulating the business drivers during the requirements phase and employing a set of tools and techniques to validate the business drivers during post-implementation. Additionally, several large suppliers are creating "value-add" clauses to contracts that entitle the supplier to a percentage of the costs savings if the goals are achieved, a real incentive to the supplier to exceed the savings goals and realize the additional revenue.

The jury is still out on the effectiveness of the value realization processes and metrics. In simple cases, such as reducing headcount, it is fairly easy to quantify and validate. However, even with these simpler scenarios, it will still require some thorough analysis to determine if the headcount was reduced and the existing team has the capacity to support the new workload, or was the headcount just shifted to another part of the organization that is now responsible for the function. The point is that it is rarely black and white.

The discussion of the overall value or perceived results of a realization session should not discourage a GDM from conducting interviews and surveys with your end users to validate that the project goals were met. In many situations, you will gain valuable insight that can be applied to future projects. Regardless of where the general market goes with the value realization proposition, there is proven value in discussing project successes with your customers during the closing phase, such as identifying embedded software features that resolved an unknown problem or listen to rave reviews of the project success and how happy they are you were assigned as the PM.

The second major objective of gaining end-user acceptance during the closing phase is to provide an opportunity to plan the next releases. More than likely, there were change requests, defects, and production tickets identified during the project that were deferred for subsequent releases. The closing phase is a great opportunity to pull those items back out and discuss and prioritize them with the client.

This section discussed the need to satisfy multiple "customers" (supplier's customers and internal customers) during the closing phase. The techniques discussed in this section will provide appropriate direction to sign off on the contract deliverables that the supplier is interested in and gain insight from the end users on the success of the project in meeting the business goals. In the next section we will discuss the process to close out and report the service levels of the project, again, a critical component that is likely tied to supplier financials.

C. Validating the Service Level Agreements

As we've seen throughout *Managing Global Development Risk*, there are many service levels and metrics collected and reported throughout the project. Many of these metrics, such as milestones delivered on time and defect injection and detection rates, cannot be accurately captured or reported until the project is completed and moved into production. During the closing phase, the offshore team will obtain the relevant data to measure the SLAs and meet with the GDM to review the results. If this is your first time collecting and reviewing the metrics, beware!

The SLA data will typically be presented in a digital dashboard (Web interface), Microsoft Excel spreadsheet, or Microsoft PowerPoint. There are also tools on the market now that facilitate the gathering and analysis of service levels. We've included a sample in Excel with the compact disk that accompanies this book, which is discussed below. A typical SLA summary sheet will have the overall score and a value or indicator (true or false, yes or no, red, yellow, green, etc.) to quickly display if the SLA was met. In Figure 8.2, we used "TRUE" to indicate the SLA was met, and "FALSE" to indicate it was missed. There is also a summary to provide an overall score or indication of the overall performance, which is measured on a weighted average or simple average for compliancy.

The fun starts with the detail sheets and data. Each SLA should have the supporting data accessible to allow the GDM to sample, compare results with internal findings, or validate and discuss specific details. A common problem is defect reporting. If everyone is using the same repository, it should be a simple query to count the number of defects injected during the supplier responsible phases and the number of defects detected during the supplier responsible testing phases. If you've had to re-read this, then you quickly see the problem. How do you know, without detailed analysis, if the injected defect or non-detected defect was a supplier responsibility? The answer is you don't, unless you enforce the defect tracking and reporting standards earlier in the process.

Remember, the goal of SLAs is to give appropriate incentives to the supplier and effectively manage the offshore operations to continue to meet business needs in a sourced environment. That means a fundamental mind shift has to occur to assign accountability to the supplier in many subtle ways. If this accountability isn't shifted and appropriately assigned (i.e., assigning root cause of defects) in the execution phases, then the ability to effectively manage SLAs will be lost in a sea of data that will be too overwhelming and cost prohibitive to validate.

The core purpose of root causal analysis is to identify causes of defects and other problems and take action to prevent them from occurring in the future. However, in an offshore, SLA-based environment, root cause analysis is also a key activity in determining SLA compliance. If the root cause uncovers that the reason for the error was a client responsibility, then it is reasonable for the supplier to remove the data point from his or her calculations.

Up to this point, the metrics have seemed very straightforward; however, that all changes when the reports are summarized during the closing phase and final numbers are reviewed, especially if there were service levels that were missed. For example, if the users report a high number of problems and the root cause of the problems were requirements (i.e., the requirements stated the new account field was 8 bytes, but to pull up old accounts, the user needs to enter 10 digits, which was never identified or tested), then the suppliers will rightly attempt to exempt the data points from the final tally.

You can easily imagine all the issues that can get pushed to this category. Unfortunately, there isn't an easy answer. Ideally, you've clearly defined supplier and client responsibilities so that once a root cause analysis is completed, the answer is easier. However, experience dictates there are many gray areas that will need to be discussed in good faith and agreed to.

Service Levels	Score	SLA
Productivity	97.20%	TRUE
Critical Milestones Delivered on Time	75.00%	FALSE
Interim Milestones Delivered on Time	85.71%	TRUE
System Testing Defect Rate	4.33%	TRUE
User Acceptance Testing Defect Rate	4	FALSE
Sev 1 Problems Detected in Production	1	TRUE
Sev 2 Problems Detected in Production	3	FALSE
Milestone Delivered to Budget	90.91%	TRUE
Customer Satisfaction	3.3	TRUE

Key Measurements	Metric
Work Order Effectiveness	89.29%	FALSE
Network Availability	95.45%	TRUE

Summary	Total	% Missed
Service Levels	9	33.33%
Key Measurements	2	50.00%

Figure 8.2 Sample SLA Dashboard

The closing phase is also the opportunity to verify that operating level agreements (OLAs) were met. OLAs are agreements between IT and the business to identify ticket response and resolution times, network-application uptimes, hours of operation, etc. If the implemented project impacts any OLA, then the supplier and GDM should jointly verify the implementation does not negatively impact any of these critical OLAs.

OLAs related to resolution time for tickets (e.g., four hours to resolve a Sev 1 ticket) are difficult to achieve when a new project is implemented. The team can be overwhelmed with issues if it is a new product or major release, or there may be a learning curve within the business and IT that slows down the normal process. The key, though, is to communicate with the business, prioritize the issues, and set realistic timelines that get the business back on its feet.

Ideally, there is a documented set of OLAs that are well understood so the teams can drive to meet them. As is often the case, though, the OLAs are more informal, and they only surface when the business user is upset because of a bad implementation and wants immediate results. As we've seen, being in a reactionary mode with a global software team is not a good situation. Time-zone differences, communication challenges, etc., can all work against you in these crisis situations. The mitigation step is to ask early in the process for the OLAs that are applicable to your project. If they don't exist, meet with the business and the supplier to identify the top three to five impactful agreements. Including the supplier helps ensure the requirements are understood and tied to the SLA and provides the supplier an opportunity to introduce additional activities, which will equate to additional costs, to better prepare the team to meet the OLAs. Activities may include additional testing, failover capabilities, fault-tolerance, and redundancy or staffing a 24/7 offshore operation until the application is stable. Each of these examples will potentially impact costs or schedule, something that needs to be clearly articulated to the executive sponsors.

D. Capturing and Applying Lessons Learned

For many years the software community has conducted post-mortems or lessons-learned meetings with the plan to uncover what went well and what didn't work well with the intent of applying these lessons to the next project. In general, these have been accepted with mixed results. With the exception of problems that plague many projects and which take multiple post-mortems to identify (e.g., we should use a version control system because we pulled the wrong design document out of my e-mail and lost five days changing the wrong module), many of the best practices and opportunities discussed in these meeting are followed by a few practitioners, but are rarely institutionalized.

This is another area, somewhat by necessity, where the offshore firms have far outpaced their onsite counterparts. Offshore firms have fully embraced the tenets of continuous improvement and in many cases have developed processes to feed back process improvement initiatives discussed in these meetings. We've seen multiple examples where offshore suppliers are conducting lessons learned after each phase or milestone, which allows them to make mid-course corrections by applying a best practice or a process-improvement idea in near real-time.

So what does this mean to the GDM? It presents a great opportunity to leverage your offshore supplier's best practices internally to learn how to make the mid-course corrections. More importantly, though, it provides a widely accepted venue to implement process improvement initiatives in a systematic, controlled manner. That is powerful. For example, if during the design phase the team noted that the client's business analysis did not require sign-off on critical documents and was not part of the review team, you can modify the process (and associated process documents and workflows) and add new tasks in the development phase to resolve this gap.

From a closing perspective, the lessons-learned meetings also give the team an opportunity to reflect on the project's successes. When appropriately implemented, the meetings can be great morale boosters, even for projects that had few problems. I've watched PMs integrate some core metrics with a key finding to highlight the effectiveness of the existing process or quality of the team and then compare the metrics with the new process or improvement idea to demonstrate the leaps that could be achieved.

It's important to conduct the lessons-learned sessions in an organized manner. Let's look at some best practices that will help you get started. Remember, though, the offshore firms have demonstrated tremendous competence in this area, so it may be a good opportunity to collaborate with them on suggested best practices.

- **Scheduling.** This needs to be completed before the team disbands, but the project should be in production or completed for a long enough time to allow problems to be detected and for people to reflect on the project's successes and failures. Scheduling the meeting 30 days after project completion is usually a good rule of thumb.
- **Data collection.** We suggest using a survey and set form to solicit input from users, key stakeholders, team members, and other interested parties at least two weeks prior to the meeting. The form should solicit some specific information from each of the users to spot trends or common concerns across the teams. Additionally, it should allow room for narrative in two key categories (things that went well, and things that didn't go well). This may reinforce some of the other data, but it also provides an opportunity to vent or praise, both of which are legitimate and help to uncover issues or goodness.

Offshore firms will generally create a closure report for the post-mortem meeting to summarize the project. This report contains general information about the project, such as the development life cycle used, business domain, and key personnel; performance metrics such as total effort, team size, number of function points,

Table 8.1   Closing Phase Checklist

Closing Phase Checklist	
■ User acceptance of final deliverables ■ Contractual acceptance of final deliverables ■ Review of final service levels ■ Complete post-mortem ■ Complete and review project closure report ■ Update project database ■ Risk defined and risk, issue, decision (RID) log updated	
Closing Phase SLAs	*Closing Phase Metrics*
None; review and sign off on final SLAs.	None; review final project metrics.
Closing Phase Risks	*Closing Phase Deliverables*
■ Key sponsors depart project before post-mortem data collected ■ Supplier has not completed all deliverables (payments impacted) ■ Supplier and client do not agree on SLAs	■ Final SLA report ■ Post-mortem report ■ Project closure report and metrics

defect information; information on tools or processes employed; and detailed information on the size, schedule, effort, and overall quality of the project. This information is extremely helpful in sizing future opportunities and helping to validate the success of the project.

Many offshore firms store this data in project databases to help them improve their overall quality. A similar practice should be employed with the onsite team. The project results should be stored and used for comparative analysis as more and more work is completed offshore. Oftentimes patterns will begin to emerge, such as average defect injection rates or similar risks, that can help improve estimates and user expectations with future releases.

E.   Summary

The closing phase validates the acceptance criteria and SLA adherence, and provides an opportunity to capture lessons learned and key project data. It is important to conduct a thorough lessons-learned meeting for each project completed offshore and to capture and analyze critical information for future projects.

The deliverables in the closing phase include the results of the post-mortem and the final project closure report. Each of these deliverables should be stored in the project repository.

There are typically not any specific SLAs or metrics captured in the closing phase. Instead, the GDM should validate the SLAs and metrics from the project closure report and look for patterns that may help improve the estimation or quality of future releases.

Chapter 9

Thinking Globally

A.   Introduction

Throughout the pages of *Managing Global Development Risk*, we have referenced multiple times the much publicized stories about the challenges of interacting with offshore resources; talented young developers who simply smile and say yes to everything. After spending several years representing a global service provider and spending a great deal of time immersed in the culture, we believe it is time to move beyond this generality and dig into why these situations continue to occur. We want to move beyond the fascination with the symptom and understand the many causes that contribute to communications challenges. Global development managers (GDMs) will need to understand when it is truly a basic communication issue or in fact a deeper, more complex issue. It is time to end this! GDMs should no longer allow global service providers to use communications and cultural challenges as a crutch. Communications and cultural differences have acted somewhat like a free hall pass when a project is not properly executed. By now, global service

> **Section IX – Thinking Globally**
> ➤ **Tools to Bridge the Cultural Divide**
> ➤ **Global Travel Suggestions**
> ➤ **Managing Global Resources On-site**

Figure 9.1   Section IX Key Concepts

providers should have these kinks worked out and if they persist, what is the value of a capability maturity model (CMM).

This is why we spend a significant amount of time providing GDMs with the tools and techniques to help their internal team as they deal with integration and alignment with their global counterparts.

For GDMs and their internal teams to think globally means to stop projecting the reality of doing business in and with other North American or European firms and understand how the majority of global sourcing firms function. We have touched on this earlier, but we need to develop a more complete understanding of the manner in which offshore firms operate BEFORE we start to look at the complexities of communications and culture.

B. The Many Levels of Cultural Misalignment

It's important to take a few moments and look at what we call "cultural misalignment." This concept explores the challenges a GDM will most likely encounter when executing a global development project.

1. User Interface

The most visible indication of cultural misalignment within a global development organization is the never-ending communication challenge. Although this is the easiest and most superficial to address, we will cover this only after we have helped you understand the environment in which this resource more than likely must operate (please note the "must operate"). Communications impacting your global development environment are built on several interesting corporate realities including the global service provider's business, cultural, and, oftentimes, religious beliefs.

2. Corporate Culture

Global service providers, in particular, in Indian and Chinese organizations, are typically controlled by a small group of executives, and we mean less than a dozen for even the largest global service providers. In fact, as a U.S.-based GDM, you more than likely have more authority and autonomy than a mid-level Indian executive.

The cultural element of doing business in and with Indian business professionals is built on a deep foundation of respect and hierarchical decision making. Did you ever think for a moment or consider that the individual sitting across from you acting as onsite coordinator does not have the same level of authority as you? In fact, you would be truly surprised to learn that most of the time, the onsite coordinator and even the offshore project manager (PM) of your global service providers have limited ability or authority to make changes. Perhaps the reason you are getting a non-committal response or, worse, believe you have agreement due to the person saying yes, is because the individual you are talking to will have to escalate the issue to his or her manager, who in turn will need to elevate to his or her director, who in turn will need to escalate to the vice president. All this time, your point of contact has no influence in the process, but may be saying yes with a reassuring smile.

3.   Corporate Process

We discussed this issue earlier in *Managing Global Development Risk* when covering project initiation and project planning. Now we want to take a look at the interpersonal dynamics behind the estimation process that may impact global development projects.

We've run into this a number of times: "Our estimates were one third that of the offshore firm!" To understand the dynamics behind the CMM estimation process, before we can truly understand how they came about, we need to appreciate the communication and authorization process executed by your global partner. It's not that the onsite global resources did not understand the project or its details; it's that they play a very specific and defined role in the global estimation process. It is not uncommon for those individuals capturing details, requirements, and specifications to have little input in the final effort estimates. As previously noted, global service providers adhere to the CMM process and development models. Combined with a very conservative nature, multiple approval, and quality assurance (QA) checks, the level of effort can be dramatically impacted. It is easy to see why estimates done by a GDM's internal staff will vary. The individuals doing the estimation are typically back in India or China and control the process based on the inputs they have been provided; not your counterpart or the U.S.-based team. Think about it. How many times have you had a live session with a project manager of an offshore firm, re-scoped the project and the associated effort, and reached agreement on the spot? Now you understand one of the possible reasons.

On several occasions we have witnessed a surprising level of distrust between the global service provider's onsite resources, which are typically employees of the U.S. headquarters, and the Indian-based wholly owned subsidiary staff back at the main development facility. Even if each individual is a citizen of India, there is a political undercurrent between the two halves of the same company. Part of it may have to do with internal transfer rates and other issues, but there seems to be a political pecking order among global delivery resources. GDMs may believe they are dealing with a decision maker from a U.S. operation, but the project is being controlled by individuals you may have had little or no contact with. In fact, you will find a "we know better" attitude permeates the global team that can impact your project in a number of different ways such as the resources you receive and retain and ultimately the size of your offshore staff.

Although we would like to believe that estimation is a very formal and structured process, there may also be political undertones. One such issue we have observed is the political importance for Indian-based PMs to be responsible for large teams and complex projects. This helps them internally demonstrate their ability to successfully manage global development projects to their executives, helping them progress up the corporate ladder. If they are able to manage multiple large projects successfully, they will be rewarded. We have firsthand experience with Indian-based PMs who hide behind the CMM estimation methodologies and their own additional review and test cycles to drive the size of the staff because they were losing ground with other PM's at their firm's offshore development center. These review calls actually get quite animated as it can be emotion driving the activity versus pure project sizing.

Needless to say, GDMs need to be aware of multiple levels or streams dealing with project issues and staffing dynamics to effectively drive the entire global effort to a successful conclusion.

4. Organizational Dynamics

Please remember this very important fact: decision-making ability and true authority tend to be centralized within a pure play global service provider. Why is this important for GDMs to understand? Because as you attempt to engage offshore PMs, you need to understand the overall dynamic of the team and the organization in which they belong. The ability to escalate issues quickly and efficiently may be the single greatest benefit for GDMs if they take the time to understand these dynamics and the true political structure.

In addition to the centralized nature of these firms, we are dealing with a very, very courteous environment where employees do not push or challenge their managers, where doing business in a new, innovative fashion is not necessarily viewed as a positive.

C. Tools to Bridge the Cultural Divide

Now that we better understand the dynamics and political dimension of a global service provider, GDMs can begin to build an action plan that will enable them to anticipate how the offshore project managers and staff will respond in differing situations. In fact, we recommend the active participation of your technical leaders and key contributors including onsite and offshore members of the global team in the creation of these action plans as a means to gain their full support and participation.

As GDMs work through the global project initiation and global project planning stages, *Managing Global Development Risk* recommends the use of some of the following items as a means to augment the global development tools and templates we have already offered. By adding these items to your project management arsenal, GDMs greatly enhance success rate and team dynamic.

We have used these tools successfully to integrate teams and achieve global development success. These tools are:

1. *Global Development Playbook*
2. Global project management office (PMO) organization chart
3. Global team rotation plan
4. GDM escalation test
5. Global project authorization map

These unique *Managing Global Development Risk* tools, when combined with the already discussed global project management tools and templates presented, provide GDMs with powerful mechanisms to manage all aspects of the project.

1. *Global Development Playbook*

There are hosts of dynamics that surround every aspect of the global development process. These dynamics shift based on the nature of the development activity (construct, test, deploy, sustain). In the case of global development, it is essential to understand the who, what, where, and when for each activity and sub-activity. To establish a clear and concise baseline for you and your onsite and offshore global team members, we suggest the creation of a *Global Development Playbook*; an essential tool that describes the exact activities and the actions to be taken in specific scenarios.

The *Global Development Playbook*, much like what a coach will provide players with at the start of the season, is a tool to identify positions, tendencies, and audibles (corrective measures) based on the situation. We recommend that the *Global Development Playbook* include the following core areas:

- Onsite team structure: Roles and responsibilities by position, including the length of the stay, visa requirements of the resource, skills requirements
- Global team structure: Roles and responsibilities by position
- Rules around staff adjustments: Utilization rate bands
- Locations
- Responsibilities by location
- Business continuity plan
- Fast track development plan
- Connectivity strategy

The *Global Development Playbook* should be created during the project initiation stage and is intended to be shared with your global service provider as well as distributed to all onsite and offshore members of the global development team.

2. *Global Project Management Office Organization Chart*

We have already talked about the formation, use, and role of the PMO in supporting successful global development operations. The purpose of mentioning this important component once again is to reinforce how the PMO can also help GDMs bridge the cultural divide by taking a look at the underlying interaction. Using the typical Indian developer as an example, a PMO and the members of the PMO are viewed with a great deal more awe than the typical U.S. developer. To take advantage of this and pull additional team members into the perceived inner circle, develop a global PMO organization chart that incorporates an additional layer or two of team participants. Although the addition may seem trivial with little formal responsibility other than an input point, by making the global PMO organization chart and having it widely distributed, GDMs gain a great deal with little effort.

3. *Global Team Rotation Plan*

Many times in a global development operation, it is the offshore team that is responsible for the rotation of staff between locations. It may appear that the onsite coordinator is responsible, but once again, we want to emphasize it is the offshore PM who ultimately organizes staff rotation and selection.

Although the majority of travel for the execution of your global development project is identified in the knowledge acquisition (KA) and knowledge transfer (KT) portion of the global development project plan, *Managing Global Development Risk* suggests GDMs look for additional opportunities to bring global resources onsite for defined task or brief periods.

In addition to helping productivity, the movement of key resources at all contributor levels (this is an important point I will touch on in a moment) enhances overall team interaction. This shifting of resources must be bidirectional: members of your U.S. or European team must head to the global development operation for extended periods of time; preferably a minimum of 3 weeks, in addition to members of the offshore team coming onsite.

Now, what we mean by key resources at all contributor levels is that typically in a global development operation, PMs and from time to time technical leaders will travel between the offshore and onsite locations. Outside of the assigned onsite team, few heads-down resources who are doing the bulk of the actual work get to enjoy this perceived perk. *Managing Global Development Risk* suggests that it is important to include this level of team member in the rotation process. It deepens the team dynamic to a true contributor level and facilitates the relationship between developers as they will be able to work side by side and then take that reinforced relationship with them. It will spill into the informal communication areas identified above and, not least of all, will help minimize attrition as very few global development operations provide this type of opportunity at the developer level.

Yes, this will increase operational cost. It will also drive enhanced productivity, which has a true bottom-line impact.

4. GDM Escalation Test (Internal and Private)

This is a concept that we highly recommend for your global development operation. It will help bridge the cultural divide, and at the same time you get to observe how your integrated team responds to a mock disaster.

We all spend a great deal of time negotiating disaster recovery plans (DRPs) or business continuity plans (BCPs), and then place the documents in a drawer hoping we never have to see them again. In parallel, we structure a PMO and an escalation process that details exactly how and at what point issues need to be escalated and who needs to get involved. Both, however, are rarely used unless there is a true need. Is this when you want to find out if your escalation process is effective?

Like the concept of a fire drill from our childhood days, decide to run a mock failure or project episode that will engage the escalation process to the very top. This will provide you line of sight on how the global team responded overall and how each level reacted. It also gives your team members the rare opportunity to see how their support team, peers, and managers react, isolating areas that need to be improved and enhanced. Like a football team (or in the case of the global development market, a cricket team), teams relax and are more productive when they know each other when the heat is on.

If you decide to execute this test, we suggest you not inform the global partner so their performance can be truly measured and judged. A good way to handle this is to take a mid-level problem and blow it out of proportion!

5. Global Project Authorization Map (Internal and Private)

Unlike the escalation guidelines contained within most contracts, the goal of an authorization map is to put parameters around authority by resource level. In our opinion, this is a very worthwhile exercise as it will help team members, particularly your U.S. and European team members, better understand the true authority and decision-making capability of their global peers.

We discussed earlier that the communication gap that exists today between U.S. and European software development PMs and their offshore partners is not simply a language incompatibility issue. Although it is certainly a contributor, many times it is our own naïve assumption that the individual we are speaking with has the authority to make a decision, when in fact nothing can be further from the truth.

GDMs need to be prepared in advance that this may be a frustrating experience to develop and document the authority of their global resources. They may be evasive or somewhat non-committal, but as you continue to probe and question, you will eventually get the information you require. In addition, you will be able to validate this authorization map when you run the escalation test. Combined, these two tools will help GDMs fully understand those dynamics that can be so challenging to uncover, in particular when dealing with a multicultural organization.

D. Team-Building Concepts

Global development organizations are under constant pressure. Time is the rarest of commodities, and implementing what might be viewed as trivial "touchy feely" activities can be questioned by your team. However, based on our experience, every moment you spend investing in team building and integration will pay dividends in overall productivity. This productivity enhancement is measurable and can be directly linked to team morale and the overall management and integration of global resources.

Managing Global Development Risk is not suggesting GDMs need to sponsor all these activities. We are sharing some of the events we have been a part of and demonstrating how much goodwill and team spirit is realized. It is important to note that this IS NOT simply just for the U.S. or European team members when global resources come to their location. It is equally important when you have a portion of your onsite team visiting your global development operations as well. Observing the laughter and joy of a group of developers in Chennai learning the basics of touch football with a mixed team of U.S. PMs is a truly great memory. It is only surpassed by watching a team of sophisticated U.S. business executives learning and playing field hockey or cricket.

So here are a few concepts that promise to add a positive and measurable dynamic to your global development operations.

1. Holiday Profile and Schedule

This is a mandatory tool for your global development organization. We have observed many organizations that have not taken the time to develop this simple tool leaving GDMs frustrated and constantly surprised. No one is at fault. It is simply a matter of not understanding or being insensitive to others.

Our recommendation is simple:

- Assign an individual from each location of your global development operation to a central team.
- Each representative is to bring forward a complete list of national, major, and important religious holidays for his or her country.

- A calendar is developed that incorporates all these dates.
- An explanation of each of the holidays or events is populated on the lower portion of the document so that people can see what the holiday is all about. There was one firm we know of that created a Web site containing photos of the events as well, to help people understand.

What is a truly simple effort, the creation of a central calendar combined with a thoughtful execution of the final product, will have far-reaching positive impact.

2. Sports Education: Cross-Team Participation

Every country is passionate about sports. Although they can be very different, it is a wonderful means to bring individuals together. Although Americans simply do not have the same appreciation for cricket or field hockey as Indians do, we appear to be equally passionate about American football, baseball, and our other major sports. In other parts of the world it is soccer (true football, I am told), rugby, and, yes, even badminton that pack the stands and dominate the conversation by the water cooler or over lunch. Take advantage of this, and get people out of the office to participate or go to a game.

3. Cooking Classes

Cooking classes can be a great deal of fun if you make certain to take a moment and understand some of the sensitivities around preparation and religious beliefs. We have seen people bring completed dishes to the office for a special buffet and have their spouse present to help explain the recipe. Another aspect not to be ignored is how people spend a meal. Is it typically a large family and a long, formal process? What utensils are used? How do you compliment the cook?

Have some fun with it!

4. Movie Nights

When you spend some time in India, you quickly sense how truly into their movie productions they are. You have probably heard of Bollywood, but to be there and experience it helps put things into context. In short, people love this form of entertainment, and it truly is an affair.

Indian movies are long, incredibly ornate productions. They also prove that the leading man does not have to be a Brad Pitt or George Clooney type, which I enjoy a great deal. However, American and European audiences can quickly lose interest. To work through this, here is what I have seen a firm do that was incredibly well received.

Indian Movie Night in the United States or Europe:

- Pick a movie that is somewhat reasonable in length or edit the film a little (DVD's work great here).
- Have a master of ceremonies introduce the movie and provide a basic plot line.
- At logical breaks in the movie, have a person explain some of the details of what people just watched as well as some of the key items they will see in the upcoming portion of the film.
- This helps everyone overcome the language and cultural differences and enjoy what they are observing.
- It also provides the opportunity for some individuals to stand in front of the group and proudly talk about their culture.

5. *Tools to Bridge the Cultural Divide: Summary*

We have spent a fair amount of time digging into this subject and looking at numerous ways to bring a globally distributed development team together. In conclusion, we urge you to consider this an ongoing component of your global operations and not simply a box to check to conclude transition. We would also advise that you take true ownership of this important facet versus outsourcing it to a third party who walks in, does a presentation or two combined with a few team-building exercises, and leaves. In our experience, although there is some value to this approach, it is far more beneficial when it is internally driven, executed, and managed. It becomes a part of the fabric versus the input or opinion of a paid consultant.

E. Global Travel Preparations

This section of *Managing Global Development Risk* may seem trivial, but we have seen large development operations absolutely brought to their knees because they did not take simple precautions. Traveling is not easy; traveling to a third world region is a significant challenge. You and your team must be prepared.

To keep our conversation focused, we will look at travel through the eyes of the GDM and your internal technical leaders who will be headed to India or another global destination. This means that your global resources have already been secured, and all contract issues and negotiations have been closed. It is now time to get the real work done as your project plan has been developed, estimates are in hand, and you are heading to India for the first time to spend three weeks making certain your global team gets off to a quick start.

We will also focus our example on traveling to India as we have found this to be very representative of many other locations throughout Asia, such as Sri Lanka,

Pakistan, and other emerging economies like Vietnam and parts of Malaysia. In our experience, in locations such as China, South America, and Eastern Europe, although each possesses a unique character and flavor, travel preparation is somewhat less of an issue for these locations, but it is still important to take the time to understand the culture. We would also like to take a moment to suggest that as you prepare, seek out information and insight from Americans who have been there. We have intercepted many PMs who were briefed for their trip by their global sourcing counterpart and were ill-prepared for what they were about to encounter.

Americans and Europeans who have visited are in the best position to help you as a first-time traveler to India. You will get a full, objective representation of what to expect.

1. Out-Bound Travel Issues

As you prepare to travel off to this great land, you quickly begin to realize that a trip to Bangalore or Hyderabad is a bit more involved than a quick jaunt to the Caribbean. In addition to making certain your passport is up to date and does not expire within the next 12 months, your trip to India will also require the following:

- **Work visa.** Typically your global service provider will be able to assist you by preparing a letter of invitation. Although the visa process is fairly straightforward for those of us in the United States, we still recommend taking advantage of a visa service to help you through the process. Although there are several quality providers, our personal experience has been with Zierer Visa Service (1-866-788-1100). There is a cost, and it can seem a bit high, but we have had too many friends and colleagues attempt to go it on their own with some disastrous results. They are very busy the day before their flight!
- **Inoculations.** In advance of your trip, we highly recommend a trip to a professional travel doctor or clinic. Checking out the Web site of the Centers for Disease Control in advance of meeting with a doctor who specializes in this area will give you some basis for understanding the recommended preventative measures. It is important to know the cities you will be visiting and the time of season being experienced at that specific region. This needs to be done well in advance of the trip, so do not delay! Challenges with a visa can impede the trip, but won't force you to lay in bed praying for the end. Yes, you will be in a world-class hotel. But you still need to be careful. We are not offering medical advice, just pointing out that the quality of your trip is truly yours to manage.

You now have passport and proper visa in hand and have taken appropriate medical precautions including necessary prescriptions and the recommended shots. Let's walk through the remaining components of the trip:

- **Try to fly Business Class.** It is a long, long trip. It will also help you when you step off the plane late at night in India as you will reach customs and immigration ahead of the crowd.
- **Jet way shock.** As you step off the plane you will be assaulted by heat, humidity, and the distinct smell of the tropics. On one trip a close friend of ours said he was having flashbacks to Vietnam when he was a young man heading to war. You will see an airport that currently seems time has forgotten. Unlike many other global sourcing destinations such as those in China and Eastern Europe, you will most likely be taken aback by the state of most Indian airports. It is our understanding that the Indian government has recently privatized the airports in an attempt to catch up with the rest of the modern world, but be prepared for a structure that is well behind current world standards.
- **Baggage claim.** Indian baggage handling can be a marvelous thing to observe if you're not in a hurry. It will most likely be very late at night or very early in the morning, so an extra 30 minutes at baggage claim will not impact your sleep very much as it is already limited. We suggest that while you are waiting for your baggage, walk around the area a little and begin to get a sense of what you have gotten yourself into.
- **Car service.** Before you start your trip, make certain the hotel has your flight information and has arranged for a car to be waiting for you. Without question, this is the critical link in the trip. Here's why. As you emerge from baggage claim and clear customs, the doors will open to an unbelievable sea of people pushing up against the railing on both sides of you. It is a very interesting collection of people trying to get your attention. Walk slowly and keep scanning both sides for the driver holding the sign with your name. It is at this point you can take a deep breath and hand over your bags as he escorts you to the car and whisks you off to the hotel. Depending on what city you have landed in, the drive could be fairly long. At the minimum, while in the back of the car, you will begin to understand a little about living conditions in the country. No matter what the time, there is a tremendous amount of activity and people to observe.

Your situation will begin to crystallize as you sit in the back of the car and observe the sights and activity outside your car window. It will almost feel as if you are watching a movie while this strange world outside your window passes by. There is so much to observe that is very different from anything you have experienced before.

Once you arrive at your hotel and enter the lobby, it can be easily said you have stepped back into a world where you are a bit more comfortable, leaving just a few steps away the scene that conjured up images of a BBC or CNN telecast. The key from this point forward is to make certain all car arrangements are made for you to get to and from your destination.

In a moment we will talk about working in India and the nuances of making your time with the development team as productive as possible, but for now take great pride in knowing you have just entered the true world of offshore outsourcing. Congratulations! Depending on the time, either flop into bed and get a few hours sleep or hit the showers and get ready for the Indian workday!

2. *In-Bound Travel Issues: Offshore Resources Coming to Your Facility*

We have just spent a fair amount of time talking about the challenges of traveling to India and the initial startling experience if it is your first visit. Clearly the environment is different from anything we are familiar with. It seems to assault every sense, and although we may be quick to judge and compare, we often neglect to think about the experience our global team members have when they come to the U.S. or Europe to work at your facility.

Let's take a moment to think about this. As GDMs we are focused on productivity. To enhance productivity, we take time to educate our internal team for the experience, but rarely do we address the other half of the equation: your offshore resources working onsite.

We are not fully certain why this is, but it is important to take a moment to think through what can be done to truly welcome and embrace your new global team members so they will become comfortable, quickly assimilate to your unique operation, and get productive. Remember, this is not easy for them either as they too are far from everything they find familiar while they are helping you execute.

GDMs need to understand that when you raise this issue to your global service provider, you will be assured that any of their resources coming to your location are fully prepared and experienced at working in the U.S. and Europe. However, we have seen and participated in this "training" and can tell you that many times it is insufficient.

When you fly to visit your Indian development operation, you will be treated incredibly well by your global partner or peer from your organization's captive operation. We can easily say it is "their gracious culture" or "we are the customer" and they should do it, but the real answer is that time after time we are amazed at how considerate and kindly we are treated when we are visiting India or other parts of the global sourcing community. Yet when these young professionals from a far-off land reach our cities, we expect the supplier to be fully responsible. The resource is to be at the desk in the morning and ready to go.

What can GDMs do to help facilitate this transition? Is it not in your best interest to have all development team members excited and productive? What will be the bottom-line project benefit if you do a little extra planning to this seemingly forgotten item?

We provide some input below on the actions a GDM can take to welcome and embrace global team members. It is truly simple common sense and a real desire to befriend. Yes, these people are contractors, and it is their job, but we believe the little extra TLC has significant impact. *Managing Global Development Risk*, as we have detailed throughout the pages of this book, recommends a technique of combining sound PM principles with sensitivity to individual team members' needs to extract excellence. Don't miss this opportunity to establish the personality of your global development operation at such a formative stage.

F. Working in India — A Guide for Global Development Managers

There are going to be times where you and perhaps several members of your team will need to visit the development team in India. We have already spoken about some of the preparation you will need to do as well as what you will experience when traveling to this part of the globe. It is now time to discuss how you can make your time in India productive versus creating unintended havoc.

It is important that we take a moment to really understand the objectives of this visit. We have observed an interesting dynamic when a GDM or internal leads are heading to India. There are times when it seems the visitor's goal is to bring back stories of inefficiencies, lack of execution, and other sorted insights to undermine the entire global development operation. At other times, it seems the team is preparing to go on vacation and focused on absorbing the culture versus having a formal agenda and action plan. As GDM, you need to be crystal clear about the intent, goal, objectives, and tactics you will employ to have your time in India be as productive as possible. You also need to be fully aware of these underlying dynamics to ensure everyone's agenda is focused on project success.

To address this issue properly, we will address this subject in two distinct approaches: working with a global outsourcing partner and working with your firm's captive center operations. The reason to do so is that in each unique setting, you need to be sensitive to how the operation works both structurally and politically.

1. Working in India — Global Outsourcing Offshore Development Center

As discussed earlier, your firm may have a partnership with a global service provider that is referred to as an Offshore Development Center (ODC), Center of Excellence, or some other marketing-created name. The important distinction here is that the resources that are part of your team are employees of the third-party global service supplier.

GDMs need to understand how to conduct themselves in this environment to get the desired long-term reaction from these resources versus confusing them, which can be very easily done. Some of the issues GDMs will encounter are the following:

- Contributor-level resources at the global development location as well as your onsite facility are extremely hierarchical. They will smile and nod yes in agreement when you are speaking, but will only take direction from their direct line manager. Make no mistake about this. Unlike a U.S. organization, directives from a superior must come from the direct line manager, and you are not that individual. We have observed this many times in the past as U.S. PMs walk around the development facility in India interacting with the team, barking out orders, or having one-on-one meetings with the developers outlining expectations. After these sessions, the Indian developer goes directly to his or her direct manager to get clarification. Remember, you are dealing with a mindset steeped in CMM process, hierarchy, culture, and an environment that does not necessarily reward independent thinking.
- While you are in India and will be a part of the local team, we recommend some combination of the following activities so you will positively impact and enhance team productivity. This is important as we have observed almost an equal split between a PM's ability to enhance the global development activity or to cause total chaos. This list may seem a bit overwhelming or unnecessary to you, but the long-term impact will be very powerful. Take a few moments. Walk slowly and notice the ground under your feet as you step!
- Don't forget the value of bringing gifts. Most ODC's established by global service providers attempt to help the resources feel as if they are part of the customer team. When you walk the hallways at the facility, you will quickly sense that people identify each other with the project they are assigned. Simple little items such as pens, coffee cups, even polo shirts help create the team dynamic at the global development location. Do not underestimate the positive impact this will achieve.

Below is a recommended communications process for GDMs while in India.

- **Step 1:** Have a private meeting with the senior-most executive responsible for your development staff — preferably over breakfast — before you engage any of the PMs and individual contributors of your team. To be clear, we are speaking of the delivery executive of the global service provider, not your project offshore PM.
  - This is an excellent time to informally discuss the manner in which he or she manages the development operation and to articulate your expectations. Although you may think you understand these subtleties, it is important to be consistent and make certain your desires are clearly

understood at this level of your suppliers. Ultimately, your offshore PM goes to this individual for approval.

- What is the driving goal of the team? How does he interact with the project managers? What are the messages they try to reinforce with the team? How do they recognize excellent work? Who has been recognized?
- Take advantage of the time and make certain to establish an open door with the executive, as it may prove helpful in the event you require rapid escalation.
- Typically this delivery executive is one or two layers away from the president or CEO of the global service provider. This is something you want to confirm.

We have a fun example of how this can work. There was a global service provider that had established a build-operate-transfer facility for a software vendor. That vendor was acquired by a larger software vendor whose executive had a very different approach to their business. Let's just say they were a little rough! Well, the executive for the software vendor walked into the typical global service provider meeting where there were a dozen key executives to welcome him. He methodically explored each individual's role until he was clear who the decision-maker was and then asked everyone else to leave the room so he could address his issues.

Although this was an extreme case, GDMs will find similar dynamics when there are a number of executives in the chain of command or critical path who have no actual authority.

- **Step 2:** Now that you have a little insight into the personality of the global development operation, it is time to meet with the offshore PMs responsible for your project in a private setting. Dig into their project areas and ask the same questions you just asked of the overall delivery executive. Look for consistency. This is a time where you need to be aware of slight nuances when individuals respond. Body language and mannerisms are a very, very important form of communication, and you will quickly realize how different this is from what you are used to.

   Make certain to ask for the names of individual team members who have performed, and learn exactly what they have done to be recognized. This will help you later as you begin to meet with teams and walk the development center facility. A compliment goes a long way in any culture!
- **Step 3:** Next, schedule the large, full team meeting. Unlike what you may experience back at the home office, in particular if this is a global service provider, individual team members are truly eager to hear from you and understand the context of the work they are doing on your behalf. This is a great time to help them understand where in the overall scheme of your firm's information technology (IT) efforts the project they are working on actually fits, and the value of their contribution and long-term potential. It is also a

great time to recognize some of the work being executed by the PMs and individual contributors by name and to list what they have done.

This is the reason why you were probing the executive and offshore PMs earlier.

■ **Step 4:** After this very large and public forum, it is time for you to work with the individual project team and receive a detailed update. Prior to leaving on your trip to India, GDMs should make certain to request that the individual teams prepare a presentation so you can understand their current state and progress to date. At that time, direct the offshore PM to have two or three individual team members actually give the presentation, not the offshore PM or technical leader. Now as you sit there, with the PM at your side, the team will present their status. This approach helps GDMs:

  – Get to know the individual team members' names.

   ■ You will see a little of the development team personality emerge.

   ■ You have an opportunity to reinforce for the team that the PM sitting next to you is being publicly recognized as a key management team member.

  – Do not minimize the benefits of this simple gesture to the PM sitting next to you and his or her team. This simple dynamic has far-reaching impact.

  We have truly enjoyed observing these sessions. Understand that you will lose some productivity in the week or two in advance of these sessions as your teams will be busy preparing, but in our opinion it is well worth it. The teams get so excited and nervous as the presentation draws near. GDMs have a tremendous opportunity to acknowledge and compliment the individuals. Probe with some tough questions to see how they respond.

■ **Step 5:** Now over the course of your visit, do your best to meet with each of the individual team members with the PM present. Spend some time getting to know the people, their aspirations, and what makes them tick. They'll be very prepared to talk about the project. They will be truly surprised when you ask them about family, hobbies, and ambitions.

■ **Step 6:** Sponsor coffee and tea for a day. Typically, each ODC has a coffee area in it or nearby. Get in the office early one morning and have the offshore PM help you pay in advance the individual who makes the coffee or tea. We have done this many times, and it is unbelievable the excitement $20 or so can create.

■ **Step 7:** On your flight home, send as many personal notes to team members, with carbon copies (cc's) to their direct manager, thanking them for their work and include something they have shared with you about their personal life.

This multi-step approach will pay massive dividends over the life of this and future global development projects. You took the time to understand the personality of the project team and setting. You then carefully demonstrated your sensitivity to the local political structure and at the same time provided all an opportunity to participate.

With this strong foundation, as GDM, you have established a strong foundation for future visits by you and your internal team members. You have observed the pace and dynamic of the global development team and became very aware of your presence and the impact it has on the global team.

Each time you return to the development center, make certain to execute the process step by step. Each time you do so, it will continue to build the relationship and boost productivity. We observed a very large development center that was running 21 various projects in parallel. Three of the PMs used this formula when they visited the global development center. These three teams had significantly higher productivity, incredibly low attrition, and team meetings that were effective and actually dynamic. It was great to watch as it became a contest among these three PMs to see who could execute better. In addition to the project benefit, they were rewarded with incredibly lasting friendships.

2. *Working in India — Captive Center*

There is only a slight difference for GDMs when they are leveraging global resources from a captive center. As we defined earlier, by captive center we mean an offshore development operation that is owned by your company. The resources on your project, although located in another part of the world, are fellow employees. As such, these global resources will have better context of the work they are doing, but GDMs cannot automatically make this conclusion. It is your responsibility to fully execute the strategies described in *Managing Global Development Risk* to ensure the team is fully informed and operational. We have observed many of the same issues surface regardless of the source of global resources. In fact, sometimes GDMs do not apply the required rigor when they are engaging their company's captive center and encounter unnecessary challenges. Be prepared!

G. Managing Global Resources Onsite

We have just worked through the suggested process for GDMs to become a productive part of the global development process while they are working from the offshore or global location. As outlined, when you do visit these locations, you will be treated incredibly well, so much so that you may think they have mistaken you for someone else! With that experience fresh in your mind, let's turn the discussion to how GDMs welcome their global resources when they reach our shore to work at your onsite location.

Our guess is that you have already connected the dots and realize that the manner in which we typically indoctrinate global resources working onsite in the United

States is insufficient and borders on being insulting. Why is this? We have spent a great deal of time in *Managing Global Development Risk* talking about process, methodologies, techniques, and templates to lead your global development project to success. We are also suggesting that the use of common sense, compassion, and being considerate could possibly be the single greatest thing you can do to achieve global productivity.

You might be saying this isn't your job, or I am beyond doing any hand-holding, but let's take a moment to walk through this and balance the investment in time with the potential benefit. As business people, we believe the return on investment (ROI) in this area is measurable and predictable.

When you initiate a global software development project, you will hear terms such as "knowledge acquisition" and "knowledge transfer." As already discussed, this is the process by which your global resources will document and relay the knowledge of your application to their offshore location. Although there is a clear process with actionable management components, the underlying emotion will add a very thin transparent layer to the work. Do you think that there will be an ever so slight difference between a technical requirement or specification document produced by a resource who has been treated well and embraced versus one who has been treated with the minimum required political kindness? When the resource returns to the offshore facility to train and guide your other team members, how will the interaction be?

So as you are getting started or are currently managing a global development project, what are the simple things you can do to help foster a positive dynamic? How can you merge your U.S. team and the global resource?

Here are some ideas on activities you can implement to welcome the resources to the United States.

1. Arrange to have someone meet the resources at the airport and get them to their hotel. Although this is probably not the resources' first time in the United States, as the team coming onsite to execute knowledge acquisition tends to be seasoned, it removes an unnecessary item of stress for them.

2. As mentioned earlier, if you have had the opportunity to visit India and your service partner, you most likely received some small gifts when you arrived at the airport and perhaps even again when you first reached the office. Do you have any company logo items that you can possibly give to your new team members?

3. The first morning they are on site, arrange to have a team member — preferably a peer — show them around and help them learn the ropes a bit.

4. Once they are a bit settled, spend time with the individuals to give them context of the overall business and IT operation. Taking the time for them to understand the overall operation and how the project they are supporting is intended to deliver benefit will be a great perspective.

5. End the first week the resources are on site with a lunch over which you seek their opinion on what they have observed so far. Also, don't miss the opportunity to learn about their families and interests, and, yes, if you have questions about their religious beliefs and practices, ask! Although this may not be viewed as politically correct, if it is a sincere interest, the response will be positive.

6. Include the offshore-onsite resources in your staff and PMO sessions. Make them aware of all issues so they can manage and respond with appropriate context.

As you can clearly see, none of these individual items requires extra effort, yet they will help provide a comfortable, open environment that will lead to greater productivity.

H. The Emerging Dragon — China as a Global Outsourcing Destination

We spend a great deal of time talking about India because it is clearly the leader in the global outsourcing community, and it appears it will remain so for the foreseeable future. But it is important to acknowledge that China has done a masterful job of positioning itself as an attractive addition to your global outsourcing portfolio. As previously discussed, China appears to be growing in a different fashion from what we have traditionally observed in India. China today has a limited number of global outsourcing indigenous suppliers of any true scale. On our most recent visit, it appeared that the majority of smaller service providers were focused on the staff augmentation needs of the major multinational corporations (MNCs) and service providers that have established offices. This being the case, if you currently have China-based resources as part of your global development operation, they are probably through a large MNC such as Accenture or the resources are part of your own captive center.

I. Traveling to and Working in China

Unlike India, the infrastructure in China is truly incredible. If you have spent a significant amount of time in India, you will be struck by the contrast the moment you step off the plane. Whether it is Shanghai or Beijing, the airports are large, clean, and organized. The highway system is impressive. Building and expansion is everywhere.

What you will also begin to realize is the command of English within a development organization is a significant challenge.

Once at the development center, the recommendations and communication techniques we recommend are identical to those for India. Our only additional recommendation is to focus on the use of language within the development center.

How can you help your team improve their skills and have some fun while they are doing it? What type of contest, scavenger hunts, or activities that require interaction can you sponsor?

We believe that, in time, China will continue its growth and become the clear second choice for global outsourcing. The ability to communicate and establish a common understanding among team members is a direct link to productivity. To us, this is the single greatest difference working in China versus other global locations, so any extra investment in time and resources will prove beneficial.

J. Other Global Sourcing Destinations

Regardless of where you decide to outsource your development efforts, it is important to recognize that there are differences between your internal corporate culture and that of your global service provider. This difference is on multiple layers as it encompasses local and corporate cultures. Although this is a difficult area (fraught with all sorts of political correctness issues), some things you want to document prior to the start of your project include the following.

1. *Holidays:* Make sure that national or other holidays are documented at the start of the project. These holidays can have a significant impact on a project, particularly because most holidays don't align well between countries. For example, November can have a lot of holidays between the United States (Thanksgiving) and India (Deepavalli) that can significantly reduce project productivity.

2. *Infrastructure*: Many areas where offshore development is conducted can be prone to infrastructure challenges. Although most industrialized countries are not familiar with these issues, brownouts and entire city power failures can and do occur in offshore development environments. In fact on a recent trip to China, the government had enforced mandatory brownouts. When selecting an offshore development partner, document how they are supported for power outages (backup generators, etc.) and whether they operate in a high-priority area for telephone and electrical services.

3. *Language*: It can take some time to get familiar with the accents of individuals from different states or counties let alone different countries. Usually this process requires time and practice so expect to see improvements throughout the life cycle of the project. Also remember that verbal communication can be more effective than written communication because writing skills in the software development industry are typically fairly weak anyway and are only exacerbated when you involve writing in a second language. I try to have a quick review of any significant correspondence before it is issued to customers or business stakeholders. This quality assurance function should be formally embedded in your project in some capacity simply to avoid any confusion (or possibly hurt feelings) caused by a language challenge barrier.

K. Summary: Thinking Globally

We realize that for many of you, the concepts, tools, and techniques described in this section may seem trivial in the overall context of running your global development project. Some of you will embrace this facet and adopt several of the concepts whereas some will not. The value here is that as you are moving through the global development process, you may encounter events or developments that will trigger your memory of reading this section. Apply these concepts and make the true shift to that of a global development manager.

Chapter 10

Summary

The words you have just read in *Managing Global Development Risk* are the byproduct of the many workshops we have conducted as well as our roles in which we have advised leading organizations in both the United States and Europe. The material, concepts, tools, and templates have proven of great value to individuals dealing with the exact issues and challenges you are wrestling with. So we know if you embrace some of these suggested approaches and put them to work, you and your team will benefit.

We recognize that during the time you have spent with this book and the accompanying CD, we have thrown a great deal of information at you. That was our intent. The book has been designed to be an ongoing reference and repository for you to go back to each time you initiate a global development project. We have found this to be extremely valuable in our own professional lives as there are times when a project can be all consuming; the opportunity to pull back a bit and review a resource such as *Managing Global Development Risk* always seems to uncover a topic or approach that will help the current project status.

So as we come to a close, we would like to offer a few words of advice as you now move forward as global development managers:

Always apply equal focus and discipline to both your internal retained team members as well as your global team members.

Over-communicating is far better than under-communicating.

Metrics and service level agreements (SLAs) are not tools to punish but unite your global team and serve as a unifying goal for the team to know when they have succeeded.

By executing the concepts within *Managing Global Development Risk*, you will achieve improved productivity through improved communications, the integration of a true global team, and positive team morale.

Good luck, and enjoy your role as global development managers.

References

Chapter 1

1. Frost & Sullivan Ltd., "Offshore Focus," *Computerworld*, February 28, 2005.
2. Moore, Geoff, *Crossing the Chasm,* HarperCollins, New York, 1991.

Chapter 2

3. Robinson, Marcia and Kalakota, Ravi, *Offshore Outsourcing: Business Model, ROI and Best Practices*, Mivar Press, Alpharetta, GA, 2004.

Chapter 3

4. *Effective Benchmarking for Project Management*, Project Management Institute, 2004, Newton Square, PA 19173-3299.
5. Dainty, Andrew, Chenh, Mei0i,, and Moore, David, A comparison of the behavioral competencies of client-focused and production-focused project managers in the construction sector, *Project Management Journal*, 36, No. 3, June 2005.
6. *The Capability Maturity Model: Guidelines for Improving the Software Process, Software Engineering Institute*, Addison-Wesley, Reading, MA, 1995.
7. Goldenson, Dennis and Gibson, Diane, *Demonstrating the Impact and Benefits of CMMI®: An Update and Preliminary Results*, CMU/SEI-2003-SR-009, 2003. Carnegie-Mellon University, Pittsburgh, PA 15213-2612.
8. Overview of the ISO System. http://www.iso.org.
9. Schmidt, Paul, The Offshore Benchmark Report, AN ODG Research Study, Denver, 2002.

Chapter 4

10. Morstead, Stuart and Blount, Greg, *Offshore Ready Strategies to Plan and Profit from Offshore IT Enabled Services,* ISANI Press, 2003, Houston, TX.

11. Jalote, Pankaj, *Software Project Management in Practice*, Pearsons Education, Indianapolis, IN, 2002.

12. *The Capability Maturity Model: Guidelines for Improving the Software Process, Software Engineering Institute*, Addison-Wesley, Reading, MA, 1995.

13. *Effective Benchmarking for Project Management*, Project Management Institute, 2004, Newton Square, PA.

14. Gause, Donald C. and Weinberg, Gerald M., *Exploring Requirements — Quality Before Design*, New York, NY: Dorset House Publishing. 1989.

Chapter 5

15. Jalote, Pankaj, *Software Project Management in Practice*, Pearsons Education, Indianapolis, IN, 2002.

16. *The Capability Maturity Model: Guidelines for Improving the Software Process*, Software Engineering Institute, Addison-Wesley, Reading, MA, 1995.

17. *Effective Benchmarking for Project Management*, Project Management Institute, 2004, Newton Square, PA.

18. Clem, Roy, Project Estimation with Use Case Points http://www.codeproject.com/gen/design/usecasep.asp.

Chapter 6

19. Jalote, Pankaj, *Software Project Management in Practice*, Pearsons Education, Indianapolis, IN, 2002.

20. *The Capability Maturity Model: Guidelines for Improving the Software Process*, Software Engineering Institute, Addison-Wesley, Reading, MA, 1995.

Chapter 7

21. Jalote, Pankaj, *Software Project Management in Practice*, Pearsons Education, Indianapolis, IN, 2002.

22. Fleming, Quentin W. and Koppelman, Joel M., Earned Value Project Management, Second Edition, Project Management Institute, Inc. Newton Square, PA 19073-3299.

Chapter 8

Chapter 9

Chapter 10

Index

W